THE AIR
TRAVELER'S
HANDBOOK

TOWER: CLEARED TO LINE UP AND HOLD ON RUNWAY TWO—EIGHT LEFT.

............TOWER: SILVERBIRD FIVE-O-ONE IS CLEARED FOR TAKEOFF

THE AIR TRAVELER'S HANDBOOK

The Complete Guide to Air Travel, Airplanes and Airports

Simon and Schuster
New York

ND TWO SIX-O AT ONE-TWO.............................

Edited and designed by
Marshall Editions Ltd,
71 Eccleston Square,
London SW1 V1PJ

Editor: Helen Varley
Assistant Editor: Patrick Harpur
Research: Helen Armstrong
                   Caroline Landeau

Art Director: Barry Moscrop
Design: Paul Wilkinson

Artwork: Arka Graphics

Consultant Editor: Bill Gunston
Advisory Editor (US): William
Garvey

Published by Simon & Schuster
A Division of Gulf & Western
Corporation
Simon & Schuster Building
1230 Avenue of the Americas
New York, N.Y. 10020

Manufactured in Spain

Library of Congress Cataloging in
Publication Data
Main entry under title:
The Air Traveler's handbook
   Bibliography: p.
   1 Aeronautics, Commercial.
   2 Transport planes
   3 Airports

TL552.F565   629.13   78-17600
ISBN 0-671-24546-5
ISBN 0-671-24393-4 pbk.

. . . . CO–PILOT: EIGHT–O KNOTS . . . .

THE AIR TRAVELER'S HANDBOOK

Contributors

Basil Arkell (Rotorcraft design consultant)

Gordon Bain (Civil Aviation Authority)

J. W. Birchall (Deputy Chief Air Traffic Controller, London Airport, Heathrow)

L. F. E. Coombs (Smiths Industries Ltd.)

Captain T. W. Cummings (Founder of Pan Am's "Fearful Fliers" seminars)

Captain Thomas G. Foxworth (727 pilot, Pan Am; ICAO Airworthiness Committee; author of *The Speed Seekers*)

Ian Goold (*Flight International*)

Bill Gunston (Associate compiler of *Jane's All the World's Aircraft*)

N. P. Harmse (KLM Royal Dutch Airlines)

Mike Hirst (Technical Editor, *Flight International*)

Bob Jackson (Flight engineer)

Judi Loach (University of Essex)

Alec Lumsden (Formerly of the British Aircraft Corporation, technical writer and Master Photographer)

Sir Peter Masefield (Chairman, Project Management Ltd., Deputy Chairman, British Caledonian Airways, Past President of the Royal Aeronautical Society and of the Chartered Institute of Transport)

Tony Osman (Science Editor, *The Sunday Times Magazine*)

Brian Tomkins (Managing Director, Airline Publications and Sales Ltd.)

Dr. Anthony Turner (Senior Overseas Medical Officer, British Airways Medical Service, Honorary Associate Physician, and Lecturer, Hospital of Tropical Diseases, London)

Ann Welch (Vice-President, Fédération Aéronautique Internationale; author of *Pilot's Weather*)

Mike Wilson (Technical Editor, *Flight International*)

David Woolley (Editor, *Airports International*)

Contents

"Rotate!"

The flight crew will be at the airport an hour before takeoff — earlier if the route is unfamiliar. Each member has to sign in, undertaking that he has read the flying regulations. Licences, vaccinations and passports must be up-to-date and all crew members must be "dry": no alcohol within eight hours of a flight, sometimes more, depending on airline rules or state laws.

Neither captains nor airlines like to deliver their customers late, so crews vie in the Flight Dispatch Office for the most favourable altitude on the shortest route. The dispatcher recommends a route; the captain may disagree. An unfavourable route may add half an hour of flying time. Over a year this could cost the company 1,750,000 tons of fuel on 350,000 flights, the number TWA flew in 1977.

The captain settles on a fuel load allowing for a possible long wait before takeoff, and for fog or some other eventuality closing the destination airport, which would mean flying to an alternate.

About 40 minutes before departure time, the flight engineer begins a walk-round check. Rules for passing a plane to fly are laid down by the book: if an air-conditioning system is less than perfect the plane is still airworthy; a malfunctioning thrust-reverser would be acceptable on a short-haul flight to a fine-weather airport, but not for a trip to an ice-bound runway. But if one of the hydraulic systems is suspect, the plane will be grounded for repair.

A captain can close his doors on late passengers, but he may wait if the delay is justified commercially. He may call the control tower while the last passengers are boarding to request clearance for start-up. If several planes are scheduled to fly the same way at the same time, the first to be cleared gets the best route.

The co-pilot calculates the maximum allowable takeoff weight. This depends on ground conditions, outside air temperature, wind speed and direction, and runway length. Last-minute changes are possible; in the Persian Gulf air temperature can rise — and air density fall — within minutes. Freight, free-ticket passengers (often airline employees), fuel and sometimes even passengers may be offloaded. If the cargo has been unevenly loaded, it affects the plane's trim and has to be relocated.

Cleared for push-back, the aircraft is manoeuvred out of the parking bay by a tug. The tower gives the taxi-route to the runway over the radio.

In line for takeoff the crew checks the flying controls and instruments, and runs through the appropriate takeoff drills.

When takeoff clearance comes, the captain pushes the throttles forward with his right hand; the flight engineer backs him up, watching the myriad engine instruments. The captain, his left hand on the nosewheel steering tiller by his left knee, steers the aircraft like a bus until the rudder becomes effective. The co-pilot holds the yoke steady, calling out the speed as the needle on his dial flickers: "Eighty knots." "Crosscheck. I have the yoke," calls the captain, taking the wheel with his left hand. His right hand stays on the throttles, ready to chop power should a sudden need to stop arise. The white centreline markings rush at them, faster and faster. "Vee-one!" The co-pilot calls out the decision speed — Velocity one; if nothing untoward has happened the captain commits to takeoff. He puts his right hand on the wheel . . . "Rotate!"

A gradual tug on the yoke and the nose rises. The ground falls away. "Vee-two – positive rate of climb." The plane is at the takeoff safety speed, calculated to produce the best

angle of climb for the weight. "Gear up," intones the captain. The landing-gears trundle into their wells.

The aircraft climbs steeply at first, at about ten to 20 degrees, to gain height as quickly as possible and so reduce noise on the ground. The crew's attention is fixed on the flight instruments — the captain maintaining optimum speed, monitored by the co-pilot who calls out any discrepancies, the flight engineer watching the engine indicators. If speed drops too low alarms blare a warning.

Once clear of noise-sensitive zones, the aircraft is levelled off, speed increased, flaps retracted and the after takeoff checks carried out. The seat belt signs in the cabin are turned off, altimeters reset and systems checked. The autopilot may be engaged, relieving the pilot of much physical workload, but he still commands the automatics to fly the correct path.

An aircraft flies from radio beacon to radio beacon overland. Crossing the Atlantic from London to New York, the captain may follow a Standard Instrument Departure routeing (SID), initially heading for the Brecon radio beacon in South Wales while he calls up the Shanwick control centre for a route to Gander in Newfoundland.

The centre, or area, controllers may question the captain's route, and he may concede a reroute, argue or negotiate with another pilot on the "pilot's band". If he has to take a longer route than he planned, or is held down at an altitude uneconomical for his aircraft's engines, he may have to make a refuelling stop. Pilots usually give consideration to the flight with the longest haul and the heaviest load.

Once the plane is cruising, a rest roster is arranged. Some captains try to visit the cabin, a courtesy still appreciated by many passengers. On long flights, the crew keeps track of weather reports, checking winds regularly against the forecast, ready to request a rerouteing to gain a better flight time or a smoother ride.

The hard work begins again about 200 miles out from the destination. At busy terminals the plane may be cleared to descend to about 13,000 feet by a specific point on the map, and then guided by radar to within five miles of the runway. At airfields with little traffic the captain may be free to make his own approach, from cruise altitude. Tower controllers do not know exactly who to expect, or when. Clearance to land is given as planes arrive.

Some aircraft are equipped to land on the autopilot, but it is usually cut out at about 1,500 feet. Sometimes in bad weather one pilot will fly the approach and the other will take over when he sees the runway clearly.

With the flaps extended and the landing-gears down the plane needs more engine thrust and is noisier, so the pilot tries to keep it "clean" for as long as he can. It must be stabilized to land by 1,000 feet; if the gears are down five miles too early, the drag may cost an extra 80 gallons of fuel. To use minimum fuel, the plane should descend slowly, like a glider.

There may be a long stay in a holding stack (where inbound traffic is directed to fly around an airport radio beacon) if there is a queue of traffic. Two minutes before touchdown, landing checks are made.

Thirty feet above the runway the pilot raises the plane's nose slightly in order to slow its rate of descent. He aims for a touchdown point — which disappears beneath the nose as he touches down at about 130 mph. Reverse thrust is engaged. Brakes are applied sparingly. As the rushing runway centreline slows in the pilots' vision to a series of separate markings, the after-landing checks begin.

Flight planning

The image of airline pilots poring over maps on long tables is archaic, and the old-style flight-planning room a relic of the past. These days flights are dispatched in a little under half an hour from an airline office filled with electronic equipment.

The crew checks in an hour or so before a flight. On some airlines crews work in teams, the same individuals always flying together, knowing each other well. Others may never have met before a brief handshake on signing in. If anyone fails to show up, a stand-in is called.

A computer, programmed by an army of personnel with data about the aircraft, its payload of passengers, freight, baggage and fuel, and updated with weather changes at high altitudes and at the destination, prints out several possible routes (minimum distance, minimum time, minimum cost) and selects the best. Several crews may want to fly the same airway at the same time; routes are allocated on a "first come, first served" basis.

The best route may ride a jet stream, a fast river of air which offers the most economical way of getting from A to B at high altitudes. It will be high above the weather, around the 250 millibar level at 34,000 feet.

Aircraft fly along designated airways. They are numbered like highways on the ground: J (for Jet) –80 is the "route 66" across the central tier of the USA. Airways do not necessarily link cities. They follow radio beams that radiate out from navigation stations sited 200 to 300 miles apart. Pilots ply these tracks in the sky from station to station, but may deviate to avoid bad weather.

A captain planning a long-distance flight may take a great circle route, the shortest distance between departure point and destination, especially if no airway links the two. The latest

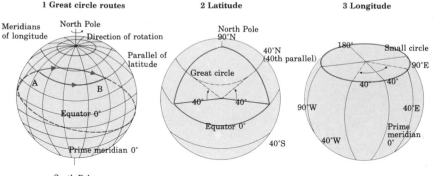

1 Great circle routes   2 Latitude   3 Longitude

The shortest distance between any two points on a sphere lies on a great circle which, marked on the surface of a globe, divides it into two equal halves. On a flight from A to B 1, since both A and B lie on the same parallel of latitude, the pilot could fly due east along it, but the shortest distance lies along the shorter of the two arcs that join the two points. If the path were continued round the Earth, along the dotted line, it would describe its diameter. Although the pilot leaves A initially heading north–east, by the time he arrives at B, he is flying south–east.

The Equator, the 0° latitude line, is the only parallel of latitude 2 that is a great circle; all other parallels are small circles. Latitude is measured north and south from the Equator through 90° in each direction. All meridians of longitude 3 are great circles. By international agreement the 0° or prime meridian passes through Greenwich, near London in the UK. Longitude is measured east and west from the prime meridian through 180° in each direction.

Pilots calculate great circle distances using simple trigonometry. Long-range radio navigation waves also describe great circles.

navigation systems that do not depend on ground stations make this possible. To avoid annoying communities with sonic boom, Concorde's crew may have to pick a route that does not overfly built-up areas.

Fuel calculations follow choice of route. The heavier the plane the higher the rate of fuel consumption, so it costs fuel to carry fuel. The amount has to be correct to carry the payload to the destination, plus a contingency amount in case of unanticipated headwinds, and enough to divert to alternate airports.

A topped-up Boeing 747 carries about 311,000 pounds of fuel — enough to fill a suburban swimming pool. It would be folly to haul so much on a short flight (New York to London is short, in modern aviation terms) or when the runway at departure or destination is short; planes must be light to take off and land safely on short runways.

But fuel prices vary from place to place and it may pay to load up with cheap fuel and burn extra to avoid filling up where fuel is costly.

Sheets of navigation and weather data, notices of conditions at destination airports and alternate routes, lists of VIPs and CIPs (a growing category: commercially important people), details of passengers' special requirements — and the flight plan — make a formidable document. When the captain has signed to accept the plan and the flight dispatch officer has confirmed it, it is filed, together with details of the aircraft's emergency equipment and procedures, with the national air traffic control service. Copies are teleprinted out to the control centres along the route.

Carrying briefcases laden with 12 pounds or so of charts and information, the crew leave for their aircraft.

One Jeppesen's high-altitude chart covers the entire USA. This section shows the area from El Paso to Albuquerque. The airways, numbered according to the degrees of the compass, converge on VOR navigation stations. They are marked with triangles and their latitude and longitude for insertion into aircraft navigation systems. The boxed numbers are nautical mileage distances between stations, and the upward-slanting lines show magnetic north. The shaded areas are military zones, forbidden to commercial and private planes. Established airways avoid them, but J-65-166 and J-108 that cross them are open at certain times.

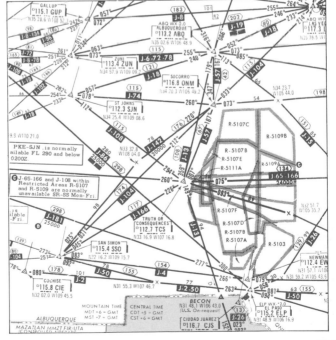

11

Predicting the weather

An airport weather office goes into high gear well before dawn, when the duty forecasters study data that has been flowing in all night from weather stations on land, at sea, in outer space, and from pilots in flight. Once fully digested by a computer, it is ready as coded hand-outs to give airline pilots the detailed information they need to satisfy themselves, as air regulations demand, that the weather is suitable for their flights.

Before takeoff pilots need to know the expected conditions for departure. Fog produces tedious delays, made more annoying when it is lying on the airport with gin-clear air only 1,000 feet up, and pilots need to know when it will clear and whether it may return. It often occurs on calm, cold nights, when warm air flows over cold sea, or during the passage of a cold front. Icing occurs in very moist air a little below freezing, and may mean that on takeoff hot air from jet engines is needed for de-icing. This will reduce takeoff power, so loads may need adjustment.

Airline pilots. must know surface conditions at airports within 30 minutes flying time. Should an engine fail after takeoff, the pilot may need a local alternative. Terminal area forecasts (TAFs) are made at major airport weather offices by meteorologists familiar with local weather patterns, and sent out by teleprinter.

Throughout the day forecasters produce synoptic weather charts giving the general weather picture for the surface and for high altitudes, and these are continuously updated. Synoptic charts warn about deep depressions and winds blowing around them. Over one side of a Low, planes encounter headwinds and use more fuel, but on the other, tailwinds shorten journey times and reduce fuel consumption. Jet streams, high-altitude tubes of air about 100 miles

Radio-sonde balloons, released at fixed intervals, provide local data on lapse rate (the fall of temperature with height) humidity, and wind velocity at different levels. Linked to a radio transmitter which emits a series of musical notes for interpretation by the ground station, the balloon takes about an hour to ascend to 60,000 ft, where it bursts. The apparatus descends by parachute and may be recovered.

Ceilometers enable airport meteorologists to establish the base height of low-lying cloud. A transmitter projects an angled light beam upwards. This bounces off the cloud base and is received by a recorder; from the angle of the beam meteorologists can calculate the cloud-base height.

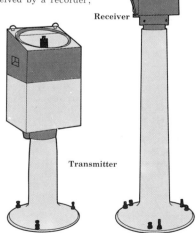

Receiver

Transmitter

wide and two miles deep which work to balance world temperatures, can produce 400-mph winds.

While fuel calculations are being made, the captain concentrates on any SIGs, significant weather reports, and may need to discuss these with the forecaster. They may warn of thunderstorms (grown from the hot, moist air and atmospheric instability which are common in warm climates) which may contain turbulence, lightning, heavy rain or hail. Thunderstorms rumbling over a destination airport mean that aircraft have to land in the turbulence and sharp wind changes — windshear — beneath massive thunderheads. Forecasters keep a close watch for adverse windshear; it can reduce a jet's airspeed dangerously, by over 60 mph. Sometimes, high in clear air, turbulence occurs with a peculiar "cobblestone" feel. Severe clear air turbulence (CAT) may cause a plane to shake noticeably and even alter altitude, but it does not last long if the captain can change flight level.

En route the crew tune into the continuous VHF Volmet radio transmission, and monitor the aircraft's weather radar (page 50), checking for storms, and endeavouring to fly above or around them. Storm lightning may not do structural damage but can burn off aerials or affect radio-navigation equipment, particularly at lower levels. Hail, especially the giant variety, is dangerous. Millions of ice golf balls bombarding a wing may damage the skin. Crews also monitor inertial navigation equipment (page 52) for windshear.

Because the weather knows no boundaries, meteorologists have developed an international language of data presentation, so airline pilots have no translation difficulties and hardly a source of information on which they cannot draw.

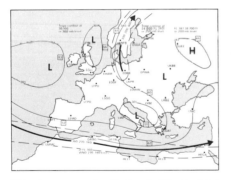

This **tropopause/vertical windshear** chart gives the altitude of the tropopause (the layer of atmosphere between the lower troposphere and the upper, almost weatherless, stratosphere) where most strong winds occur. It varies from 20,000 ft high over the Poles to more than 40,000 ft high above the Equator. For better engine performance, jet pilots fly in the cold air high above the relatively warm conditions near the tropopause. They avoid turbulent air in the high and low pressure contours where the tropopause penetrates the stratosphere, and around the jet streams, marked by arrows. The dotted lines, superimposed from a SIG chart of the same date, mark areas of CAT.

The **Earth's weather** can be clearly seen from European Space Agency (ESA) satellites. Launched under the auspices of member countries of the World Meteorological Organization, five satellites have been sent up over the Equator to give an accurate global picture of prevailing weather conditions. The ESA satellites are geostationary: they move around the Earth in 24 hours, over fixed points on the surface. They transmit infra-red photographs of cloud formations over a large area of the Earth's surface.

The control tower

The control tower is the nerve centre of an airport. At the busiest international centres controllers may direct up to 2,000 aircraft movements a day, more than one a minute during the busiest hours.

The tower has to be tall enough to give controllers an unobstructed view across the airfield. It may be a small double-decker cabin at a club airfield, from which one controller directs aircraft along a single airstrip, or as large as the 260-foot monolith at Charles de Gaulle Airport, from where a team of seven or more command a view across a runway complex of 11 square miles.

Control towers in the largest airports have two control rooms. Controllers in the visual control room at the top are responsible for aircraft taking off, for aircraft taxying, and for final landing instructions. Assistants log aircraft departure and arrival times, from which landing charges are prepared, and man the computer, which prints out the estimated times of arrival of each flight and scheduled times of departure. A ground movement planning controller books slots (available times) along the airways for departures.

An atmosphere of cool urgency prevails in the dimly-lit approach control room, usually located below. Here, approach controllers, working in the orange glow from their radarscopes, guide inbound traffic to the runways. Should a runway inspection, or a change in landing direction caused by a wind change, or overloading at peak hours, cause a delay, aircraft are fed into holding stacks, flying around a radio beacon until given landing clearance. The approach controllers integrate the flow from two or more stacks, handing them over to a radar director, who weaves the streams into a single line stretching out along the approach path. A safe separation distance of three to four miles between incoming flights provides a landing interval of about one minute. Aircraft overflying the congested airport zone are controlled by a separate radar director.

The radar screens are ringed with concentric circles, called range marks, representing distances of two, five or ten miles from the antenna. With the aid of a compass rose superimposed on the radarscope, controllers can accurately calculate aircraft positions. Dotted and solid lines encircle radio-navigation reference points. The "blips" or "targets" pinpoint each moving aircraft. In modern alphanumeric displays, each target is labelled with the flight number, and the aircraft's altitude and routeing, for rapid identification. The blip continually fades, then brightens as a new position appears.

Intense concentration is needed to track dozens of aircraft moving at speed within a small area, and controllers take a 30-minute "winddown" break after a maximum of two hours' work on the radarscopes.

Saarinen's pagoda-like control tower at Dulles International Airport is 193 ft high. The glass-enclosed "cab" at the top is surmounted by obstruction lights as a warning to low-flying aircraft at night. A radome protects the short-range radar scanner and an FM radio antenna keeps controllers and pilots in contact.

The visual control room (the "cab") at the top of the tower at Chicago O'Hare Airport **above** is rounded to give the controllers an unobstructed view of the runway complex. The glass walls are angled outward so that reflections of the room's interior are not visible, and the glass is tinted to absorb solar heat, and reduce glare.

Radar controllers in approach control scan the skies for up to 50 miles around the airport on short-range radar **below**. Radarscopes can be adjusted to eliminate interference from rain or snow, and to give a close-up view of a small area. Computer-aided radar can be set to monitor airspace at different altitudes.

Runways

Although modern jet airliners are less affected by crosswinds than propeller airliners used to be, planning a new airport still includes a climatographical survey of a large area around the site. A wind rose, often drawn up by a computer, ensures that the runways are orientated to take advantage of prevailing winds.

Formerly, runways were laid out in a triangular pattern, like those at London's Heathrow Airport, so that one was always pointing roughly into the wind. Seen from the air it looks like the pattern made by a snowflake on black velvet.

Intersecting runways enable planes to take off from one and land on the other, but only alternately. Sets of parallel runways, the usual configuration at new airports, can be used simultaneously, even at busy times. A subsidiary runway may be built at an angle for use by small aircraft.

The hotter the climate and the higher the airfield above sea level, the longer the runways have to be. Air density decreases with altitude and heat, so aircraft need longer distances to generate thrust and lift for takeoff. The 15,000-foot long runway at Doha on the Persian Gulf is one of the longest at a civil airport.

Aircraft need a long takeoff run, too, to lift the heavy fuel loads needed to fly long distances. New York's John F. Kennedy Airport has one 14,572 feet long. But 6,000 feet or less may be enough for planes on short-haul services, and in remote places turboprop aircraft and even small jets use gravel, grass or even dirt strips.

An aircraft landing may weigh up to 400 tons and touch down at more than 125 mph. It takes some stopping. Surfaces must be strong and carefully graded for drainage, and scored with grooves to prevent aquaplaning, skidding on a film of water. Grooves are made two inches apart by a diamond-cutting wheel, or moulded during construction when still plastic, and have to be renewed every six to eight years at a cost of more than £50,000 ($100,000). In rain, ice and snow, friction meters towed at speed measure the runway's braking action and the information is relayed to pilots.

Runways cost up to £15 million ($30 million) to build and equip.

The runway centreline is marked by a broken white line. Distance-to-go markings, 500 ft apart, indicate the final 1,500 ft at either end.

Two-figure runway identification numbers, multiplied by ten, give centreline bearings to the nearest 10° measured from magnetic north. Parallel runways are marked "L" (left) or "R" (right). The letters are 30 ft long and ten ft wide.

Threshold markings

500 ft

500 ft

Porous friction asphalt

Pavement quality concrete (14 in)

Lean concrete (6 in)

Sub base

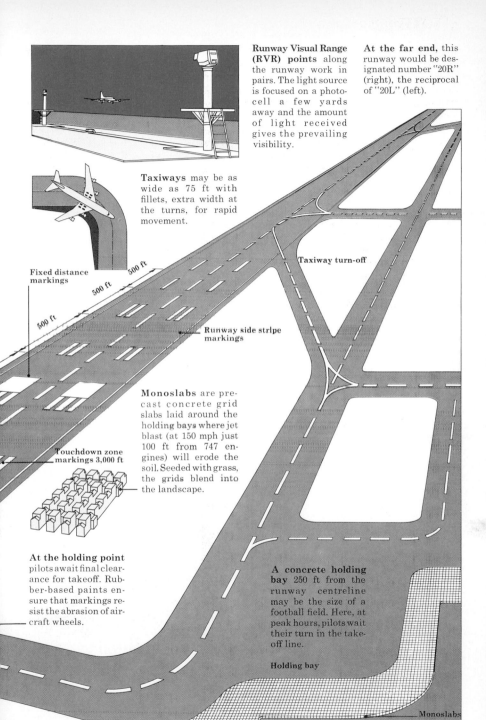

Runway Visual Range (RVR) points along the runway work in pairs. The light source is focused on a photocell a few yards away and the amount of light received gives the prevailing visibility.

At the far end, this runway would be designated number "20R" (right), the reciprocal of "20L" (left).

Taxiways may be as wide as 75 ft with fillets, extra width at the turns, for rapid movement.

Fixed distance markings

500 ft

500 ft

500 ft

500 ft

Taxiway turn-off

Runway side stripe markings

Monoslabs are precast concrete grid slabs laid around the holding bays where jet blast (at 150 mph just 100 ft from 747 engines) will erode the soil. Seeded with grass, the grids blend into the landscape.

Touchdown zone markings 3,000 ft

At the holding point pilots await final clearance for takeoff. Rubber-based paints ensure that markings resist the abrasion of aircraft wheels.

A concrete holding bay 250 ft from the runway centreline may be the size of a football field. Here, at peak hours, pilots wait their turn in the takeoff line.

Holding bay

Monoslabs

17

Ground control

The flight plan is put into operation from the moment the crew makes contact with air traffic control (ATC) by calling for permission to start up the engines using the appropriate radio frequency. Congestion along the route will mean a delay until there is space for the flight on the airways. The crew is given a "slot" time during which the aircraft must become airborne; if it misses the slot it has to request a new one, and this may mean further delay.

Changing radio frequency, the co-pilot calls the ground movement controller (GMC) to request taxi clearance. From a "nose-in" stand he asks for "push-back" clearance, but before issuing either, the controller must consider the effect of the man-oeuvre on an airfield crowded with aircraft already taxying, or about to begin. A simple push-back clearance may mean that another flight will have to be rerouted to a stand or runway, and one wrong decision can mean chaos.

On the taxiways, monitored by the GMC through binoculars — or perhaps on a ground radar screen — the captain is given airways clearance. At most airfields this is in the form of a Standard Instrument Departure (SID), and a "squawk". A SID is a routeing telling the crew which levels and airways to take to start the journey. SIDs include noise abatement routeings to avoid annoyance to communities lying beneath the flightpath.

The squawk is a four-figure number code which the crew sets on a transponder, a radio receiver that can transmit an incoming signal in a different form. It is displayed as an identification number beside the flight's "blip" on the air traffic controller's radar screen.

At the holding point the aircraft is transferred to an air traffic controller whose job is to guide the aircraft into the air.

6
"Silverbird five-o-one is cleared to line up and takeoff. Wind two-sixty at twelve"

5
"Silverbird five-o-one hold short of the runway"

Using the ground movement monitor board **above** the GMC monitors and controls the runway lights. The airfield surface movement indicator, the ASMI **right** depicts the airfield.

1	2	3	4	5	6	7	8	9
P1340		R330	B747/K		T410	EGLL	UG1	KJFK

BA1620 / BCN /12/ /T1330/ 5263 102

14 13 12 11 10

This **flight progress strip** gives all relevant flight plan details on departing aircraft.

1 **Expected flight plan departure time**

2 **Actual time the flight becomes airborne**

3 **Requested cruising level for the flight in hundreds of feet**

4 **Type of aircraft operating the flight**

5 **Type of transponder carried**

6 **True air speed filed on the flight plan, expressed in knots**

7 **Departure airport four-letter code**

8 **The airway the aircraft will be flying on**

9 **Destination airport code**

10 **ATC computer identification**

11 **Transponder identification code**

12 **Time (GMT) within which the aircraft must become airborne**

13 **SID: the departure routeing**

14 **Flight call sign and flight number**

7
"Silverbird five-o-one now climb to six thousand feet. Change to one-one-nine point three"

3
"Silverbird five-o-one requesting taxi clearance"
"Silverbird five-o-one taxi to runway two-eight left via the outer"

4
"Listen out on one-one-eight point seven for takeoff clearance"

2
"Silverbird five-o-one is cleared to the John F. Kennedy Airport. Your initial routeing is to Brecon twelve"

1
"Ground control from Silverbird five-o-one on stand Juliet one-five requesting start-up clearance"

Air traffic control assistants prepare a flight progress strip for every inbound and outbound aircraft **left**. Aircraft movements are monitored by air traffic controllers **above**.

Air traffic control

The sky around an airport is full of different kinds of aircraft flying at different speeds in different directions, crossing over each other at different heights. Keeping them separated is the main task of the air traffic (or tower) controller.

There is usually a minimum separation time of one minute between two aircraft of the same type taking off in different directions. If they are taking off in the same direction, the time gap is two minutes, and a light aircraft taking off behind a wide-bodied jet may be held back by ten minutes to avoid the turbulent air it leaves in its wake.

When a flight has been safely separated and is climbing away on its SID (Standard Instrument Departure) the air controller will transfer it to the care of the first radar sector (departure) controller for further climb clearance toward its cruising level.

Aircraft usually follow the airways, which are divided into three main altitude layers. The highest altitudes, from 45,000 to 75,000 feet (the limits of usable airspace) are used by supersonic and high-flying business jets; below them, subsonic airliners occupy the lower airways and the levels below are generally used by slower turboprops and propeller-driven aircraft. Many sectors are restricted to military use, and civil airways are channelled into the often narrow gaps between them.

Along the lower airways, means to avoid bottlenecks are essential in busy areas above the VOR navigation beacons where airways intersect, and this is provided by area controllers, not necessarily operating from airport ATC centres, but in charge of vast sectors of airspace. One covers the whole of Belgium. Area (or centre) controllers watch dozens of aircraft at once on huge radarscopes. The instructions they radio give pilots altitudes and headings (called "vectors") to fly to avoid aerial traffic jams.

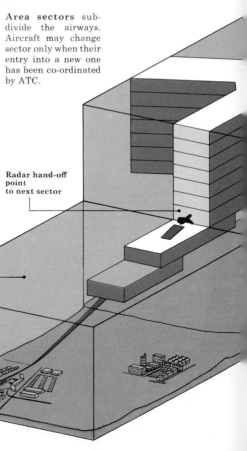

Area sectors sub-divide the airways. Aircraft may change sector only when their entry into a new one has been co-ordinated by ATC.

Radar hand-off point to next sector

The airport control zone is the airspace around the airport. Its limits, and the degree of control, vary with the importance of the airport, but large airports may have a control zone extending up to 20 miles around them. All aircraft arriving and departing, and those crossing the zone, are subject to local controls and regulations.

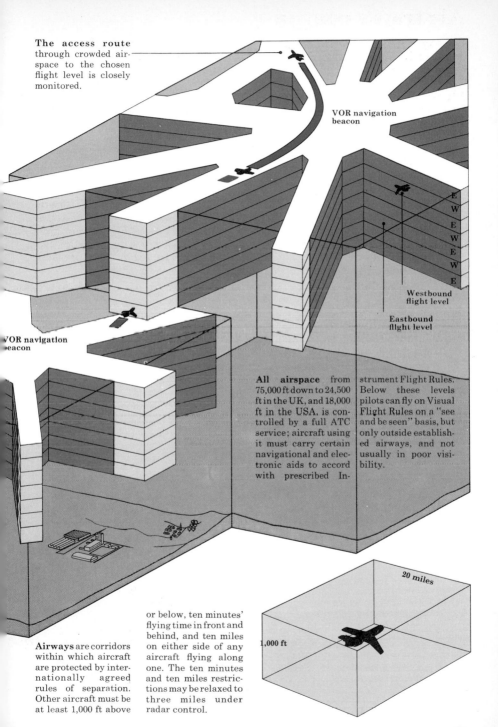

The access route through crowded airspace to the chosen flight level is closely monitored.

VOR navigation beacon

VOR navigation beacon

Westbound flight level

Eastbound flight level

E
W
E
W
E
W
E
W
E

All airspace from 75,000 ft down to 24,500 ft in the UK, and 18,000 ft in the USA, is controlled by a full ATC service; aircraft using it must carry certain navigational and electronic aids to accord with prescribed Instrument Flight Rules. Below these levels pilots can fly on Visual Flight Rules on a "see and be seen" basis, but only outside established airways, and not usually in poor visibility.

Airways are corridors within which aircraft are protected by internationally agreed rules of separation. Other aircraft must be at least 1,000 ft above or below, ten minutes' flying time in front and behind, and ten miles on either side of any aircraft flying along one. The ten minutes and ten miles restrictions may be relaxed to three miles under radar control.

20 miles

1,000 ft

The rules and regulations of air travel

From the routes that an airline is permitted to fly to passengers' legroom, from fares to air crews' training standards, from noise levels around an airport to charges for in-flight movies — all may be subject to regulation by national and international organizations. In the long run these groups have the same aim: the good of civil aviation. In the short term, aims may conflict.

In 1944, 52 nations signed the Chicago Convention, which established the International Civil Aviation Organization, ICAO. This UN agency recommends international standards (usually to do with safety) on technical and operational matters. For example, many countries are currently applying Annexe 16 of the Chicago Convention, regulating takeoff and landing noise, even though this is forcing the retirement of elderly, but airworthy, aircraft.

Freedoms of the air

The Chicago Convention defined "freedoms of the air", which are put into practice as a result of bilateral agreements between pairs of countries. The first freedom is the privilege of overflying a territory without landing. The second freedom is the privilege of making a "technical" landing, to refuel or repair. Most air traffic is third-freedom or fourth-freedom; that is, carried between two countries by the airlines of those countries. Under fifth-freedom rights a US airline, for example, can carry passengers from Rome to Bahrain on a New York–Rome–Bahrain flight.

Most bilateral agreements have been modelled on the 1946 Bermuda Agreement between the UK and the USA. This classic agreement was ended by the British in 1977. Ten minutes after its expiry, hectic bargaining resulted in a new agreement. For example, the UK gained the right to fly the direct London–San Fran-

cisco routes, while the USA was permitted to open direct services from certain American cities to London. The USA also agreed to limit the routes on which it would allow two US airlines to compete, and agreed to control the growth in numbers of seats offered. Bermuda-style agreements aim to give "fair and equal" commercial opportunities to the countries involved regardless of the strength of their airline industries.

IATA, the International Air Transport Association, is the trade association of airlines offering scheduled services; charter operators have their own association, IACA. Traditionally, not only fares but such things as baggage allowances, service, seat space and travel agents' commissions are decided by IATA. All recommendations must have the unanimous approval of IATA's 100 or more members, but are binding only when they have been incorporated into the bilateral inter-governmental treaties.

The Warsaw Convention

IATA also sets conditions of carriage for passengers and baggage, stemming from the Warsaw Convention of 1929. For most journeys the Convention limits an airline's liability for loss of or damage to checked-in baggage to about £5 or $9 per pound, or to £200 (about $400) for unchecked hand baggage. Higher figures apply on US flights.

Compensation for injury or death is also set by the Warsaw Convention at about £5,000 or £10,000 ($10,000 or $20,000) on flights wholly outside the US. But for any flight involving a stop in the US, an airline has a maximum liability of $75,000 (about £40,000) including legal costs. These figures represent a "strict" liability: the claimant does not have to prove negligence by the airline. Agreements such as the Hague Protocol and the Montreal Agreement increase the maximum liability of airlines.

It is impossible to generalize about the contract a passenger enters into in buying a ticket. Passengers willing to brave a legal struggle might be able to prove in a US court that an American-built aircraft was unsafe. The manufacturer is not protected by the international insurance conventions. Record awards were made after the world's worst in-flight accident, the 1974 crash in France of an American-built aircraft belonging to a Turkish airline. There were over 340 victims, of a score of nationalities. The dependants pursued a joint action in California against the aircraft manufacturers, one of their sub-contractors and the airline. After nine months of preliminary hearings the defendants, while not admitting liability, decided not to contest it. Four years after the accident, $26 million had been paid out, with 20 suits still undecided.

Price warfare

In 1977 the IATA system came under attack. Laker Airways, a non-IATA airline, started its Skytrain service between London and New York, offering minimal facilities and only a few hours' advance booking. It was licensed after years of opposition from the major airlines and after legal battles with the British government. Laker's competitors responded with reduced stand-by fares (for seats still unsold at the last minute) and more favourable long-term advance booking fares. Airlines watched the experiment anxiously. If prices were not controlled, the choice of flights could be greatly reduced.

US airlines had other reasons to worry; their internal fares were set by the Civil Aeronautics Board, and they had been allowed to take part in IATA price-setting through a special exemption from the American anti-trust laws. Under a new administra-

tion, the CAB threatened to lower internal fares and forbid the airlines to negotiate fares through IATA.

Air safety

The civil aviation board of the country in which an aircraft is registered (such as the Federal Aviation Administration (FAA) in the US and the Civil Aviation Authority (CAA) in the UK) fixes and enforces stringent air-safety standards for airlines and air crews. Manufacturers' tests are carried out to schedules laid down by the boards, and some may be repeated by them. The boards' pilots make tests in addition, to ensure that the aircraft operates safely in manoeuvres well beyond normal limits.

When the aircraft type has been awarded a certificate of airworthiness, each model must be certified as complying with the type specification. Samples of newly delivered machines are tested by the board, and in service they must be maintained by authorized procedures.

Consumer organizations, such as the Aviation Consumer Action Project in the US and the International Airline Passengers' Association speak for the passenger. Governments fund groups such as the UK Air Transport Users' Committee. IATA supports their efforts to persuade authorities to streamline immigration and Customs controls and improve airport service. They can also press the airlines to, say, compensate passengers denied seats because the airlines have overbooked.

Many safety regulations are promoted by the professional associations of air crews and air traffic controllers. Lobbying by IFALPA, the International Federation of Airline Pilots' Associations, has contributed to the adoption of many procedures and devices that are now commonplace, such as improved runway lighting and flight recorders.

Takeoff

When he pushes the throttles forward to begin takeoff, the pilot of a big jet has 100,000 thrust horsepower at his fingertips — the power a heavily laden Boeing 747 needs to accelerate to 180 mph so that the wings can haul its mass free of the ground.

The amount of lift an aircraft needs to generate for takeoff depends on its weight — the more the wings have to lift, the higher takeoff speed must be. All aircraft have a maximum takeoff weight, determined by the manufacturer, but other factors may limit the allowable takeoff weight. These have to be considered at the planning stage of the flight.

Most major airports have runways two or even three miles long to provide room for the speed-gathering needed for flight. If the runway is shorter, the aircraft's capacity for passengers, freight and fuel will be limited. Because wing lift depends on air density, jets at airports in the tropics, or at high altitudes where the air is thin, have to generate higher speeds for takeoff, and runways need to be correspondingly longer.

A pilot's logical choice for takeoff is a long runway aligned into the wind. Since lift depends on air speed, the bonus of a 20–mph headwind means that an aircraft need only accelerate to 160 mph to achieve an airspeed of 180 mph. Sometimes, though, a short runway, or one aligned across or even downwind, has to be used to direct departing traffic away from noise-sensitive communities.

Before liftoff, the pilot has to make the commitment to take off. The point

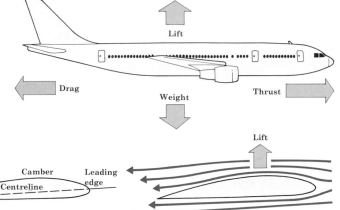

Four counterbalancing forces act on an aircraft in flight. *Lift*, generated by the airflow over the wings, overcomes *weight;* and *drag*, caused by the resistance of the air, opposes the *thrust* of the engines. When an aircraft is in straight and level flight thrust counterbalances drag, and lift counterbalances weight.

Lift

Drag

Weight

Thrust

Lift

Camber Leading edge

Trailing edge Centreline

The cross-section of a wing—the aerofoil—shows the curved shape that is the key to flight. A classic wing is cambered, or curved more sharply on the top than on the underside, and more strongly at the leading than at the trailing edge. Lift is generated only when the aerofoil moves forward, so a plane needs speed to fly. Its shape causes the streamlines, caused by its passage through the air, to be close together above the top surface, and farther apart below the bottom surface. The laws of physics state that fluid flow accelerates through a constriction, and where the velocity is high, the pressure is low. Above the wing there is constriction, high velocity and low pressure; below there is low velocity and high pressure. Low pressure above and high pressure below constitute an upward force, which is lift.

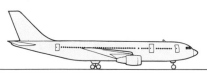

along the runway at which he makes this decision is determined by speed, and this is termed "decision speed" or "velocity one" (V_1). If an engine fails, or a warning sign or klaxon indicates a systems failure, he can abort the takeoff up to this point by applying maximum brakes, retarding throttles, raising wing spoilers and engaging reverse thrust. All rules governing takeoff performance are based on the assumption that an engine *will* fail at the worst possible moment; if this happens after V_1, he can still climb, fly a circuit and reroute to join the inbound traffic, and land again with one engine out.

At takeoff speed, the precalculated "velocity-rotate" (V_R) speed, he pulls back the control column, lifting the aircraft's nose until it rises to an

angle of about 12 degrees. The plane lifts off and the landing-gears are retracted by moving a single lever on the flight-deck console. Aircraft climb out at "velocity two"(V_2), the speed that produces the best angle of climb for the weight. But if a steep climbout after takeoff is necessary to avoid high ground, that can limit takeoff weight.

The airborne plane climbs steeply, the nose 15 to 20 degrees up, speed at V_2 plus about 10 mph, to 1,000 feet or more, where the power may have to be cut back for noise suppression. Speed increases and the wing flaps are retracted, often in stages. By the time the flaps are finally retracted, a 747 will be flying at around 280 mph, about 250 knots, the unit in which aircraft speeds are usually measured.

A **wing stalls** when its angle of attack is too great: the airflow over its surface becomes turbulent, and lift is lost. The greater the load on the wing (this increases in a turn) the higher the speed necessary to avoid stalling.

Lift increases as the angle of attack (the angle at which the aerofoil meets the airstream) increases. The upper airflow is forced to make a longer detour and the downward acceleration of the airflow increases.

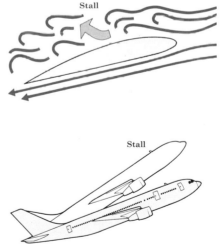

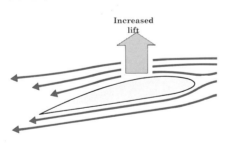

An airliner "rotates" to take off. When it has passed V_R, the optimum speed for takeoff, the pilot raises the nose; lift increases with angle of attack, overcoming the aircraft's weight.

The angle of climb is a compromise between conflicting requirements. The noise disturbance to nearby communities is least when an aircraft climbs steeply, but fuel consumption and the risk of a stall are least when the climb is shallow. The control column vibrates vigorously to alert the pilot if a stall is imminent.

Flight

A railway locomotive has one freedom of motion. Directed by its track, it can only go forward or backward. A car, under the direction of its driver, has two freedoms of motion, it can also turn left or right. But an aircraft has three freedoms of motion, it can be made to climb or dive.

Within each of the three freedoms of motion, an aircraft has two others. It can pitch nose-up or down about an imaginary line stretching from wing-tip to wing-tip — its lateral axis. It can roll about a line from nose to tail — the longitudinal axis; and it can

yaw, left or right, about the vertical axis.

The fuselage and wings alone would, like a dart without flights, be too unstable to fly. An aircraft has to be stabilized about its three axes of rotation by adding a tailplane (horizontal stabilizer) for pitch, a fin (vertical stabilizer) for yaw, and by setting the wings at a positive dihedral angle (an angle raised from the horizontal plane) for roll.

Control about each axis is provided by manipulating hinged control surfaces on the aircraft. Elevators on the

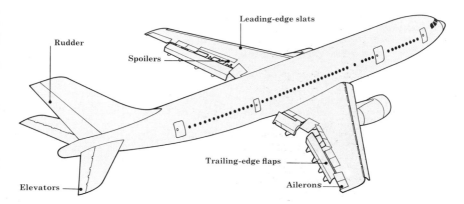

Leading-edge slats

Rudder

Spoilers

Trailing-edge flaps

Elevators

Ailerons

The elevators are lowered or raised by moving the control yoke forward or backward to dive or climb.

To move the rudder left or right, the pilot depresses corresponding left or right rudder pedals at his feet.

The ailerons are moved by turning the control yoke left to cause a roll to the left, and vice versa.

The area and camber of the wings increase when leading – and trailing-edge slats or flaps are deployed.

Straight wings give good lift at low speeds so the flaps and slats are simple, but they produce excessive drag at high speeds.

Sweptback wings cause minimum drag at high speeds, but they need complex flaps and slats for lift at low speeds.

Delta wings, streamlined for supersonic speeds, have elevons, combined elevators and ailerons, on the trailing edges.

When an aircraft changes speed, lift alters and the angle of attack must be changed to compensate, by adjusting the elevators. The pilot uses a "trimming" system to take the strain of holding them against the airflow. This is done by operating tabs on the elevators, which use the force of the airflow to hold the elevators in position.

tailplane control pitch. Raising them causes a down-load on the tailplane, which drops, and the nose pitches up; the reverse happens if they are lowered.

The rudder controls yaw exactly like the rudder on a boat. Swinging it to the right forces the tail left and the plane yaws to the right; swinging it left has the opposite effect.

The ailerons are moved in opposite senses to make the plane roll. Lift is lost on the wing where the aileron is raised, but it increases on the side where the lowered aileron increases the camber of the wing.

On modern jets almost the entire leading and trailing edges are taken up by lift-increasing flaps and slats for takeoff and landing. Ailerons are smaller than on the older jets, and they are aided by spoilers mounted on the tops of the wings. When a spoiler is raised, the wing on that side drops. When both are raised, overall lift falls and drag increases, so the aircraft descends.

Like a bicycle, an aircraft turns by banking. To turn left, the pilot deflects the ailerons so that the left aileron goes up to make the left wing incline downward, and the right aileron goes down to make the right wing tilt up. The lift force is pulled inward, away from the vertical. The elevator, tilted upward slightly, increases the down-load on the tail. Centrifugal force plays a counter-balancing role, pulling the aircraft outward, to the right; held in equilibrium, the aircraft turns smoothly.

The rudder plays a secondary role. During a turn it is used to prevent yawing. If a pilot tries to turn with the rudder alone, centrifugal force makes the aircraft skid out sideways. Often the rudder is controlled in flight by one or more automatic yaw dampers, robot devices which, together with many others, handle corrections on modern airliners.

As an aircraft approaches higher speeds, close to the speed of sound the trim will be changed automatically to keep the fuselage level. This compensates for a backward movement of the lift forces as shockwaves develop.

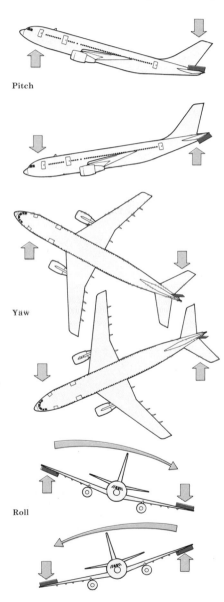

Pitch

Yaw

Roll

Aircraft design

Aircraft in a variety of shapes took to the air after World War I. Some were more efficient than others, but their speed, around 90 mph, was not too testing of their design and structure. Gradually, as cantilever monoplanes proved their efficiency, less economical designs were discarded, and aircraft took on a more stereotyped look. The last important piston-engined airliners, the Lockheed Constellation (1943) and the Douglas DC–6 (1946) were basically similar.

In 1954 the celebrated Boeing 707 established a basic configuration for the four-engined jetliner and serves to illustrate the classic shape. From a distance it looks just like its close rival, the Douglas DC–8.

The classic sweptback shape enables jets to fly up to a speed of Mach 0.8 (about 550 mph) and to slow down, using complex flaps and slats, to speeds safe for takeoff and landing. The cruising speed is unlikely to be surpassed by airliners designed for subsonic flight; the extra strength and weight a faster jet would need to resist the onset of shockwaves caused by flying close to the speed of sound — around 660 mph — would be reflected in its running costs.

The 707 needed four turbojets to travel intercontinental distances. If one or even two engines failed, the plane could still fly. But today's turbofan engines are so powerful and reliable that four may not be justified

Classic jet wings are swept back at an angle of around 35° so they can reach Mach 0.8 (about 550 mph) before drag becomes excessive. Much less sweepback would slow them down, and more may cause flutter at speed and reduce lift on landing and takeoff.

Wings as thin as 7% of their chord, or width from leading to trailing edge, bend noticeably up and down

in flight. This is normal; their high elasticity smooths out the worst of the bumps in turbulent conditions.

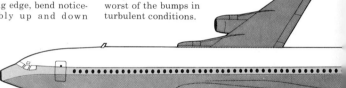

The classic tricycle landing-gear, still the most common configuration, consists of a dual-wheel nose gear and two dual-tandem wheel main gears. To minimize drag each platform or bogie bearing four main landing-gear wheels is retracted inward after takeoff into an unpressurized well in the lower fuselage. The nose gear can be steered up to 60° to either side. It retracts forward into a well beneath the flight deck.

The fuselage tube has a constant diameter over most of its length, making it cheap and easy to produce in quantity because all the bulkheads and frames are the same shape and size. It can be made longer or shorter by adding or subtracting

"plugs"—extra sections—as the customers and the traffic require. The cabins of high-flying jets are pressurized up to more than three times the pressure of the thin air outside.

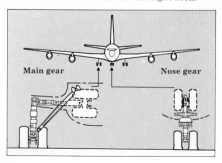

Main gear   Nose gear

in future airliners. The newest medium-range airliners have two engines, and medium and long-range planes have three.

In 1955 the Caravelle appeared with two engines attached to the rear of the fuselage. This configuration became another classic formula. The bow-wave, the region of disturbed air around aircraft engines, could damage a tailplane (stabilizer) if the engines were located near it, so tailplanes of rear-engined aircraft are mounted above the jets, often above the fins (horizontal stabilizers).

The most noticeable innovation in recent years has been in the size of subsonic jets, but the Boeing 747 looks like a scaled-up version of the trend-setting 707, and designers of other wide-bodied jets have not deviated from the classic norm.

The long narrow delta shape of supersonic aircraft is an example of aesthetic functionalism, an extreme form of streamlining that is essential to minimize drag. Experience in supersonic flight is modifying subsonic aircraft design. The Airbus, perhaps the most advanced subsonic airliner in use, has wings designed so that lift is spread along their breadths. They give a better performance, with less sweepback, at high and low speeds.

But it is unlikely that the shape of subsonic aircraft will change radically in the foreseeable future.

The tailplane and fins (the stabilizers) are, in effect, miniature wings. They are swept back to minimize drag in flight.

Wings set low on the fuselage allow the wing-mounted landing-gears to be shorter than on high-wing aircraft, and relatively lightweight.

The cross-section is an egg-shape in which all interior space can be used both for seats and cargo. The floor beams in tension take the pressure loads.

Engines in pods help to improve the lift of the wings. Mounted on thin pylons ahead of and just below them, they are accessible for servicing from the ground, and a sudden fracture of part of an engine will not damage the vital wing structure. Together they act as a balance preventing flutter at high speeds, and so reduce the need for stiffening, whose weight would lower the payload or range.

The introduction of the Boeing 707 began a decade of intense competition among manufacturers. Boeing and McDonnell Douglas produced "families" of airliners of varying lengths, all designed to fly at around 40,000 ft high in the stratosphere (where the thin air offers less resistance, reducing fuel consumption). The McDonnell Douglas DC-9 had several "stretched" versions of the original model, the DC-9-10.

"Stretched" versions

1954: Boeing 707-120 (145 ft 1 in)

1959: Boeing 707-320B (152 ft 11 in)

1960: McDonnell Douglas DC-8 Series 50 (150 ft 6 in)

1966: McDonnell Douglas DC-8 Super 60 (187 ft 5 in)

1965: McDonnell Douglas DC-9 Series 10 (104 ft 4¾ in)

1979: McDonnell Douglas DC-9 Super 80 (147 ft 10 in)

Aircraft structure

A modern airliner flies more hours in one year than pre-World War II aircraft flew in their entire lifetime. The Junkers G.38, the "Jumbo" of the thirties, carried 34 passengers; the Boeing 747 carries 500 and its airframe has to withstand the stresses of takeoff and landing with loads 16 times as great. A modern airframe has to take the strains of flying through turbulence, and of pressurization to some nine pounds per square inch at cruising height, as well as those of normal flight and landing.

An aircraft's strength lies in its monocoque construction: though reinforced by a supporting frame, the skin takes most of the flight loads.

Aircraft are subject to more extreme changes in temperature than any other form of transport. An hour or so in the hot sun of the tropics can heat an airframe to over 120 degrees Fahrenheit, yet within 30 minutes of takeoff it will be cruising at high altitudes where the temperature may be 100 degrees below freezing. Aluminium-copper alloys are the lightest materials able to stand up to this treatment. They account for more than 95 per cent of the structure of most modern jetliners. Highly-stressed parts such as the landing-gear are made of forged steel whose extra weight is more than offset by its greater strength. A 747 making a hard landing will impose upon them three times its 400-ton loaded weight.

Parallel frames of aluminium alloy, like large hoops, define the shape of the fuselage cross-section. They are held in place by long strips or stringers which run along the length of the fuselage. A skin of light alloy, $\frac{1}{16}$ in to $\frac{1}{8}$ in thick, is stretched around each section and the floor is bolted to the frame. Here, the lower centre fuselage of a Trident is under construction.

The centre section of the aircraft, where the wing passes through the fuselage, is the strongest part of any airliner. Here the weight of the entire fuselage is transferred to the wing during flight. Long metal spars stretching from one wing-tip to the other take the bending loads in flight, and on the ground the weight of the whole plane is channelled down to the landing-gear.

Airframes are as lean as they can safely be. So that aircraft can take off with as big a profit-making load as possible, all excess weight is pared away with computerized precision. Wing skins are chemically milled in acid baths to exactly predetermined strength and weight requirements; control surfaces are often stiffened with light honeycomb structuring and floors are based on strong metal frames. CFRP (carbon-fibre reinforced plastic) is a new material often used in Boeing 747 floor beams because it is much lighter than the alternatives. Composite materials of glass, carbon or graphite filaments in an adhesive matrix are superlatively light, strong and heat-resistant, and may prove themselves in the future.

Today's airliners fly ten to 12 hours a day for 20 years or more. The stresses produced by continual movement, and even intense noise, cause fatigue, the cracking and breaking that occurs in metals under constant flexure. Fatigue is an aging process that cannot be avoided, but weak points such as holes and joins can be reduced by using adhesives instead of rivets and bolts, and by casting wing skins in gigantic panels. Fatigue can start from a scratch, so surfaces are polished and sharp corners rounded off. Safe limits are set to the lives of susceptible components, and frequent testing and replacement ensure that catastrophes no longer happen.

The Airbus is built in segments by several companies located hundreds of miles apart. Its assembly in Toulouse, shown here, takes just a few weeks.

Each Airbus wing has three upper and three lower skin sections. They are machined out of huge slabs of 2 in-thick aluminium-copper alloy. Milling processes remove most of the metal leaving a sheet tapering to about $\frac{1}{16}$ in thick with integral strengthening corrugations as deep as the original slab. These are laid over a framework of ribs and spars which give shape.

Propellers

In the gradual invention of the flying machine one of the most important advances was to separate lift from propulsion. Only when flapping wings had been discarded could the flying machine be made to work. A rigid wing gives lift, and propulsion is effected by accelerating an airflow backward. Until the jet era, this was done with a propeller.

The propeller is simply a rotating wing. It generates lift exactly as a wing does, but the blades direct the air backward so lift becomes propulsive thrust. The faster it turns, the greater the thrust. A propeller would have the effect of rotating the fuselage and wings in the opposite direction. The aircraft's shape and the use of the control surfaces counter this

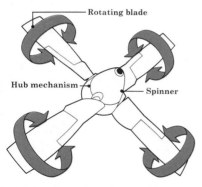

Rotating blade

Hub mechanism

Spinner

The blades of a variable-pitch propeller are adjusted—usually hydraulically—to any chosen angle by the hub mechanism, which is covered by a streamlined spinner. If an engine fails, the propeller is feathered (turned edge-on to the air) to minimize drag.

torque reaction, and some twin-engined aircraft have handed (counter-spinning) propellers.

The propeller's pitch — the angle of its blades to the airflow — decreases from root to tip so that it acts through the air as a screw through wood. The pitch is a measure of the distance it will travel through the air in one revolution. Like the thread of a screw the blade pitch may be set fine for takeoff, matching a fast-running propeller, and can be reset to coarse for cruising speed, matching a slow-running propeller.

Fixed-pitch propellers are effective at one forward speed, but constant-speed propellers adjust pitch automatically. They keep the engine rpm at a constant-speed setting, permitting it to be used at its most efficient (and economical) speed at all stages of the flight and, twisted into reverse pitch on landing, act as a brake.

Fast-running propellers are noisy, so modern propellers are being made to run more slowly to reduce noise. To maintain the same thrust they are made longer, as on the DHC Dash-7, or more blades are added, as on the Shorts 330. The ducted propulsor, pioneered by Dowty-Rotol in the UK but not yet in airline service, has many short blades surrounded by a streamlined duct, and is quieter than any conventional propeller. Glass fibre, steel sheet, alloys and compressed wood veneers have replaced hardwood in propellor construction.

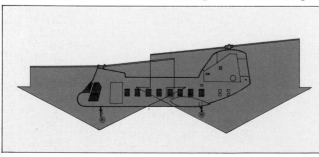

Helicopter rotors are giant propellers set along a vertical axis. Lift is generated by increasing the pitch of the moving blades. To move forward, the rotor is tilted forward so that lift is inclined away from the vertical. A counter-spinning rotor counters the torque reaction.

Piston engines and turbojets

Nineteenth-century airships and would-be planes had propellers driven by steam, compressed air or electricity, but every *successful* airliner has had one or more internal-combustion engines. A tiny fraction have had diesel engines, but almost all use the Otto-cycle (four-stroke piston engine) or the gas turbine.

Aviation piston engines are similar to car engines, but larger and more powerful — usually with six or eight cylinders, air-cooled and arranged in horizontally opposed pairs.

Each pair drives one crankpin, via two connecting rods, and the front of the crankshaft is geared down to a slower-running propeller. The rear end of the crankshaft drives accessories and may be geared up to a fast-running supercharger which pumps extra air (to burn more fuel) into the engine as the aircraft climbs into thinner atmosphere; alternatively there may be a turbocharger, a supercharger driven by a small turbine spun at high speed by the white-hot exhaust gas.

Fuel — gasoline (petrol) — is dyed different colours according to type, and the type varies from top-grade motor fuel in light aircraft, up to 115/145 octane in bigger engines. Only small aircraft, and those needing tough low-speed propulsion at low altitudes, for agricultural work and fire-fighting, still have piston engines.

In 1939 the turbojet brought an entirely new method of propulsion. In this engine, air is converted, by burning fuel, into a blast of hot gas moving at high velocity.

The core of a gas-turbine engine works quite simply: a compressor sucks in air, compresses it and delivers it to a combustion chamber. Kerosene-type fuel is sprayed in and burned to convert the high-pressure airflow into a column of white-hot gas. Fixed, curved blades direct this gas onto the blades of a turbine rotor, spinning it like a windmill. The turbine converts the energy in the gas flow into shaft-power, which drives the compressor. In a turbojet it extracts just enough power to drive the compressor while the rest of the high-velocity gas roars out of the exhaust nozzle to jet-propel the plane.

The axial compressor of a turbojet increases pressure by forcing air through rows of blades like small wings rotating between fixed stators.

Combustion takes place in separate flame tubes or alternatively, in an annular (ring-like) chamber encircling a smaller and lighter engine.

Nozzles are profiled to extract maximum thrust from exhaust gases. For vertical takeoff they swivel downward to convert thrust into lift.

In the Comet, the first jet airliner, **above** engines were in the wing roots: on later jets they were mounted below the wings or on the rear fuselage.

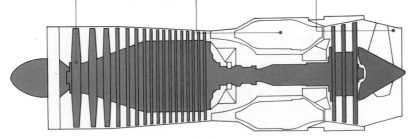

Turboprops

In a turboprop engine, the main thrust comes from the propeller and only a small proportion from the jet exhaust. A turboprop handles a larger airflow than any other aircraft engine and so (at low speeds) generates the largest thrust for any given rate of fuel consumption. But, as forward speed increases, thrust falls away until, at about 450 mph, propeller efficiency is seriously impaired as the blade tips approach the speed of sound. A turbojet, therefore, is more suitable at higher speeds.

In 1945, Rolls-Royce made a turboprop by scaling up the supercharger of a piston engine to form the compressor, and adding a combustion chamber, turbine and gearbox. This was the Dart engine and it is still being produced 30 years later. Four Darts were used in the first turboprop airliner, the Vickers Viscount, which flew a year earlier than the turbojet-powered Comet (1948), but did not enter airline service until 1953.

Many types of helicopter are powered by a turboshaft engine, which is essentially a turboprop minus the propeller. The horizontal output shaft spins at about 6,000 rpm, as in a turboprop. Through a gearbox on the airframe, the shaft turns the main rotor at about 200 to 300 rpm.

The Hawker Siddeley 748 is powered by twin Rolls-Royce Dart turboprops.

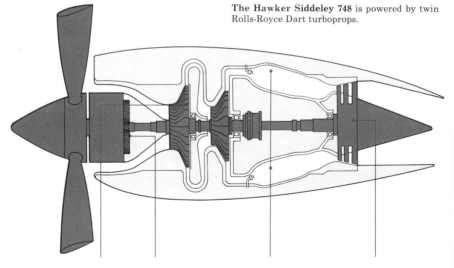

This turboprop engine, the Rolls-Royce Dart, uses a centrifugal compressor which accepts air at the centre and flings it off at high speed to compress it. Replaced by axial compressors in modern turboprop airliners, it is still used in light aircraft.

Turboprop turbines have more stages than those in turbojets, to extract enough energy from the gas flow to drive both compressor and propeller via a reduction gearbox. Compared to the thrust from the propeller, the exhaust gas plays a negligible part.

Separate flame tubes are often replaced by annular combustion chambers, some located at the back of the engines to reverse the air/gas flow. A turbine can then be conveniently placed next to the gearbox and propeller, making a more compact engine.

The extra stages on the turbine have developed into a second turbine, rotating independently of the first on a concentric shaft to drive propellers separately from the compressor. This is a common arrangement and is called a free-turbine turboprop.

Turbofans

Modern airliners use turbofan engines, which incorporate the best features of the turbojet and turboprop. Early turbofans, called by-pass jet engines, were simply turbojets with oversize blades in the first few stages of the compressor. The surplus air compressed by the tips of these blades was ducted round the rest of the engine — "by-passing" it — and discharged through the jet pipe. The resultant slowing-down of the final jet did not reduce power because it was compensated by the increased volume of airflow. But, in comparison with an ordinary turbojet (or "straight jet", as it became known) there were other vital reductions in fuel consumption and, most important, noise. Since noise varies as the fourth power of jet speed (twice the speed of the jet means 16 times the noise), ways had to be found to quieten the jets. Early turbojets experimented with special nozzles — some were shaped like the petals of a flower, others had as many as 21 pipes to mix the jet with the atmosphere quickly. But no method was as effective as the high by-pass ratio turbofan. This engine has revolutionized air transport, dramatically reducing airline fuel bills and noise, with no loss in aircraft operating speeds.

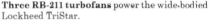

Three RB-211 turbofans power the wide-bodied Lockheed TriStar.

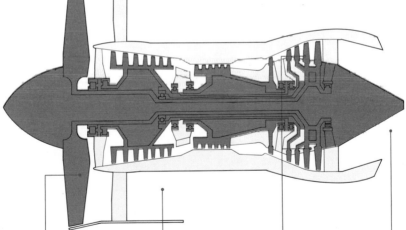

The large-diameter fan, located at the front in a profiled duct, acts like a propeller to supercharge the core engine on the one hand, and to by-pass air around it on the other. Future fans may well have variable-pitch and reverse-pitch blades.

Early by-pass engines had a by-pass ratio of less than one (the air by-passed around the core was less than the flow through it). Today's turbofans have by-pass ratios of between four and seven — they by-pass four to seven times the core airflow.

The turbine, powered by the small fraction of airflow passing through the core, drives the fan. In some smaller turbo-fans, the turbine is so tiny and the fan relatively so large that it has to be coupled via a gearbox, just as the turbine is in turboprop engines.

The colossal airflow handled by wide-bodied airliners such as the 747 may approach a ton per second for each engine — enough to fill about twenty average living-rooms. Virtually all of this is discharged as a giant, relatively slow-moving propulsive jet.

Supersonic aircraft

Most jets cruise at a subsonic speed of 550 mph, about 50 mph slower than the world land speed record, and slower than the speed of sound in the surrounding air. Their passage through the air causes a disturbance which sends out pressure waves in all directions, like ripples in a pond, though the waves are spheres, not rings.

The relatively small pressure differences transmitted ahead of a plane moving at subsonic speed act as warning signals to the air in front, giving the molecules time to move out of the way and flow smoothly round the wings and tail.

Supersonic aircraft cruise at the muzzle velocity of a .303 rifle bullet. As they approach the speed of sound, Mach 1, the warning signals become shorter. The molecules have less time to move out of the way as the plane catches up on the pressure waves ahead, compressing them until at Mach 1 (around 660 mph at 50,000 feet) they form into a vertical wave, a shockwave, more violent than a sound wave. Its pressure rises instantaneously, and near the source it sounds like the crack of a whip.

As the aircraft accelerates beyond Mach 1, the shockwave forms a cone, with the aircraft at the vertex, "towing" it along. Because supersonic transports (SSTs) travel faster than sound only at high altitudes, the shockwave cone has time to expand enormously before it reaches the ground, where it is weak enough to be heard as a dull boom. Even so, many people are concerned that shockwaves may damage human ears or even buildings. There is usually more than one shockwave in the cone, one from the nose and another from the tail 200 feet farther back, giving a double boom, or continuous air disturbance sounding like thunder or a distant explosion.

The fuselage of an SST is streamlined to a point at the nose, and the

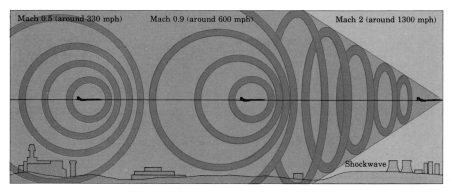

Mach 0.5 (around 330 mph)   Mach 0.9 (around 600 mph)   Mach 2 (around 1300 mph)

Shockwave

The boom carpet is the strip of ground over which the audible part of the shockwave cone passes. It may be 40 miles wide, so SSTs are allowed to go supersonic only over seas and thinly populated areas, although Tu-144 flights over the USSR are unrestricted.

SSTs are designed with a thin-sectioned, long, slender fuselage and slim delta wings to fit inside the shockwave cone, causing least air resistance and giving maximum ease of handling for pilots and the smoothest possible ride for the passengers.

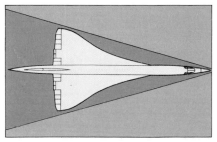

slender delta wings are very long, reaching from nose to tail. The sharp leading edge is so shaped that at takeoff or landing the air swirls over it to create an extremely powerful vortex (a writhing column of air) which gives increased lift. Passenger windows are smaller than usual to reduce the possibility of fatigue in the highly pressurized cabin.

Passengers are not aware of transonic acceleration, and since supersonic cruise at Mach 2 (over 1,300 mph) takes place at a height of 50,000 feet, the ground seems to go by at the normal speed. But from a supersonic aircraft the clouds look very, very far below. Identifiable features on the ground look tiny and passengers can see a fantastic distance. The sky is a blackish-violet shade, and the horizon is obviously slightly curved.

Supersonic cruise

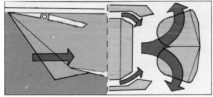

Reverse thrust

The engines, called powerplants because of their complexity, are mounted in easily-accessible nacelles or casings under the wings. To increase the airflow to the engine, and so give extra thrust for takeoff and transonic acceleration, ramps in the roof of the huge air intakes automatically lift up and a spill door opens. The front ramp closes to achieve normal thrust when the plane is cruising at supersonic speeds.

The exhaust assembly alters in area and profile, in time with the engine, to accommodate the aircraft's wide speed range. Two variable geometry "clamshell buckets" on the rear of the powerplant are partly closed at takeoff, "fishtailing" or squashing the jet stream to reduce noise. They open fully in normal flight but, shut tight, they act as thrust reversers on landing to slow the aircraft down as rapidly as possible.

Rolls-Royce Olympus turbojet engine

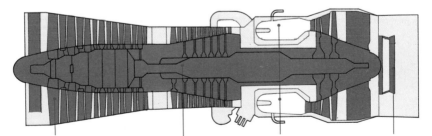

Concorde's Olympus two spool turbojet engine preceded Concorde by more than 20 years. It broke the world altitude record in 1953. Heat-resistant nickel-based alloys and titanium, which will withstand fierce heat, ice and bird strike, are used in the engine's manufacture.	**The two spools** act like two engines in one. The low- and high-pressure compressors raise the temperature of the intake air so that less fuel is needed to generate up to 40,000 lb of thrust (equal to the horsepower of 10,000 small cars), four times that of the first Olympus.	**The annular (ring-like) combustion chamber** was an improvement on earlier variants. Together with a new vaporizing fuel injector system, it burns the fuel/air mixture so completely that Concorde is one of the most smoke-free aircraft in present-day service with airlines.	**An afterburner** or re-heat system is a thrust-booster. Placed between the turbine and the exhaust nozzles, it gives extra thrust for takeoff, and to overcome air resistance on transonic acceleration, by igniting fuel in the jet pipe's hot exhaust gases. The system is costly in fuel.

37

Rotorcraft

Helicopters can take off and land vertically on a space little bigger than the diameter of their own rotors. Their value, therefore, is in their ability to operate from conveniently small heliports, saving journeys to and from out-of-town airports.

But helicopters will never replace airliners for long-distance travel because their speed is limited to below 250 mph, at which speed the rotor tips are whirling round at almost 500 mph. Any faster and they approach the speed of sound, overstressing the blades. And helicopters are short-haul vehicles. Most of the energy, and fuel consumed, is used for lift; an airliner with the same engines could travel twice the distance at more than twice the speed for the same fuel consumption.

A rotating-wing aircraft is an old idea only recently developed by complex engineering. Leonardo da Vinci designed a starched-linen *helixpteron* (literally "screw-wing") in 1490, but made no allowance for torque reaction, a force familiar to anyone who has felt an electric drill turning in the opposite direction to the spinning motor. This force is neutralized in modern helicopters by the side thrust of a tail rotor (whose variable-pitch blades also permit it to be used as a rudder) or by two counterspinning main rotors.

Igor Sikorsky, a Russian-born American, designed and produced the first practical helicopter in 1939. The versatile Sikorsky S-61 is now produced in various military and civil versions. It flies at an average speed of 138 mph over a range of 450 miles.

The rotor head revolves at a virtually constant speed of just over 200 rpm (just over three turns a second).

Two turboshaft engines drive both main and tail rotors; only a small amount of energy is used for thrust.

The universally-mounted swashplate can be tilted forward, causing the rotor plane to tilt. The blade advancing through the forward sector of the rotor disc reduces pitch and flies low, and then increases pitch and flies high through the rear sector. This effectively tilts the whole rotor, and so moves the aircraft in the direction the pilot wants to fly.

The cockpit is similar to that of a fixed-wing aircraft, but the pilot sits on the right.

The cabin, in elongated passenger versions, can seat up to 28. S-61s are often used for inter-city terminal connections.

A freight compartment in the hull can be used for baggage. All-cargo versions carry over 6,000 lb.

The most complex aerodynamic problems of rotorcraft were solved by a Spanish engineer, Juan de la Cierva, who designed the first autogyro. It looked like a propeller-driven monoplane topped by a large rotor. An autogyro's rotor is set in motion by the engine, but continues to turn in the air by the action of the slipstream through the blades, employing the principle Cierva called autorotation. Similarly, if the power supply of a helicopter fails completely, it will not stall. When the angles of pitch of the rotor blades are reduced to a minimum, aerodynamic forces maintain their rotation in the same way as a falling sycamore seed spins gently to the ground.

A helicopter cockpit has two main controls. The floor-mounted collective pitch lever increases the pitch of all the blades simultaneously to provide vertical control. The machine climbs when the angle of pitch of the blades is increased and more engine power is applied to overcome the extra drag created. The cyclic pitch stick, the equivalent of the airliner pilot's control stick, can vary the angles of pitch of the rotor blades alternately as they pass round the rotor disc. The alternating pitch change tilts the rotor plane in whichever direction the stick is pushed to move the helicopter forward, backward or sideways.

A fixed tailplane, mounted on the tail boom, gives stability in forward flight.

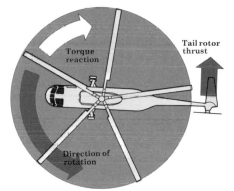

A swashplate transfers control lever movements to the rotor head. Its upper part revolves with the head, tilting the rotor.

The pitch change hinge gives control of the rotor in flight by allowing the blades to be twisted, to increase or decrease their angle to the horizontal. Together with the flapping hinge which allows the blades to rise and fall, and the drag hinge on which they can move forward and backward slightly, it forms a kind of universal joint to give the blades free motion about three axes.

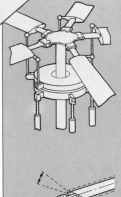

The rotors generate and also control lift. In hovering flight, the speed of the main rotor and the angle of pitch of its blades combine to direct a slipstream downward that exactly balances the aircraft's weight. The tail rotor counteracts torque, the tendency of the fuselage to rotate in the opposite direction to the main rotor.

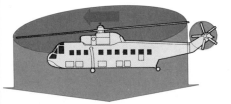

To move forward, the rotor is tilted forward. Most of the airflow is directed downward to give lift, but some is directed backward. Its reaction moves the helicopter forward.

Hovercraft

In 1954 an experiment with coffee cans finally solved a stubborn engineering problem: how to overcome the resistance that water imposes on the speed of ships. Christopher Cockerell, a British electronics engineer, forced air with a vacuum cleaner through a simple plenum ("full") chamber, made from two cans, to create an annular jet, and tried the idea out on a punt and a motor launch before producing the first successful air-cushion vehicle (ACV).

This had a hoverheight of less than two inches; the flexible skirt, which retains air to make a deeper cushion, was the vital development that made the hovercraft practicable.

The hovercraft is amphibious, able to ride over waves, ice, sand, mud and marsh. It is not built to negotiate slopes, and steering, effected by moving the fins and pylons to alter the thrust of the propellers mounted on top of them, can be unwieldy, especially in crosswinds. But hovercraft cruise at around 70 knots (80 mph), twice the speed of passenger ships, and need no special harbours.

Gigantic new hovercraft can accommodate 400 passengers, and over 60 vehicles. The French Sedam N500 has three engines for propulsion and two for lift, and no transmission, reducing vibration and noise. Lift is created by air directed down many "miniskirts", each having its own air supply, but under unified control, and this may give them greater resistance to crosswinds.

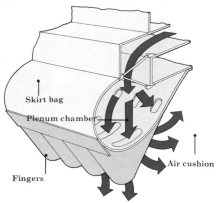

Skirt bag

Plenum chamber

Air cushion

Fingers

Flexible skirts make the hovercraft amphibious, acting as giant shock absorbers enabling the craft to clear obstacles up to 8 ft high. They cushion the impact of waves before it is transmitted to the hull, so high speeds can be maintained in rough seas.

The bag, or upper part of the skirt, is made up of segments. The flexible extensions, or fingers, attached to these, extend and contract with the undulations of the surface, providing an air seal.

The SRN4 is powered by four turbine engines **1**. The airflow from the intakes **2** is pumped by lift-fans **3** into an expandable plenum chamber **4**, and is fed through jets which direct it inward to form the air cushion **5** and downward for stability.

40

Seaplanes, skiplanes and flying boats

Encouraged by the vast amount of open water available for natural runways, the development of seaplanes began soon after the first successful land flights. Seaplanes have two major advantages over wheeled aircraft: they take off from, and land on, water and need no specially prepared landing site; small seaplanes need only 500 yards or less of unobstructed water. During the 1930s these aircraft were the world's fastest machines.

Seaplanes present unique design problems. Not only must they be able to float on water, but they must also be able to skim along the surface at high speed. They are supported on floats (and are often called float-planes) which are much heavier and cause greater drag than wheels because they cannot be neatly retracted. Hydroskis, light retractable surfaces like waterskis, have solved some of the problems of lift and drag.

Skiplanes are designed specifically for landing on snow and need no special landing strip. They have no brakes, but in mountainous areas they usually land on upward slopes. They "weathercock" in wind, making steering a highly skilled technique.

Flying boats, used extensively in the 1930s and still found on some inter-island airline services, have large hulls which create extra drag, but are necessary to keep the wings and propellers clear of the water. The hulls are surmounted by wings with floats at the ends.

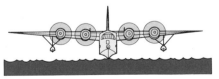

Floats are like miniature boat hulls, aerodynamically designed to give lift. Retractable wheels make this DHC-2 Beaver amphibious.

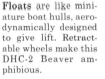

Amphibious flying boats, such as the Grumman Mallard left are still used in the Americas. Like ships, flying boats are designed so that the centre of gravity is below the centre of buoyancy. The hull bottom is V-shaped above to push the water downward and outward and improve lift. It is stepped upward at the rear, forming a platform (the "step") which carries the aircraft's weight as it planes—skims over the water, prior to liftoff. The floats provide stability during taxying.

The flight deck

Inside the flight deck there is calm. The engines can only just be heard and the sensation of movement comes mostly from the sound of air round the nose of the aircraft. Above the cloud layers, the view is far-ranging but dazzling, particularly when flying into the sun. At high altitudes other aircraft are hard to distinguish against the bright light and dark blue of the stratosphere.

The flight deck is designed to allow both pilots to reach all the essential controls and switches without moving from their seats. There may be up to 150 instruments, some with digital readouts, most with the familiar circular dial, but not all have to be watched at once. Pilots rarely concentrate on one particular instrument, but scan them all at intervals. Immediately in front of each pilot is the

Basic T, aviation's standard arrangement of the four principal readings, showing speed, height, attitude and heading. The instruments are arranged so that the most important are closest to the pilot.

Aviation has its traditions. In the early years, influenced by the keep-right rules of the road and at sea, aircraft also kept right on the airways. For ease of visibility captains chose to sit on the left.

All the primary instruments and controls are duplicated and for some there is even a third stand-by instrument. In the unlikely event of one of the pilots collapsing, the other has all the controls needed to fly safely. In flight, each pilot can monitor the other's instruments, and ensure that they are giving the same indications on both panels.

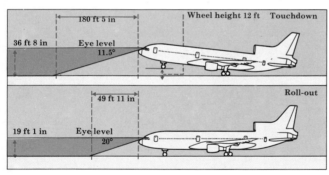

A pilot's groundward view is limited by the small window area in a pressurized aircraft. In the TriStar downward vision during touchdown is about 11.5° and on the ground is 20°. Lateral vision at 232° is almost equal to that from a car's front windows.

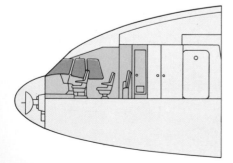

The flight deck is planned for visibility, utility and comfort. Curved windshields and insulation cut down outside noise. Oxygen masks and smoke goggles are near to hand; a built-in ladder leads to an escape hatch. In the nose a weather radar scanner sweeps left and right through 30°.

The flight deck of a TWA Boeing 747 (the co-pilot's seat has been omitted for a clearer view)
1 Overhead switch panel
2 Navigational radio selector
3 Autopilot engage switch
4 Basic T arrangement
5 Inertial navigation warning lights
6 Thrust reverser lights
7 Pitch trim controls
8 Nose gear tiller
9 Landing-gear control handle
10 Water injection control
11 Speed brake handle
12 Thrust levers
13 Inertial navigation controls
14 Brake pressure
15 Computer selection switch
16 Stabilizer trim levers
17 Flap lever
18 Pitch trim wheel
19 Parking brake levers
20 Engine start levers
21 Central console containing: weather radar controls; ADF (automatic direction finder); radio equipment; aileron and rudder trims; intercom switches
22 Observer's seat

There is also a highly sophisticated centralized warning system on the main instrument panel. Red or yellow illuminated squares accompanied by loud buzzing indicate immediately any failure of any part of the aircraft and its control systems. The strident sound of any of 18 different warning signals could disturb the serenity of a flight deck.

All airlines may shortly adopt a feature at present only used in some civil airliners and military aircraft — electronic headup display (HUD). Height, speed and heading, and a picture of the runway, can be projected electronically onto the windshield so the pilot can look "head-up" to see the picture merging with the real runway during a landing approach. This system saves the essential two or three seconds the pilot loses in adjusting his vision from the instruments to the runway.

The windshield 23 is nine in high at the centre. Made of laminated glass and plastic with a hard coating, it is $\frac{5}{8}$ in thick.

The flight engineer's panel 26 contains the main circuit breakers and the environmental and engine-monitoring systems.

Pedals 24 are pushed to control the rudder. Only slight movements are needed to turn the aircraft or keep it level.

The control column 25, pulled and pushed, lowers and raises the elevators hydraulically. The wheel controls the ailerons.

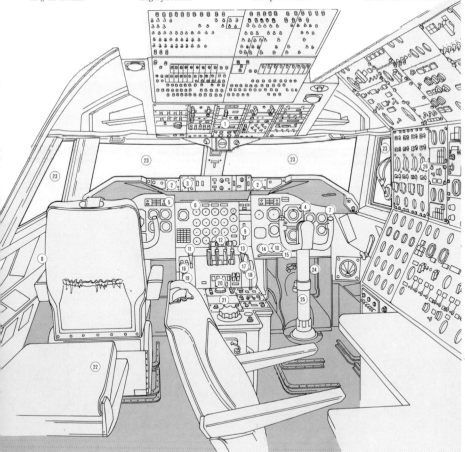

The control panel

A striped pointer indicates maximum permitted airspeed according to altitude

A Mach scale aligned with the pointer indicates Mach 0.35

A pointer indicates an airspeed of 180 knots

The airspeed indicator (ASI) gives the plane's speed in knots and Mach number. A sensor—the pitot probe—leads from the ASI out into the airstream at the nose; the faster the aircraft, the greater the build-up of pressure in the sensor. Airspeed determines the lift generated.

A clear digital read-out is easily scanned

Altitude shown in ft

The large pointer completes one revolution for every 1,000 ft of altitude

The standard setting of 1013.25 millibars is sea level pressure on a normal day

Knob to set surface pressure

The altimeter is an aneroid barometer connected with the atmosphere via a vent on the aircraft's outer skin. The pilot sets the surface pressure before take off and subsequent changes, detected by the instrument as the plane climbs or descends, appear as altitude.

Distance to radio beacon

Command track counter in degrees

Fixed lubber indicating magnetic heading

Command track pointer showing new heading

Position relative to radio beam

Systems failure warning flags

Aircraft symbol

The horizontal situation indicator (HSI) displays an aircraft symbol set in the centre of a revolving compass card. It indicates the aircraft's position relative to radio navigation and instrument landing beams, and the bearing and distance in nautical miles to a selected radio beacon.

Artificial horizon

Aircraft symbol and flight director

Angle of pitch

Systems failure warning flag

Pointer indicating angle of bank

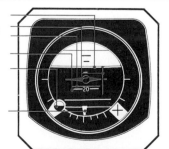

The attitude director shows the attitude (pitch and roll) of the aircraft relative to the Earth's horizon. The aircraft symbol remains fixed and the artificial horizon moves, so that the aircraft symbol seems to climb, dive, bank and turn in tail view, in step with the aircraft.

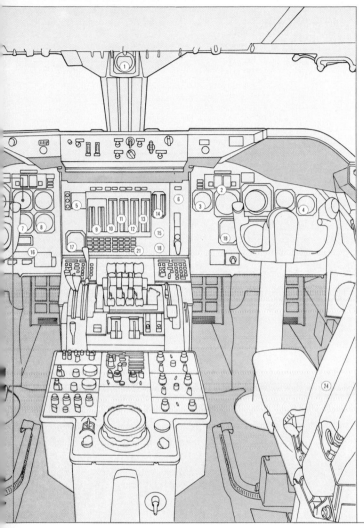

The flight director converts the attitude director into an instrument that tells the pilot how to fly the plane. Its computer processes the attitude and heading information displayed on the other instruments, and by means of two pointers superimposes directives on the artificial horizon. Whenever the aircraft, and consequently the pointers, move out of alignment, the pilot simply has to manoeuvre his plane exactly as the flight director indicates until the pointers cross, and he will find himself flying back onto the required heading. In the diagram, the plane is seen diving and banking to the right. The artificial horizon responds by moving above, and inclining to the left of, the aircraft symbol. The vertical pointer indicates that the pilot must fly still farther to the right; the horizontal pointer below the aircraft symbol indicates that he must descend a little more before intercepting the ILS beam.

The autopilot

In May, 1914, a Parisian crowd saw Laurence Sperry, son of the American inventor of the first autopilot, fly a biplane low overhead. He was holding his hands in the air while his companion walked along the wings.

Uncontrolled, an aircraft will not immediately fall out of the sky but, even in calm air, it will gradually bank, turn, climb or dive. Sperry's system overcame those tendencies.

An autopilot is essentially a stabilizing system which takes over the controls during the climb, cruise and descent-to-destination phases of a flight, leaving the pilot free to concentrate on surveillance and communications. In turbulent conditions it relieves him of the fatiguing task of maintaining a smooth ride.

Sophisticated modern autopilots feed essential flight information from electrically-driven gyroscopes, pressure sensors and accelerometers (which measure vibrations and accelerations) into a computer. The data is processed and fed to servomotors (mechanisms which respond to electrical command signals, converting them into hydraulic signals) and these move the aircraft's control surfaces.

Signals to the autopilot computer may be caused by influences within the aircraft. Pitch can be affected as the fuel load lightens, or by people crowding to the back of the cabin to watch a movie. The autopilot compensates by moving the elevators and trimming the aircraft to hold it level.

On the flight deck the pilot merely monitors the trim indicators and keeps an eye on the flight director. Switched to autopilot, this no longer issues commands as in manual flying, but depicts the aircraft movements that the autopilot is bringing about.

Except for a switch lit up on the control panel, the autopilot cannot be seen. But the control column moves as if operated by invisible hands.

The autopilot control panel, mounted at the top of the instrument panel, can be reached by both pilots. From left to right the controls include: a setting knob and course indicator in compass degrees; automatic speed controls; auto approach and landing and flight director buttons; dual autopilot control channels (AP1 and AP2); a press bar (TURB) to reprogramme the computer for turbulence; heading selection controls; controls for the altitude at which the autopilot will hold the aircraft; a warning system for a descent below 10,000 ft.

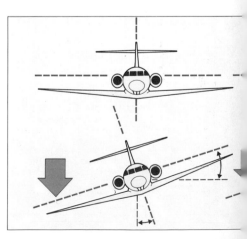

The sensing unit contains pressure sensors, accelerometers and three gyros mounted on different axes.

Weather radar scanner

The autopilot moves the elevators for correct pitch and trims them to hold the aircraft steady on its path.

The rudder is moved by servomotors activated by signals from the autopilot.

Wind

Any deviation from the pre-set flightpath is sensed by the autopilot, which adjusts control surfaces accordingly, compensating for drift.

Compensatory manoeuvre

The pilot has only to dial in a new altitude on the autopilot controls and the aircraft will climb automatically to the appropriate new level.

A computer in a briefcase-sized black box processes flight information to provide the next control action.

Autopilot control of ailerons and other surfaces can be cut out instantly by a button on the control column.

When locked onto **radio navigation beams** the autopilot can be set to avoid turbulence via the horizontal situation indicator.

Radio beacon

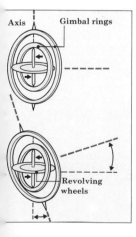

Axis   Gimbal rings

Revolving wheels

The axis of a gyroscope's rapidly spinning wheel will remain fixed in the direction it is originally spun irrespective of the aircraft's attitude. Any deviation of the aircraft from its flightpath is reflected in the movement of a gimbal ring in which the wheel is suspended. The amount and rate of deviation is measured and electrical signals sent to servomotors which instantly move the appropriate control surfaces.

The autothrottle is a refinement which can control speed automatically while the aircraft is climbing, cruising and landing.

Aerial navigation/1

To be able to find his way around the skies, a pilot needs to know his position and his direction. Finding direction is easy using the simple magnetic compass, and there is at least one of these on every flight deck. Another kind of aircraft compass uses a gyroscope. Modern aircraft compasses are complex and highly efficient. Finding position is more difficult for a pilot than finding direction, and needs complex aids.

Air travel was always limited as long as pilots had to navigate using only compass bearings, maps and visual pointers. Planes equipped with radio have the aviator's equivalent of the mariner's lighthouse to find position, with one advantage: radio waves do not need to be visible to be effective. They can travel all over the world either in long waves — used in

Dead-reckoning (sometimes called "ded" — for deductive — reckoning). The oldest and simplest form of aerial navigation is still used by pilots of light aircraft. It depends on recognizable ground landmarks. The pilot plots his track on the map before takeoff and, using his compass, flies in the right direction. Knowing his speed will enable him to calculate when he should fly over certain landmarks, and so check his progress.

The wind, carrying the aircraft off course, or causing sudden speed-ups or slow-downs, upsets such simple navigation. By relating his last known position to the direction he has flown, and his speed, the pilot will determine an approximate position several times during the flight. This becomes the centre of a circle, called a circle of uncertainty, whose radius is about ten per cent of the distance flown since the last landmark.

Astro-navigation

Above clouds or over featureless country when the sun or stars are the only familiar sights around, pilots can make use of astro-navigation techniques. Using a sextant (this measures the angular separation of objects by means of adjustable mirrors) the pilot takes azimuth and elevation readings at a given time. To do this he measures the sun's angle relative to the aircraft's flightpath

and to the horizon, and calculates the aircraft's latitude and longitude on the world's surface. An accurate measure of the time of each observation, by chronometer, is essential.

On a clear night astro-navigators use the Pole-star in the northern hemisphere and the Southern Cross in the southern. It is rare for commercial pilots to use astro-navigation techniques today, but military crews are still familiar with them.

Position-fixing

True position will gradually become masked as small measuring errors accumulate and as the aircraft moves. As the illustration shows, a pilot flying an aircraft equipped with radio will take readings from, say, three radio beacon signals, and plot position-lines on a map. Where these intersect a small triangle is formed and the aircraft's position is assumed to be within this so-called cocked-hat.

The best results are obtained when all the measurements are taken within a short period; a one-minute delay in taking a position-reading at jet speed can introduce a ten-mile error. Automatic radio systems, and other modern systems, take almost instantaneous readings and so minimize this problem. Radio beacons register on the pilot's radio magnetic indicator or horizontal situation indicator.

long-range navigation — that curve around the Earth's surface, or in short waves which tend to travel in straight lines and are used in short-range navigation systems.

But even the most sophisticated radio navigation system has something in common with the simple method of leaning out of the cockpit to take a visual bearing on a church or river: both depend upon ground-based aids. Ultra-modern devices such as Doppler radar and weather radar are entirely self-contained, and so are the inertial guidance systems whose accurate measuring devices can record barely perceptible accelerations in aircraft speed.

In future years these systems will be completed by a network of very low frequency Omega radio stations, by laser devices and by satellite systems.

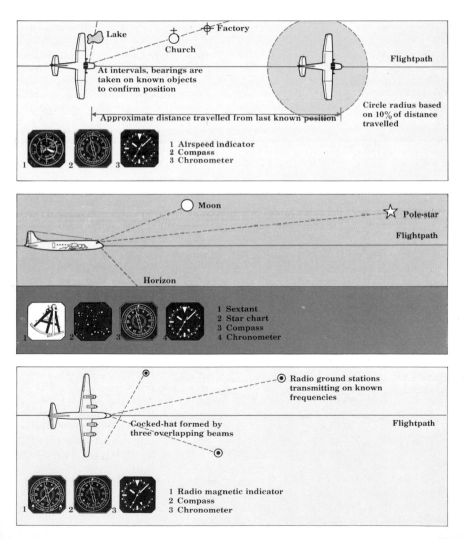

Lake   Church   Factory

At intervals, bearings are taken on known objects to confirm position

Flightpath

Approximate distance travelled from last known position

Circle radius based on 10% of distance travelled

1 Airspeed indicator
2 Compass
3 Chronometer

Moon   Pole-star

Flightpath

Horizon

1 Sextant
2 Star chart
3 Compass
4 Chronometer

Radio ground stations transmitting on known frequencies

Cocked-hat formed by three overlapping beams

Flightpath

1 Radio magnetic indicator
2 Compass
3 Chronometer

Aerial navigation/2

Radio Range and NDB

A Radio Range system consists of a station transmitting two morse letters: A $(\cdot -)$ and N $(- \cdot)$. As the signals merge into a continuous note the pilot knows his aircraft is on the centreline of a designated airway. But this system can give a pilot guidance along up to four routes only, and has been largely superseded.

An alternative is the non-directional beacon (NDB), a station emitting a continuous signal, usually with an identifying message in morse that is repeated at frequent intervals. This can be received by aircraft homing onto the station, just as they would follow the beam of a lighted beacon, from up to 50 miles away. Without a compass a pilot following the signal cannot tell from which direction he is approaching the radio station. The direction to the beacon is displayed on the HSI.

VOR

Very high frequency omnidirectional range is the most commonly used radio system. Each VOR beacon transmits a continuous signal with morse-code identifying letters superimposed. By regulating the frequency of the signal it can be received in different forms by aircraft heading towards it from different directions. A processed signal is displayed on the horizontal situation indicator. Range is determined by distance-measuring equipment transmitting a signal to a VOR station and triggering an automatic reply. The time interval, translated into distance, is read off in nautical miles. At large airports VOR stations guide inbound aircraft to where an NDB, located about five miles from the runway on an extended centreline, enables the pilot to home onto the Instrument Landing System.

Long-range radio navigation

Until recently long-wave radio signals were only reliable to a range of about 2,000 miles. Now they extend even farther, and their accuracy is such that a pilot can be sure of his position to within two to five miles. Because it is impractical to build conveniently sized aerials to carry direction-related long-wave information, a number of simple radio stations, one called a master and the others called slaves, are sited about 200 miles apart. Together they transmit synchronized pulses or continuous radio waves whose regular interference with one another sets up a complicated but predictable pattern of interference. This is always stationary relative to the ground even though the aircraft is moving, and so provides a reference against which an aircraft's radio receiver can automatically establish its position.

Weather radar

Nose-mounted weather radar is carried by many airliners. Though very simple — it is a safety device rather than a navigation system — it can be used to make navigation decisions. Its beam, sweeping across the sky up to 200 miles ahead (only 20 minutes away in a jet airliner), reflects off water droplets and detects weather that could be uncomfortably rough or even dangerous to fly through. A pilot usually changes course to avoid severe weather. The display unit in the flight deck gives a phosphorescent map of rainfall ahead, and the strength of the radar returns is approximately equivalent to cloud turbulence levels, but clear air turbulence cannot, unfortunately, be detected by radar. Most weather radars can be tilted downward to give a rough outline map of the terrain beneath the aircraft.

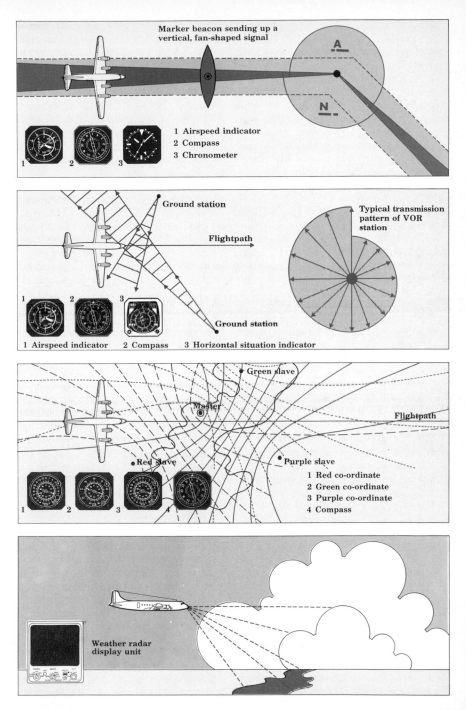

Marker beacon sending up a vertical, fan-shaped signal

A

N

1 Airspeed indicator
2 Compass
3 Chronometer

Ground station

Flightpath

Typical transmission pattern of VOR station

Ground station

1 Airspeed indicator   2 Compass   3 Horizontal situation indicator

Green slave

Master

Flightpath

Red slave

Purple slave

1 Red co-ordinate
2 Green co-ordinate
3 Purple co-ordinate
4 Compass

Weather radar display unit

Aerial navigation/3

Doppler radar

The Doppler system is entirely self-contained. In this navigation system the radar splays up to four beams at a known frequency onto the ground beneath the aircraft. As they are reflected back to the aircraft the frequencies of the forward beams are increased, and the frequencies of the rearward beams are reduced, in proportion to the component of the speed in each direction. By analyzing the frequency of radar energy scattered back from the ground the radar's computer can determine data such as the speed of the aircraft across the ground and the angle of drift caused by winds. Recently, such information has also become available from devices such as Omega and inertial navigation systems (INS) that are considerably simpler — so Doppler radar is tending to disappear from commercial aircraft.

INS

The heart of an inertial navigation system is a carefully-balanced platform, held level by gyroscopes, on which three accelerometers are mounted, each pointing in a different direction: fore and aft, up and down, left and right. They measure the aircraft's slightest acceleration, and this is automatically converted to velocity and then to distance covered. On takeoff the system is given the aircraft's exact position, and thereafter a panel display shows position continuously throughout the flight. The INS can also determine how winds are affecting the aircraft. A drift of one mile an hour is typical.

It is usual for large airliners to carry three INS sets so that the crew can check any discrepancies; by comparing the three position indicators they can tell immediately whether one of the systems has failed.

Omega

A recently introduced navigation system whose accuracy surpasses that of the INS, the Omega system is already being used on all types of aircraft. The illustration shows the positions of the Omega transmitters in each hemisphere, each sending out powerful long-wave radio signals that can be picked up by aircraft and also by ships and submarines. Within a ten-second interval, each station transmits three pulses, each on a different radio frequency and lasting for approximately one second. All the signals are synchronized, and super-accurate atomic clocks keep their transmissions in time. On the aircraft a miniature computer, whose many thousand components can fit onto a thumb-nail-sized circuit board, analyzes the signals and calculates its position anywhere in the world to within two miles.

Laser navigation

Laser "gyros" may soon provide a navigation system with no moving parts; three, mounted in an aircraft, can detect the slightest movement. They consist of triangular tubes with mirrors at each angle. Two laser beams, transmitted in opposite directions, take the same time to travel round the triangle, but when rotated by aircraft movement one beam takes longer to complete a circuit.

Satellite navigation systems

Navstar, several of its satellites already in orbit, is one of various satellite systems under development. It may be fully operational by the 1990s. Its final 24 satellites, orbiting simultaneously 10,000 miles high, will provide continuous high-quality position fixes. When perfected, the system will enable a pilot to know where he is within 20 ft, the width of a Boeing 747.

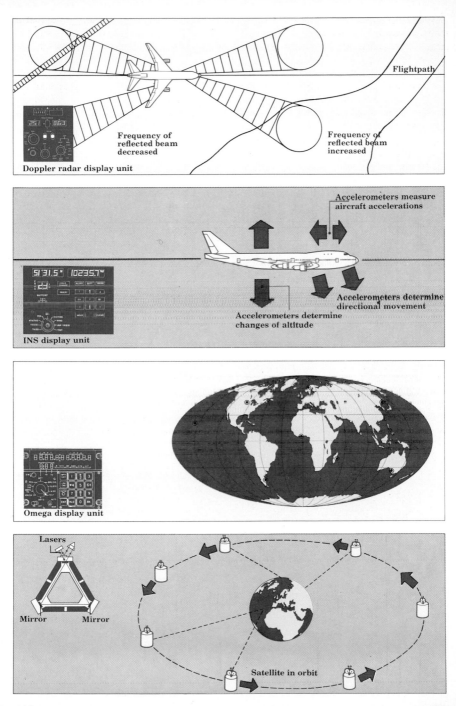

Frequency of
reflected beam
decreased

Frequency of
reflected beam
increased

Flightpath

Doppler radar display unit

Accelerometers measure
aircraft accelerations

Accelerometers determine
directional movement

Accelerometers determine
changes of altitude

INS display unit

Omega display unit

Lasers

Mirror   Mirror

Satellite in orbit

The fuel system

A long-range jet airliner carries 100 tons or more of fuel, enough to drive a small car about 50 times round the world. Of necessity, the earliest of all the complex aircraft systems to evolve was the fuel system.

Light aircraft have piston engines much like those of cars, burning aviation-grade petrol (or gasoline). This is pumped into the tanks, flexible neoprene-rubber bags fitted into the wing compartments or fuselage, via a gravity filler.

Jet airliners burn various grades of jet fuel of the kerosene (paraffin) type. There is often no separate tank. Instead, the aircraft structure — the spaces between the wing spars, parts of the body, or the fin — is coated

with layers of rubbery sealant to form a series of fuel-tight compartments. These stay absolutely leakproof even though the structure twists and bends in turbulence or on rough airfields. Baffles in the tanks stop the fuel sloshing about, and one-way valves prevent it from running uncontrolled from tank to tank. The space above the fuel is not filled with combustible air but dry nitrogen, which is inert.

All fuel can serve any engine, the tanks being linked by pipes with one-way or pilot-controlled valves. These allow it to flow no matter what the aircraft's attitude, and they control the flow of fuel or gas through the system to balance out pressure differences at varying altitudes. Vents,

Fuelling sockets may be in the fuselage, as in the BAC One-Eleven **above**, on the landing-gear bays, or under the wing as on the Boeing 747 **below**. They can usually be reached from the ground, but the 747 needs a lifting platform.

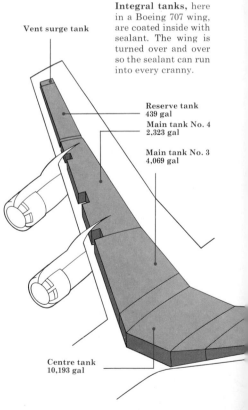

Vent surge tank

Integral tanks, here in a Boeing 707 wing, are coated inside with sealant. The wing is turned over and over so the sealant can run into every cranny.

Reserve tank
439 gal

Main tank No. 4
2,323 gal

Main tank No. 3
4,069 gal

Centre tank
10,193 gal

usually at the wing tips or tail, keep the pressure constant.

The fuel is pumped out of each tank by electric or air-driven booster pumps at the lowest point. Multi-engined aircraft have special proportioners to distribute the fuel accurately between the engines, and high-pressure pumps on the engines.

Extreme care is taken to eliminate water from the fuel, which would freeze at high altitudes and cause blockages, but heated filters melt any ice crystals that do form.

Even though the aircraft's skin may heat to 120 degrees Fahrenheit (49 degrees Celsius) on the ground at hot airports or due to friction at supersonic speeds, the fuel must never be allowed to boil and produce bubbles, despite the fact that it may serve as a "heat sink" to which nearly all unusable heat is rejected, as it does in Concorde. Lightweight reticulated foam usually insulates each tank.

In subsonic aircraft, fuel is consumed evenly throughout the system to make the centre of gravity shift by as little as possible. In Concorde it is used to change the centre of gravity, to counteract trim changes between subsonic and supersonic flight.

Refuelling an aircraft, particularly the new-generation, wide-bodied airliners, needs special equipment. Giant mobile tankers and fixed airport fuel hydrants can refuel a wide-bodied aircraft in less than half an hour.

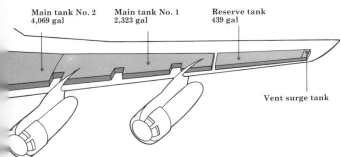

Main tank No. 2
4,069 gal

Main tank No. 1
2,323 gal

Reserve tank
439 gal

Vent surge tank

Pressure-fuelling has replaced gravity fillers. Fuel is pumped aboard at a rate of up to 2,000 gals (2,400 US gals) a minute through high-pressure couplings which seal automatically when the hefty hose is uncoupled. Anti-static fuel additives, and an electrical bonding wire between hose and aircraft, prevent sparks.

The hydraulic system

A pilot of average strength can exert a muscle force of perhaps 100 pounds. This was adequate to operate the wire-controlled ailerons, elevators and rudders of the first airliners, but when flaps and retractable landing-gears were invented, and aircraft began to weigh 50 tons or more, pilots needed mechanical assistance.

Hydraulics provide the muscles that work the moving parts of a large aircraft. The principle is the same as in the brakes of a car: pumps driven by the engines force fluid through pipes and valves.

Most hydraulic fluids used in aircraft are mineral oils, but increasingly, water-based non-inflammable compounds are used. They are virtually incompressible, providing not only an immediate operative force, but a lock, preventing unguided movement in any part of the system.

Airliners usually have two or more hydraulic systems in case one should fail. Some aircraft have control surfaces divided into separate sections, each controlled by a separately signalled hydraulic power unit. Others couple several systems to single items, with a "majority rule" to overpower any system containing a fault.

Aircraft power steering is so responsive that resistance is built into the column so that pilots can gauge how much pressure to apply.

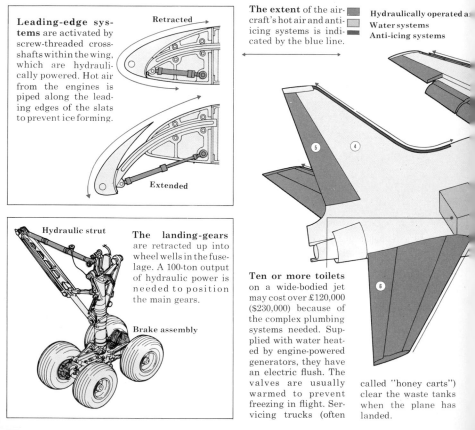

Leading-edge systems are activated by screw-threaded cross-shafts within the wing, which are hydraulically powered. Hot air from the engines is piped along the leading edges of the slats to prevent ice forming.

Retracted

Extended

The extent of the aircraft's hot air and anti-icing systems is indicated by the blue line.

■ Hydraulically operated a...
□ Water systems
■ Anti-icing systems

Hydraulic strut

The landing-gears are retracted up into wheel wells in the fuselage. A 100-ton output of hydraulic power is needed to position the main gears.

Brake assembly

Ten or more toilets on a wide-bodied jet may cost over £120,000 ($230,000) because of the complex plumbing systems needed. Supplied with water heated by engine-powered generators, they have an electric flush. The valves are usually warmed to prevent freezing in flight. Servicing trucks (often called "honey carts") clear the waste tanks when the plane has landed.

Anti-icing and water

The first airliners were dangerously affected by ice formation during flight. It increased their weight, starved the engines of air and even changed the shape of the wings by forming along the leading edges.

Alcohol sprays and brush-on pastes were the first attempts at anti-icing during the 1930s, but the rubber pulsating boot, still common on slow aircraft, was the first really effective de-icing system. Tubes along the leading edges of the wings and tail alternately inflate and deflate by air pressure, breaking the ice so that the slipstream can carry it away.

On jets, extremely hot air is ducted from the engine compressors along the wing and tail leading edges, and to engine inlets and windshields. Electric elements, embedded in rubber or plastic, heat the windshield and other surfaces until they are too hot to touch. Heated anti-icing fluids protect grounded aircraft.

Only since 1950 have clear drinking water, running water for washing, and flushing toilets been installed in all airliners. The increasing popularity of air travel made them indispensable, yet the apparently simple problems of freezing waste pipes at high altitudes, and surge in water tanks during turbulence, needed complex engineering before their efficiency was assured.

The water system is controlled by the flight crew, who can switch off the supply by depressurizing the water tanks if a leak occurs.

The flight-deck windshield may be heated through a conductive gold film.

The Lockheed Tri-Star has four totally independent hydraulic systems supplied with fluid by four separate engine-driven pumps. Combinations of the systems control:
1 Inboard leading-edge slats
2 Outboard leading-edge slats
3 Spoilers
4 Tailplane (horizontal stabilizer)
5 Rudder
6 Elevator (geared)
7 Inboard trailing-edge flaps
8 Inboard aileron
9 Outboard trailing-edge flaps
10 Outboard aileron

Pressure couplings, connected to a water service panel under the fuselage, usually near the tail, fill the potable water tank as part of the servicing. A wide-bodied airliner holds 250 to 300 gals, a narrow-bodied jet holds around 100 gals.

Heated water, pumped into wash basins from the main tanks, is suctioned down to the lower fuselage as waste. Sprayed out into the atmosphere, it forms a shower of ice crystals.

Pressurization and air-conditioning

The higher a plane flies, the colder the temperature of the air around it. At 35,000 feet and above, the outside air is around minus 70 degrees Fahrenheit (minus 50 degrees Celsius) far, far colder than an icebox.

As an aircraft climbs, atmospheric pressure falls too, from about 15 pounds per square inch at sea level to around four pounds per square inch at airliner cruising height, which may be 10,000 feet above the highest altitude that will sustain human life. Cabin pressure is usually allowed to fall gently to the equivalent of 8,000 feet, and maintained at that level by pressurizing the fuselage.

Piston-engined aircraft and turbo-props have air compressors to maintain cabin pressure. Jet engines handle so much air that pressurization supplies can be bled from them under great pressure, and already very hot. These are cooled in a heat-exchanger, from where some is fed to the cabin and the excess expelled. Full pressurization can add a ton of weight to a Boeing 747.

Oxygen masks are installed above passenger seats for emergency use in the event of pressurization failure.

Fresh air for the environmental control system (ECS) is heated in the same heat-exchanger, humidified and fed into the cabin to air-condition it to a constant level of comfort.

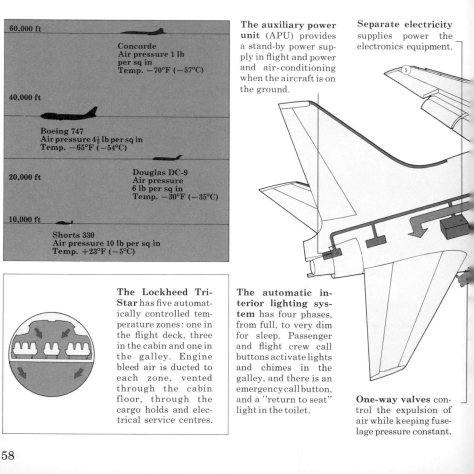

60,000 ft

Concorde
Air pressure 1 lb per sq in
Temp. −70°F (−57°C)

40,000 ft

Boeing 747
Air pressure 4½ lb per sq in
Temp. −65°F (−54°C)

Douglas DC-9
Air pressure 6 lb per sq in
Temp. −30°F (−35°C)

20,000 ft

10,000 ft

Shorts 330
Air pressure 10 lb per sq in
Temp. +23°F (−5°C)

The auxiliary power unit (APU) provides a stand-by power supply in flight and power and air-conditioning when the aircraft is on the ground.

Separate electricity supplies power the electronics equipment.

The Lockheed Tri-Star has five automatically controlled temperature zones: one in the flight deck, three in the cabin and one in the galley. Engine bleed air is ducted to each zone, vented through the cabin floor, through the cargo holds and electrical service centres.

The automatic interior lighting system has four phases, from full, to very dim for sleep. Passenger and flight crew call buttons activate lights and chimes in the galley, and there is an emergency call button, and a "return to seat" light in the toilet.

One-way valves control the expulsion of air while keeping fuselage pressure constant.

Electrics and electronics

Simple one- or two-seater planes have a direct current (DC) system to run the radio and navigation lights; large airliners usually have other kinds of current on board, suited for specific purposes. They have over 15,000 electric and electronic devices, served by systems as complicated as those of a complete city. They generate most of their electric power as AC (alternating current), the same as a house supply, by alternators on each engine. For emergency use there are other generators: a ram air turbine (a windmill spun by the slipstream), and an auxiliary power unit (APU) which can either be used in an emergency or on the ground when the engines are not running. AC is used for all the heavy loads: for anti-icing the airframe (needing the largest AC supplies) for powering hydraulic systems, for heating ovens in the galley, for powering radio masts, toilet and galley drains, and accounts for about half the total power.

The avionics (aviation electronics) use about one-twentieth of the power, but need a precisely controlled frequency of AC current generated by alternators which turn at the right speed no matter how fast the engines may be turning. Absolute integrity of these supplies must be guaranteed; they have total priority over non-essential loads.

Engine-driven generators turning at precise speeds supply current to the avionics (aviation electronics).

The galleys are served by separate AC electricity supplies.

From the room-sized service centre, electricity is routed to all aircraft systems.

AC supplies to vital electronics systems have priority in emergencies.

Windshields are electrically heated to prevent misting and ice formation.

The ECS is governed by three separate air-conditioning packs.

Punkah louvres, controlled from the seat consoles, supply cooled air to each passenger. Cabin air flows continuously at a rate of 6,000 cu ft a minute, giving a complete change of air every three minutes, dissipating odours rapidly.

Pressurization air supplies enter through a ram air inlet. They are compressed and then warmed and are fed to the cabin, which can be held at sea-level pressure up to 22,000 ft. At 42,000 ft cabin pressure is equal to 8,000 ft.

Aircraft have exterior lights for night-flying:
1 Landing/taxi lights on nose gear
2 Wing-scan lights for ice-detection
3 Runway turn-off lights
4 Landing lights
5 Wing-tip navigation lights
6 Upper anti-collision lights.
7 Wing-tip navigation lights.
Aircraft should also have tailplane (stabilizer) navigation lights, and lower anti-collision lights, and some have a light to illuminate the logo.

Cabin layout

An airline's profit depends upon each of its aircraft carrying as many passengers as possible. The less cabin space devoted to passenger seating, the more expensive the air ticket will be. The designers of aircraft are therefore required to accommodate the largest number of seats, while retaining reasonable comfort.

In the early days of airline operation, during the 1920s and 1930s, aircraft could carry few passengers. The wooden-winged Fokker F.XII which flew KLM's Amsterdam to Batavia (now Djakarta) service, the longest air route in 1931, carried only four. As the technology of air travel advanced, seats were positioned one behind another, usually with a side aisle.

When long-distance air travel became established, after 1930, aircraft were fitted with sleeping compartments. As late as the 1950s, the Douglas DC-7, which operated the first regular non-stop transatlantic services in 1956, taking about ten hours, was fitted with "slumberette" reclining seats and bunks. These were not needed in later, faster jets.

The economic significance of high-density seating was soon exploited, and a line of seats on each side of a central aisle became the classic configuration; the second-generation jet airliners had rows of five (three plus two) or six (three plus three) seats.

Not all airliners have alternative economy (coach) and first-class accommodation. Some commuter and shuttle aircraft, charter operations and small island-hoppers have a single class. The distinction is most evident in the different seat layouts.

In narrow-bodied airliners, the economy-section rows of triple-seat units usually give way to two plus two rows of double-seat units in the first-class cabin. In the wide-bodied airliners the standard seating pattern

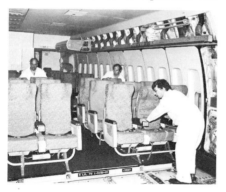

The inside wall of the passenger cabin, which appears solid to the passengers, is completely removable **above.** Walls, ceiling and floor are made up of lightweight panels which can be removed individually or *en bloc*, enabling maintenance engineers to service the systems behind and beneath, replace damaged fittings and examine the windows. Storage units, galley and toilet walls and doors, partitions and bulkheads are also removable. Wall panels are one-piece vacuum mouldings made from lightweight synthetic materials, and floor panels are constructed from plastic honeycomb panels bonded between glass-fibre or carbon-fibre skins.

Airbus A300   Douglas DC-9 Super 80

The Airbus A300 single-class layout has nine seats abreast. The mixed-class layout has eight abreast in economy and six abreast in first class.

The DC-9 Super 80 seats 12 first-class passengers in rows of two plus two, and 125 tourist-class travellers in rows of three plus two.

consists of rows of up to nine or ten abreast with two aisles: two plus five plus two in the Douglas DC-10, or three plus four plus three in the Boeing 747. The first-class seating pattern is usually two plus two, with extra luxury provided in the additional lounge areas.

Although an airliner is a parallel tube for most of its length, the cabin tapers at each end, most noticeably in wide-bodied jets, so in the front and back of most aircraft the number of seat rows is reduced.

Ultimately the number of seats is determined by the number of seat rows. Seats are usually spaced about 34 inches apart in first class, 32 inches apart in the economy section. This distance, measured from the front of a seat to the same point on the one behind, is known as the seat pitch. To keep fares low, in charter flights, seats may have a pitch of only 29 inches, much closer than for the (more expensive) scheduled services on which an airline's reputation is built.

Most major airlines will permit passengers to select the seats they prefer on mixed-class scheduled flights, as long as they book early enough. A seat at the front is likely to be in a no-smoking area, and in small airliners especially, may give a view into the flight deck. Smokers are located at the back because the smoke drifts backward, although air-conditioning changes the cabin air once every three minutes. Window seats on the side away from the sun give the best view, and seats with most leg-room are by the doors or emergency exits where seat-pitching is most generous. A few airlines mark off a "business end" for executives, and most aircraft have special cot-holders, where babies should be stowed whenever the "Fasten seat belts" sign flashes up.

Business jets like the Hawker-Siddeley 125.700B **above** can be fitted out more or less to a customer's requirements, with customized interior colour schemes, materials and furnishings. Five-, eight- or ten-seat configurations are available, but most business jet interiors are designed as lounges, the seats arranged to make the most of the available interior space. Optional luxuries can include stereo tape and radio units, bars and even beds. An air-to-ground telephone/telex link, desks, tables and electric typewriters can turn a small jet into a flying boardroom or office.

Concorde

Beechcraft B99

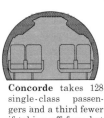

Concorde takes 128 single-class passengers and a third fewer if taking off from hot or high airports.

The Beechcraft B99 commuter aircraft carries up to 15 passengers in single seats flanking an aisle.

Cabin comfort

Wicker garden seats were fashionable in the smoking lounges of Imperial flying boats of the 1930s. Modern seats may be less elegant but they are safer; and the handful of manufacturers who supply all the world's airlines ensure that the core of comfort provided by adjustable backrests and cushioned upholstery is surrounded by all possible conveniences: plug-in or fold-away meal trays, ashtrays, magazine racks, footrests and luggage restraint devices.

The world's civil aviation authorities set the safety standards. To be able to take the strain of severe air turbulence, or of an emergency stop, passenger seats must be able to withstand several times the normal takeoff acceleration and landing deceleration rates. The UK and US authorities demand that an occupied seat be able to withstand an acceleration of nine times that of gravity (a mass of one pound accelerated by 32 feet per second per second) forward, and one and a half to four and a half times gravity rearward, sideways, upward and downward. Extensive testing ensures the strength and resistance of all welds, bolts and safety-belt anchorages. Adjustable backrests break forward on a sudden stop so that passengers in the seat

Passenger seats are designed in twin, triple and quadruple units. The main frame assembly is made of tubular steel. The legs are braced for extra rigidity and the "feet" lock into seat rail-tracks on the floor so that no forward, backward or sideways movement is possible. Seat units can be removed to give maintenance engineers access to underfloor systems.

The centre seat of a triple unit may have a table built into the contoured backrest. This folds down and locks onto the armrests, converting the centre seat into a centre table.

The backrest should be upright for takeoff and landing. In this position it locks securely enough to resist a sudden deceleration.

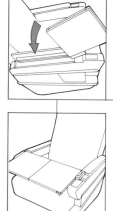

In some seat designs an integral folding table is stowed in the armrest. It can be slid upward and locked into place across the two armrests, turning an empty seat into a side table.

Recline control button

Underseat baggage restraint unit

Tip-up centre armrest

Life-jacket

Flip-top ashtray

Stewardess step

behind will not hit them if thrown forward on a sudden deceleration.

Most passenger seats face forward, toward the aircraft nose. Backward-facing seats would be safer: passengers would be supported by the backrest during sudden deceleration instead of forward against the seat in front, unrestrained except for the seatbelt fastened across the abdomen.

Because passengers would rather see where they are going than where they have been, airlines have refused to alter this practice but, significantly, whenever military use is made of civil aircraft, seats are turned around into the safer position.

Lifejackets are usually stored beneath each seat where they are readily accessible. Above the passengers' heads, or sometimes released from the seat in front, oxygen masks drop down automatically if the cabin pressure should fall below the optimum level. Seats are upholstered in flame-resistant materials. On some airliners the cushions can be removed

and used as floating life-preservers.

In structure and standard of upholstery there is little difference between first and tourist (coach) class seating. But there is an obvious difference in size. First-class seats are larger and are farther apart, and contoured backrests, often fitted with "slumber" headrests, provide a little extra luxury.

Noise levels vary little between different points on an aircraft, although passengers near a galley or toilet may be disturbed frequently. The engine noise is more noticeable at the back of a rear-engined airliner; the first-class cabin is located away from the engines. From a seat positioned near the landing-gears, the sound of the doors locking into the up and down positions can be disturbing, but noise from the wheels on the runway tends to be transmitted throughout the fuselage. Aircraft could be made quieter, but a level of mechanical noise diffuses the sound of 400 passengers talking at once.

Direction of nose

To protect themselves in an emergency, forward-facing passengers **left** must brace themselves in a forward-leaning position, head protected by the arms and cushioned on the knees. Rear-facing passengers **right** are more protected and need only brace hard against the seat back.

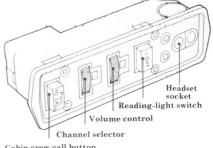

Headset socket
Reading-light switch
Volume control
Channel selector
Cabin crew call button

Released by a latch, a meal table slides or folds down from the seat in front.

Individual control units, set into the armrest of each passenger seat, enable passengers to call the cabin crew, operate individual light and fresh-air units, and listen through headsets to the variety of music usually offered by major airlines. One of the channels gives the film soundtrack, which may be available in alternative languages. The film projector, generally located below the ceiling storage units, aims the picture at a mirror which produces an almost horizontal beam, preventing distortion. Screens are located on the cabin bulkheads, or arranged so that they hinge down from the ceiling.

Cabin service

Before the first airlines had found their own identity, they mimicked the stately luxury of the great sea-liners. During the 1930s, graceful airships and elegant flying boats were staffed with a full complement of chefs and stewards who served leisurely meals in grand dining rooms.

But mass travel, and the pursuit of speed rather than comfort, brought the need for mass catering: a large airline such as TWA serves over 16 million meals in flight every year, and Singapore Airlines ("Airline of the Year" in 1977) invests about £63 million ($120 million) or 5.9 per cent of its budget in cabin services.

Airline food is prepared in vast catering centres, often leased at airports at both ends of the routes.

Catering may be contracted out to large hotels or restaurants, or specialized companies contracted to load flights 20 to 40 minutes before departure with pre-cooked meals ready for reheating, and trays of cold food. Only pre-browned steaks are cooked on board, in ovens powered by the aircraft engines. Frozen meals take 30 seconds to defrost in microwave ovens. Frozen meal packs are essential on flights to airports with inadequate catering facilities. Fresh food would not survive delays, but the use of frozen food and powdered instead of fresh milk (which sours quickly in a pressurized cabin, and is not readily available in some parts of the world) limits the standards of airline catering. Yet airlines go to great lengths to plan varied menus, and to transport delicacies such as coffee beans, tropical fruit, fresh fish and even caviar for first-class passengers, from distant parts of the world.

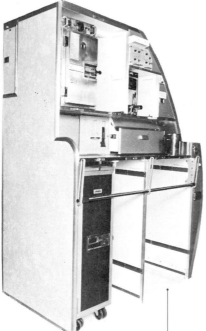

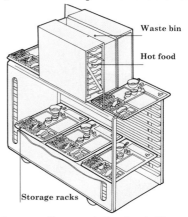

Waste bin

Hot food

Storage racks

Meal tray trolleys are designed to hold more than 30 meals. A BAC One-Eleven configured for 99 tourists **below** can provide a full meal service from one galley.

Galleys are fitted with self-contained food replacement units that can be slid along the seat rails to the door for easy loading.

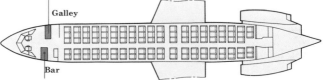

Galley

Bar

Singapore Airlines have spent £15 million ($30 million) developing a new-style in-flight kitchen.

National dishes vary the "international" sautéed chicken and steak: most Eastern airlines provide an alternative national menu; British Caledonian Airways serves a British breakfast on transatlantic flights and haggis on Burns' Night; Pan Am serves turkey and cranberry sauce on Thanksgiving Day. Some airlines have speciality dishes, not always listed on the menu, for passengers who do not like the standard menu.

On average, economy meals cost about £5 ($10) a head; first-class meals cost about twice as much, and as a rule, only first-class passengers are offered free drinks. Some airlines present free gifts to first-class passengers. The crew may be served a more varied menu. For fear of food poisoning the captain and co-pilot usually eat different meals and shellfish may be banned to them.

Passengers on special religious or medical diets can ask for vegetarian, Moslem, kosher, Hindu, salt-free, dietetic ulcer, diabetic or slimming meals when they book their tickets. Children may be served special meals and infants' bottles will be made up by the cabin crew.

Mealtimes depend on departure times, and follow an international clock. They may be changed to avoid service during turbulence. Heating and serving are timed so that no passenger is served lukewarm food.

The catering trucks are usually the first servicing vehicles to arrive at the aircraft parking bays. Catering staff remove soiled utensils and waste, and reload the aircraft. British Airways handles over 500,000 items of cutlery, 168,000 glasses, 50,000 tray dishes and 40,000 cups and saucers, and launders around 100 tons of linen and blankets a week.

Some bar-service trolleys have cold storage units chilled by gas-activated dry ice. Aircraft bars are installed and sealed by Customs. A mixed-class Boeing 747 configured for 385 passengers **below** needs six galleys to provide a full meal service.

On the cabin interphones, the crew can call other stations in different parts of the aircraft, and override an existing conversation to contact the flight crew in an emergency.

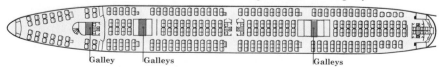

Galley Galleys   Galleys

Emergencies

Accidents do happen, and when they do, crew training, aircraft equipment and the good sense of the passengers may be fundamental to survival. To be alert to (but not obsessed with) the possibility of an emergency increases the chances of surviving it.

Aircraft seat belts, like the seats, are designed to withstand sudden deceleration. Work out how to fasten and unfasten them quickly. Cabin crews check that they are fastened at takeoff and landing, and that babies are installed in special cot-holders.

Do not, unless you are well versed in them, ignore the safety demonstrations at the beginning of a flight. Learn how to put on a lifejacket, and how to use the emergency oxygen masks stored above the seat or in the back of the seat in front: should depressurization occur suddenly at high altitudes, there will be very little time to find out how to put them on. In each magazine pocket is a card of safety instructions in pictures. It gives the positions of the emergency exits. Each of these has a sign giving the operating instructions in one or more languages, so they can be opened by passengers.

Fire extinguishers and sometimes axes are stowed at the cabin crew stations. Life raft stowages are usually near each main exit; in wide-bodied jets they are extensions of the escape slides, and in aircraft such as the VC10, 707 and 747 they are stored in the ceiling above the aisle. The survival, first-aid and polar kits are

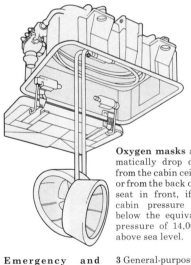

Oxygen masks automatically drop down from the cabin ceiling, or from the back of the seat in front, if the cabin pressure falls below the equivalent pressure of 14,000 ft above sea level.

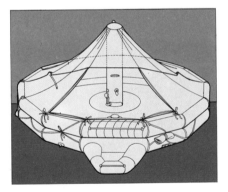

This self-inflating life raft holds 26 people. It is stocked with lifejackets, floating cots, supplies, a floating non-puncture knife, a lifeline, paddles and a drogue (sea anchor), and may have a radio transmitter. The canopy acts as a rain-catcher.

Emergency and evacuation equipment carried on the McDonnell Douglas DC-10 includes:
1 Asbestos gloves
2 Axe
3 General-purpose fire extinguishers
4 Door barrier straps
5 Carbon-dioxide fire-extinguisher
6 Survival packs
7 Escape ropes
8 Flashlights
9 First-aid kits
10 Floating baby-survival cots
11 Spare lifejackets
12 Oxygen masks for portable bottles
13 Megaphones
14 Oxygen bottles
15 Oxygen bottles with face masks
16 Extension seat belts
17 Smoke goggles
18 Paddles

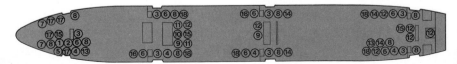

usually found near, perhaps attached to, the life rafts or exits.

If the "fasten seat belts" signs flash on in flight, obey them quickly; the aircraft may be about to enter turbulence and passengers walking about, especially at the back, could be thrown around.

Extinguish cigarettes immediately the "no smoking" signs go on (in the ashtray, never on the floor). *Never* smoke in the toilets where inflammable materials are invariably used in the furnishings. Between 1946 and 1976, 316 accidents were caused by in-flight fires or smoke; many began in the toilets.

In an emergency, obey the cabin crew without question. They will order passengers to fasten seat belts, extinguish cigarettes and brace themselves (bracing positions are illustrated on the "safety instructions" card) for sudden deceleration. They man the exits when the aircraft stops, instruct passengers on the procedure, and collect emergency equipment and supplies. If doors are inoperative, they activate the emergency exits, ordering passengers to unfasten seat belts, leave everything behind, and make for the designated escape chutes indicated by the cabin staff.

At the doorway, jump or slide down the chute to the ground (or into the life raft). Then get away from the aircraft. Move fast, and *forget your belongings.* In a fire, stragglers may be overcome by toxic fumes released by burning cabin furnishings.

Polar suits are replacing the fur coats carried on Arctic flights. Big enough to fit anyone, they are made of fire-resistant, water repellent material and are insulated on both sides with aluminium coating. They weigh half a pound.

On the Lockheed TriStar, all emergency exits are located clear of the wing for the safest evacuation of passengers directly onto the ground, or into life rafts. Four exits on either side enabled 345 passengers plus a crew of ten to be evacuated in 82 seconds during demonstrations conducted for US Federal Aviation Authority certification.

Escape chutes, doubling as life rafts, are stowed in the cabin doors, and inflate when released. Passengers are despatched onto them every one and a half seconds.

Standard survival packs contain food and water, water-purifying tablets, a first-aid kit, a baler, a 72-ft lifeline, a torch, a whistle, a heliograph, distress rockets and survival booklets.

Skyscape

As an airliner climbs through city smog or wintry murk into the clear sunshine of the upper air, the world and its weather spread out below like a map. In bright sunshine the shadow of the aircraft can sometimes be seen on the clouds below, with a rainbow halo all around it. The Earth may be ringed by a sharp horizon, or, in warmer climates, obscured by the dazzling peaks and purple ravines of 30,000-foot-high thunderstorms. The aircraft may travel through wispy ice-cloud cirrus that patterns the sky

clouds usually lie far below a jet; they rarely grow above 12,000 feet even in warm sub-tropical skies. Light aircraft fly in the smooth air just above their tops, and seldom below them in the turbulent thermals, the currents of rising warm air that produce them.

Pilots of small aircraft also avoid flying through the dark hearts of thunderstorms, though the crew of a jetliner may not always clear their pinnacles. These cumulo-nimbus sometimes grow so fast they can be seen "boiling" upward and wearing

The Earth may be dappled with puffs of fine-weather cumulus **above** which make shadows on the fields beneath; ground features can be easily identified as the plane comes in to land.

A peak of the English Cumbrian hills breaks out from a mass of hill fog **right above.** Thunder-clouds **right** are easily recognized by the anvil-shaped clouds on their tops.

like translucent lace, or grey banks of cloud that give only brief glimpses of the ground beneath.

The clouds have information to give. Light puffy cumulus is made in rising warm air and grows more quickly over land than sea; on a featureless ocean crossing a cluster of distant cumulus can indicate islands still hidden by the curving Earth — a navigational aid used by Viking and Polynesian sailors.

Clouds come in every shape, and are not difficult to identify. Cumulus

small eyebrow-shaped clouds called pileus on their heads. Because they grow so tall, thunder-clouds remain bathed in golden sunlight after it has become dark on the ground.

The long-distance jet flies above most of the clouds, giving passengers a grandstand view of the world's weather in all its moods. On windy days strange lens-shaped lenticular clouds may be spotted hanging in the sky above mountains or even solid cloud. They grow to the lee of mountains like gigantic versions of the

68

ripples that form downstream of rocks in a river. These waves of cloud may go as high as Concorde, to 50,000 feet. Pilots flying smaller aircraft are wary of such massive streams of up and down air.

In high latitudes at night, the spectacular aurora borealis, northern lights from outer space, may be visible from the cabin window. Often in the form of an arc, sometimes with rays shooting skywards, this eerie display of greenish light is caused by electrical discharge more than two

miles high, in outer space.

The degree of latitude affects the length of twilight. The northern sun's low path gives a long half light, but toward the tropics, where the sun is high and plummets steeply at the end of the day, dark — and dawn — come rapidly. Travelling westwards across either hemisphere in summer, passengers at jet speed have the impression that night has disappeared.

Few passengers realize how easy it is to identify the fascinating geography over which they fly, but from six miles up on a clear day so much can be seen that an airline route map or a pocket atlas can make a long flight more interesting. High over the incredible blue of the Mediterranean the Greek islands, Cyprus or Malta are unmistakable, and it is easy to visualize the ships of the ancient civilizations voyaging between them. Quite different are the Pacific islands, or the American Florida Keys linked into a great curve by the roads and bridges of a new concrete world.

In the dark, cities below look like islands; 25,000 feet from the ground they show up so clearly that it is sometimes possible to see streets lighted as brightly as runways, and even large buildings. Mercury vapour lights are bluey pinpoints with coloured halos, and sodium lights make a yellowy-orange glow. The aircraft lights, reflected off a million water droplets, may dazzle passengers as the plane flies through a cloud.

Watching the aircraft in flight can be absorbing. Seats at the front may give glimpses into the flight deck. The propellers of short-range aircraft may be seen to change pitch when speed is altered. There is a wispy vortex from propeller tips at takeoff if the atmosphere is moist. Wingtip vortices may be visible in a turn, but Concorde's are quite spectacular. After takeoff, when the jet is at a steep angle, a huge cloud forms at the front of the wing and rolls back along the leading edge in the form of a thin tube. In flight, it seems to trail after the wing tip in a stream.

Aircraft wings are designed to flex up and down in flight, helping to give a smoother ride. The flaps, slats and spoilers can be seen working as the plane climbs, turns and descends. Back seats give the best view of the flaps and spoilers working together when landing. Passengers near the wing may be able to see right through it when they are full out.

Holding patterns

A pilot on a long-distance route starts his descent more than 100 miles out, but long before he reaches the last stage of the flight, preparations for guiding him in are already being made.

As the incoming flight shows up, a bright "blip" on his radar screen, the area controller contacts the destination airport's approach controller by direct communication link to give a "release". He identifies the flight by its flight plan details and confirms the altitude that the pilot will descend to and the radio beacon that he will be told to head for.

By the time the inbound crew contacts approach control, the controller has already decided where the aircraft will be positioned in the sequence of other inbounds, outbounds and overflights. This he does by using his minimum separation of 1,000 feet vertically and three miles horizontally on radar. Using speed control he regulates the constant flow of fast jet and slower turboprop and piston-engined aircraft.

At the beginning of the descent, he tells the pilot of the inbound flight the type of approach to make to the designated runway, and gives a resumé of local weather conditions.

At most major airports, aircraft make a radar controlled approach to the Instrument Landing System for a particular runway. For the approach the pilot is guided by the radar controller, who will put him into a "hold" if the airport is busy. The hold is an area of airspace in the airport's control zone where aircraft are kept flying safely around a radio beacon until they can be cleared to start the approach to landing. In no-wind conditions a properly-flown holding pattern should take the form of a racetrack, and take four minutes from beginning to end, but if the wind is strong, one side of the racetrack will elongate and the other shorten as the aircraft fly before or into it.

Guided into the uppermost level, each flight descends in turn, layer by layer, 1,000 feet at a time, until it reaches the lowest level. The busiest airports may have four or five stacks, smaller airports have two. Aircraft may be held for up to an hour.

Traffic inbound from the hold is separated according to the runway configuration at the destination airport. If there is only one runway, used for both landing and takeoff, landing aircraft must be spaced six miles apart. In good weather conditions, aircraft landing at airports with a separate runway for landings only will be brought out of the stack in a steady stream, three miles apart. But they may be spaced six miles apart in gusty, turbulent conditions. The controller ensures that the first aircraft is clear of the runway before the next one touches down.

At a range of nine miles and a height of 3,000 feet, the aircraft intercepts the ILS glidepath. Under the instructions of the air controller in the tower, the captain starts his final descent to the runway.

The progress of each flight, from takeoff to roll-out, appears in alphanumeric display on the approach controllers' radar screens, and is automatically video-recorded. In the event of an accident, the stored tapes can be played back and studied by investigators.

8 "Roger, seven-three-two. You are cleared to land two-eight-right"

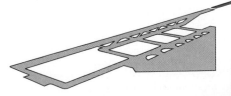

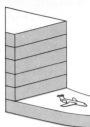

1 "Heathrow Approach, Worldair seven-three-two is descending to FL one-o-o and estimating Ockham at time two-four"
"Roger, Worldair seven-three-two. Continue descent to FL eight-o and enter the Ockham hold. Short delay only and landing runway two-eight-right"
"Roger. Descending to FL eight-o"

2 "Approach, Worldair seven-three-two is over Ockham entering the hold level at eight-o"
"Seven-three-two, next time over Ockham leave on a heading of o-seven-o degrees and descend now to FL seven-o"
"Roger. Heading o-seven-o and leaving eight-o for seven-o"

3 "Seven-three-two is over Ockham heading o-seven-o level at seven-o"
"Roger, seven-three-two. Descend to three thousand feet on QNH one-o-two-four"
"Seven-three-two leaving seven-o for three thousand feet on QNH one-o-two-four"
"Seven-three-two, that's correct. Contact radar director on one-two-o point four"

4 "Seven-three-two changing to one-two-o point four"
"Director, Worldair seven-three-two is with you passing four thousand for three thousand"

5 "Roger. Seven-three-two, continue to two thousand feet. Reduce speed to one-seven-o knots. You are fifteen miles from touchdown"

6 "Worldair seven-three-two, turn left heading three-two-o degrees and report established on the localizer two-eight-right"
"Seven-three-two is established"
"Seven-three-two is twelve miles from touchdown. Contact tower on one-one-eight point four"

FL 8,000 ft

FL 7,000 ft

FL 6,000 ft

FL 5,000 ft

FL 4,000 ft

FL 3,000 ft

Flight level (FL) 2,000 ft

7 "Tower, the Worldair seven-three-two is established. Leaving two thousand feet on the glidepath"

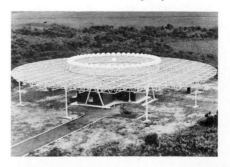

The hold, which may be as much as 20 miles away from the airport it serves, passes over a VOR beacon. A pilot locates it by following the radial leading to it. This shows up on the VOR receiver on his control panel. Looking like a broad-brimmed white top hat, the VOR station **right** broadcasts its signals from frequencies 108 to 118 on the FM dial.

Landing

As the descent begins, the calm relaxation of the flight crew changes to intense concentration. Between staccato bursts of radio talk and crackle, the captain makes critical decisions with precision.

His choice of approach speed is defined in exhaustive specifications made by the aircraft's manufacturers. They determine a minimum speed for final approach under ideal conditions, "V_{ref}", for which they guarantee landing performance data. Actual approach speeds are higher, 120 to 160 mph for a subsonic jet.

The heavier the aircraft, the higher the V_{ref} and the longer the distance needed to stop. For various gross weights and an approach speed of V_{ref} the manufacturers calculate the required runway length by measuring the distance from the point at which the plane is 50 feet high to its stopping position, and multiplying this by one and two thirds.

But more than this distance may be necessary on wet and slippery surfaces and the captain has to limit landing weight correspondingly.

Airliners approaching touchdown follow a shallow glideslope, miles long. The more steeply they descend, the less noise disturbance they cause to nearby residents. Just before the final descent the pilot lowers the landing-gears and extends the flaps fully, to slow the aircraft while maintaining lift. Unnecessarily early extension of the gears and flaps causes high drag and thus higher fuel consumption and noise levels.

Crossing the runway threshold, he "flares out", lifts the nose slightly to reduce the rate of descent, and gently throttles back. He aims for the VASIs, the Visual Approach Slope Indicators; but a 747 pilot, his eyes some four storeys above the wheels, aims at the 1,500-foot point to ensure adequate wheel clearance. Runways with no visual aids are difficult, especially at night or if the runway slopes, and heavy rain can cause insidious optical illusions from its prismatic effect on the windshield.

As the aircraft sinks down onto the main wheels, the captain raises the spoilers, "dumping" lift. Because of their drag, they also act as air brakes. He engages reverse thrust and ap-

Reverse thrust buckets, basically similar to these clamshell buckets used on Concorde, are used to slow aircraft down after touchdown. In normal flight they are open; when they are shut, exhaust gases are deflected forward and outward, providing a backward thrust that helps the wheel brakes to kill the landing speed. The wheel brakes alone are able to slow an aircraft in an emergency, but they may become dangerously overheated. To reduce the danger of explosion, nitrogen is used to fill aircraft tyres.

All high-lift surfaces are extended on this Airbus A300B2 as it lands. Slats have been extended from the leading edge along the full wingspan, and Fowler flaps have been run out along the tracks visible at the trailing edges. This configuration, needed to lower a plane weighing around 120 tons gently onto the runway, creates high drag, but each of the General Electronic turbofan engines has a full 51,000 lb of thrust to accelerate the aircraft in case the landing has to be aborted.

plies the wheel brakes by gently pressing the tops of the rudder pedals. Maximum wheel-braking capacity is applied only in an emergency. With multiple fixed and moving discs between the wheels, modern brakes can absorb well over 60 million foot-pounds of energy.

On a slippery runway the brake pedals can be fully depressed. The sophisticated anti-skid system senses when each tyre begins to slide, releases the brakes momentarily to allow the wheel to grip again, then reapplies them. This occurs several times a second maintaining an optimum slip ratio for stopping.

The worst hazard of wet runways is aquaplaning (hydroplaning) when wheels may "ski" on the film of surface water, losing adhesion. Runways can be grooved, like highways, with transverse slits a quarter of an inch deep give stopping characteristics almost equivalent to dry conditions on a wet runway.

Slowing a heavily-laded 747 to a safe taxying speed is equivalent to bringing 6,000 family cars to a halt from over 40 mph.

Slats on the leading edge and flaps on the trailing edge are extended in low-speed flight to increase lift and drag. Air channelled through the slots holds the main airflow to the wing and flaps, maintaining lift.

Raising a spoiler disturbs the airflow over the upper wing surfaces. The resulting increase in drag slows the aircraft and is useful in controlling a steep descent. One spoiler can also be raised to bank the plane.

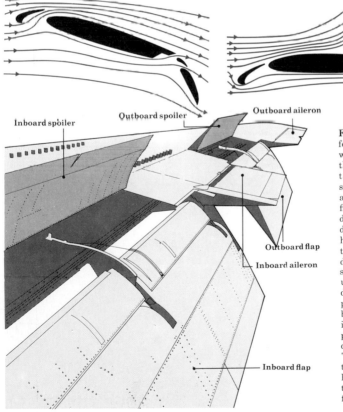

Inboard spoiler

Outboard spoiler

Outboard aileron

Outboard flap

Inboard aileron

Inboard flap

Flaps and spoilers festoon a Boeing 707's wing. During landing they provide the drag that the plane's streamlining eliminates during cruising flight. The flaps are driven backward and downward on rails, and have to be forced into the airstream by hydraulic power. The spoilers, sometimes used as air brakes during the fast early part of the letdown, before the aircraft intercepts the glide-path, are fully raised during roll-out to "dump" lift and put the weight onto the landing-gears so the tyres will grip more firmly.

Runway lighting

The distinctive pattern of lights marking the runway approach says "home" to the pilot who may have flown his aircraft through long hours of darkness. Two lines of lights along the runway sides give the perspective for judging the angle of approach and round-out for touchdown, such essential guidance that airports still keep at hand portable lighting units for emergencies.

Sophisticated, expensive lighting systems are also essential for a rapid alignment check during daytime approaches if visibility is poor. For a pilot breaking out of low cloud, high-intensity approach lights are the only visual clue that the ground is near. In fog, even approach lights may hardly be visible, but the bright runway lights will guide the roll-out after touchdown.

Fog-plagued airports may have individual lights that peak at an intensity of 30,000 candelas (twice the illumination of a set of car headlamps). To prevent dazzle they can be dimmed — from 100 per cent for sunlight or fog, to one per cent for a clear night.

On the taxiways the pilot follows blue edge lights and sometimes green centre lights marking the route. Red stop bars may appear when another plane crosses the path.

Failure of the electricity supply could be catastrophic to a landing jet, so most civil airports have emergency systems that switch in automatically within 15 seconds of a failure, and those with all-weather facilities have a stand-by system that switches in within one second.

National differences have made the standardization of airport lighting systems difficult. London's Heathrow Airport is among the most complex, with 28,000 individual lamps, but the American system, illustrated here, is widely used.

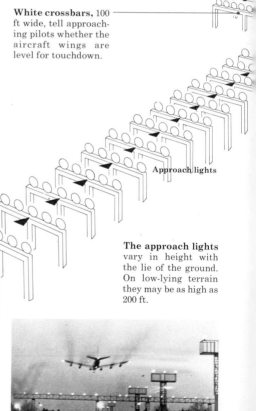

White crossbars, 100 ft wide, tell approaching pilots whether the aircraft wings are level for touchdown.

Approach lights

Sequence flashers, lines of white strobe lights, illuminate in sequence to guide the pilot's eyes towards the runway centreline.

Sequence flashers

The approach lights vary in height with the lie of the ground. On low-lying terrain they may be as high as 200 ft.

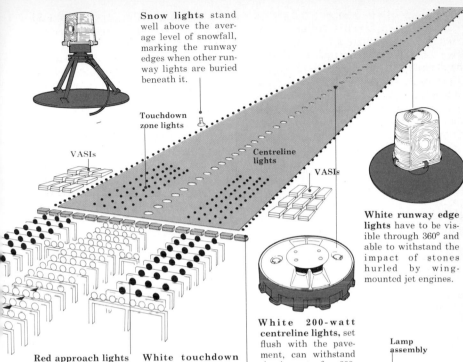

Snow lights stand well above the average level of snowfall, marking the runway edges when other runway lights are buried beneath it.

Touchdown zone lights

VASIs

Centreline lights

VASIs

White runway edge lights have to be visible through 360° and able to withstand the impact of stones hurled by wing-mounted jet engines.

White 200-watt centreline lights, set flush with the pavement, can withstand the impact of a 300-ton jet landing squarely on them.

Red approach lights mark an undershoot zone 1,000 ft long in which approaching aircraft should not land.

White touchdown zone lights give depth to the pilot's perspective view of the runway, and mark the 2,500-ft long touchdown zone.

Lamp assembly

Filter assembly

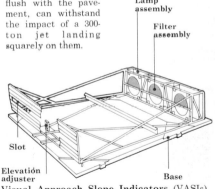

Slot

Elevation adjuster

Base

Approach lights have frangible stems that snap off if accidentally hit.

Threshold lights may be bidirectional, showing green to pilots landing and red on the reverse side, marking the runway end for pilots taking off.

Visual Approach Slope Indicators (VASIs) indicate the pilot's angle of approach and help to prevent overshoot or undershoot in all but the poorest visibility. They consist of two parallel rows of lights angled to project a white beam above the ideal approach path, and a red beam beneath it. If the pilot is approaching at the correct angle he sees red lights above white. If all the lights are white he is too high and if they are red he is too low. Runways used by Boeing 747s need a three-row configuration because of the height of the flight deck above the wheels. The individual unit illustrated in this cutaway diagram is mounted on a frangible stem, and is strong enough to withstand jet blast.

75

Automatic landing

Breaking out of cloud at a height of 200 feet, a jet pilot has 20 seconds or less before touchdown. Finding himself immediately at decision height (the point where he has to decide whether it is safe to land, or whether he should put the aircraft into a go-around climb) he has a last few critical moments in which to assess instrument readings and take corrective action. But he loses vital time refocusing his eyes on the runway to identify his position in relation to the centreline and glidepath.

The prevalence of fog, mist and low cloud at British and European airports (where, for instance, British Airways makes over 200,000 landings a year) led to the development of an automatic landing system.

An autoland system is a super-autopilot which detects and responds to Instrument Landing System (ILS) radio beams. In fog or poor visibility, it guides aircraft onto the runway accurately and safely, and in good visibility it gives a more consistent and therefore safer approach and landing than might always be possible under manual control. By guiding flare-out accurately, it can lower the decision height for a safe go-around to less than 20 feet.

The ILS consists of a localizer beacon whose beam, radiating along the straight line of approach to the runway, guides the aircraft onto the centreline, and a glidepath transmitter, set about 450 feet to one side of the runway, with a beam, angled at about three degrees to the horizontal, that guides aircraft down at an even rate of descent.

The position of an aircraft in relation to these beams is shown on the flight director. Once the autopilot has locked onto the ILS beams, the pilot has no need to touch the controls until the aircraft is on the runway.

Glidepath signals are usually "captured" by aircraft at a height of about 1,000 feet. Pilots fly either manually

A localizer, left, transmits two radio beams on either side of, and overlapping, the extended runway centreline for horizontal guidance.

The glidepath transmitter, right, sends beams above and below the descent-path centreline, to intersect localizer beams at a 3° angle, for vertical guidance.

The main gears touch down first, followed by the nose gear, and the pilot engages reverse thrust. Autoland control is cut except on the rudder, which guides the aircraft down the runway until speed has dropped to 85 mph.

At 12 ft, three radio altimeters, measuring the rate of descent, cause automatic adjustment and alignment for landing.

Localizer

Glidepath transmitter

Inner marke

Flare-out at 65 ft raises the aircraft's nose to arrest descent.

or on autopilot toward the airport's navigation beacon until they intercept the ILS radio beams and follow them down to the runway. At 65 feet, radio altimeters trigger flare-out, raising the nose so the aircraft sinks gently onto the runway.

The first passenger-carrying autoland was made in 1965. Subsequent refinements improved the system, but ILS beams bend if they pass over buildings, stretches of water, or even highway traffic, making the system unsuitable for many airports.

The new Microwave Landing System (MLS) is gradually being adopted at major airports. This system transmits a radio beam from left to right and right to left across the sky. By automatically timing the intervals between successive interceptions of the sweeping beam, the landing system can accurately calculate an aircraft's position relative to the runway. It is cheaper than the ILS to install at airports (although the aircraft equipment is more costly) and, because the beams spread more widely, it offers a number of alternative approach paths.

To date, only about 1,000 out of 4,000 major world airports are equipped with ILS suitable for autoland, and only about ten runways have the most accurate versions enabling aircraft to land safely in zero visibility with a less than one in 1,000,000 probability of failure.

ILS-equipped aircraft have more than one set of radio beam receivers, computers and control circuits which cross-monitor each other to ensure safety from the point the aircraft intercepts the ILS beam to its final deceleration on the runway. Pilots check their display panels, ready to take over manually if the system fails.

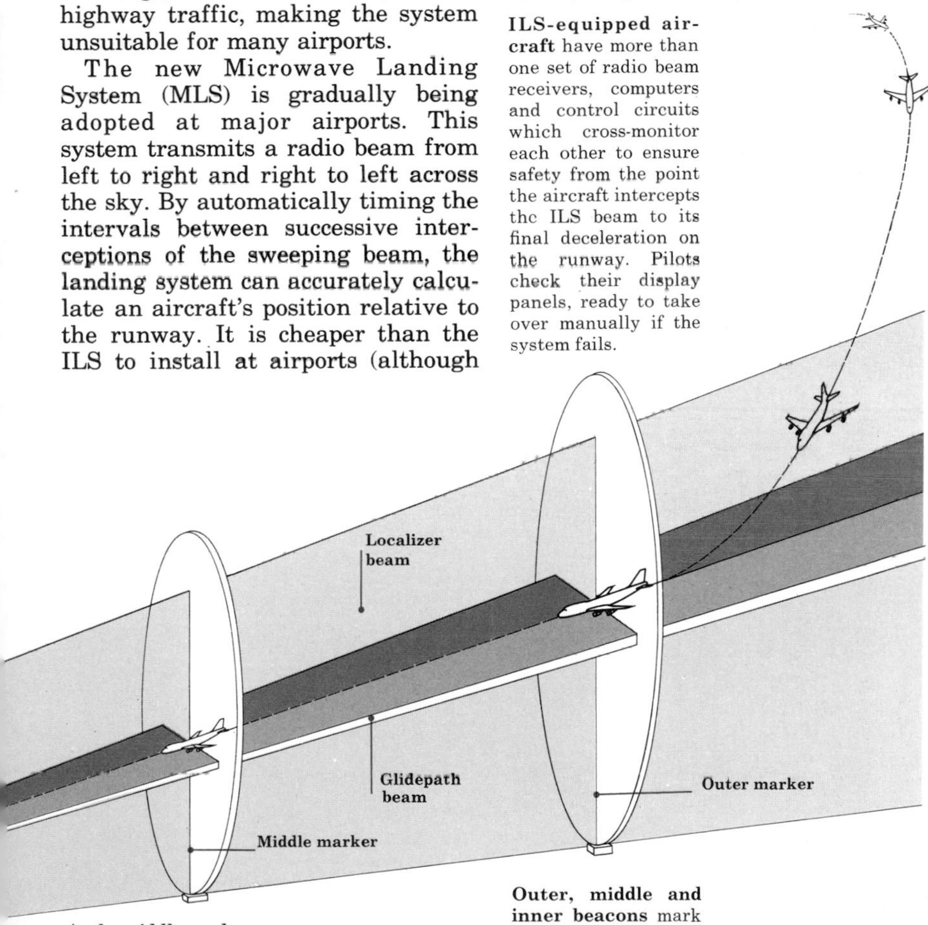

Localizer beam

Glidepath beam

Middle marker

Outer marker

At the middle marker, ideally half a mile from the runway, the aircraft is just 15 seconds from touchdown.

Outer, middle and inner beacons mark the distance to touchdown. The aircraft is safely locked onto the beams as it passes the outer marker.

After touchdown

An airliner landing at a large airport may have to negotiate a mile of taxiways to reach a stand or parking place. Pilots usually have maps of the airport layout, and taxiways are marked with lights and other signals. But if a pilot loses his way despite the radioed directions of controllers in the tower giving him the route to be taken, an airport truck with a large "Follow me" sign may be sent to lead him in.

Lines painted on the concrete apron adjoining the taxiways lead the pilot to his final positioning; he will aim to keep his nosewheel on the appropriate line, and the aircraft's stopping point must be precise if the airbridges (the telescopic walkways joining aircraft to terminal) are to reach the doors. Various optical or electrical signs assist the manoeuvre: some of these are illustrated.

Moving walkways are often installed to speed passengers disembarking; each stand can be as much

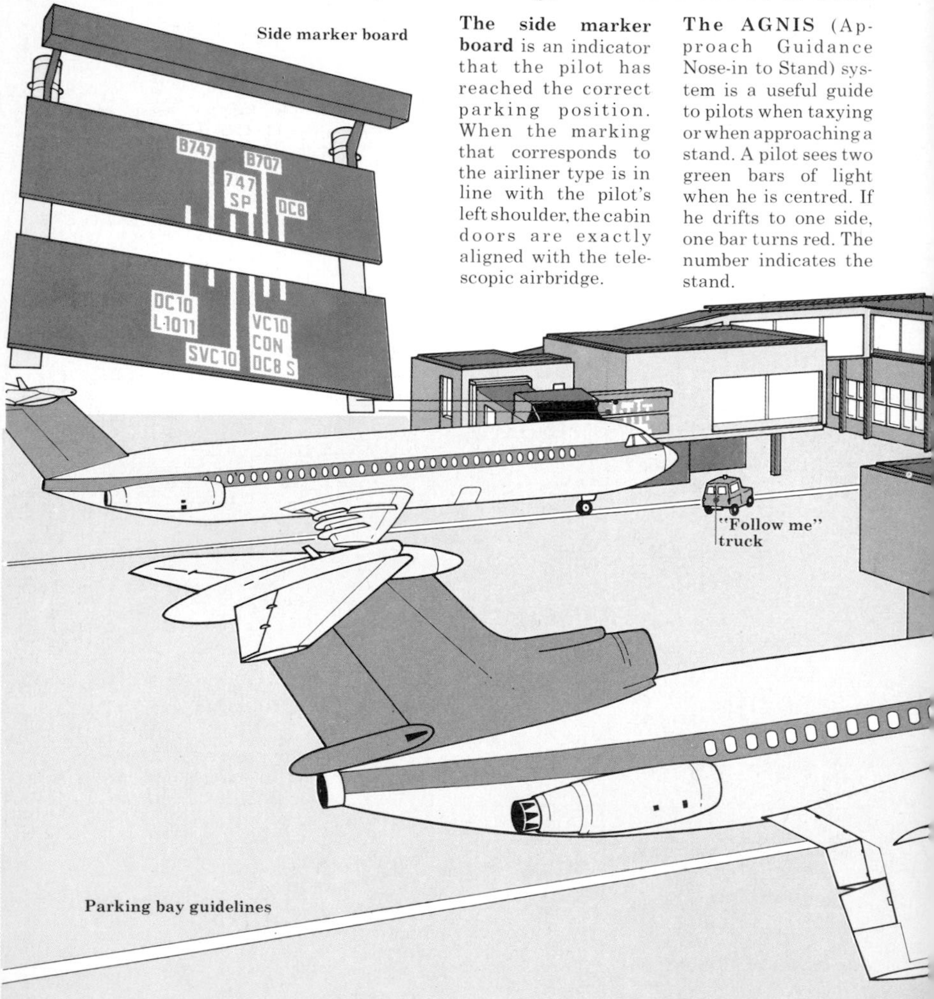

Side marker board

The side marker board is an indicator that the pilot has reached the correct parking position. When the marking that corresponds to the airliner type is in line with the pilot's left shoulder, the cabin doors are exactly aligned with the telescopic airbridge.

The AGNIS (Approach Guidance Nose-in to Stand) system is a useful guide to pilots when taxying or when approaching a stand. A pilot sees two green bars of light when he is centred. If he drifts to one side, one bar turns red. The number indicates the stand.

"Follow me" truck

Parking bay guidelines

as 200 feet wide, and a pier that can accommodate half a dozen planes will be hundreds of yards long.

If the airliner has to park at a stand remote from the piers, mobile passenger steps are driven out to the aircraft and passengers will be collected by bus, or by a mobile passenger lounge, perhaps capable of holding 150 people. Such lounges are mounted on hydraulic "stilts" whose height can be changed so that the exit aligns with the doors of any type of plane and with the terminal doors. An airline may choose to save the expense of a ramp disembarkation and bus passengers to the terminal.

Immediately all passengers have disembarked the airliner can be refuelled and reloaded with cargo, galleys replenished, toilets emptied and the systems checked. Turnaround may take only 20 minutes for an airliner plying a short-haul route.

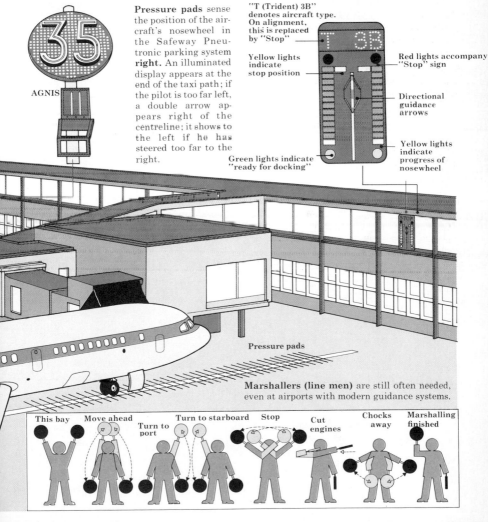

Pressure pads sense the position of the aircraft's nosewheel in the Safeway Pneutronic parking system **right**. An illuminated display appears at the end of the taxi path; if the pilot is too far left, a double arrow appears right of the centreline; it shows to the left if he has steered too far to the right.

AGNIS

"T (Trident) 3B" denotes aircraft type. On alignment, this is replaced by "Stop"

Yellow lights indicate stop position

Red lights accompany "Stop" sign

Directional guidance arrows

Yellow lights indicate progress of nosewheel

Green lights indicate "ready for docking"

Pressure pads

Marshallers (line men) are still often needed, even at airports with modern guidance systems.

This bay   Move ahead   Turn to port   Turn to starboard   Stop   Cut engines   Chocks away   Marshalling finished

Aircraft spotter's guide

During the 1930s, thousands of aircraft spotters at Croydon Airport in the UK used to crowd the terminal roof and a special enclosure on the airfield. Many more thousands of enthusiasts recorded the development of aviation in the USA. With the advent of the diesel locomotive, disenchanted steam-engine spotters turned to aircraft and a new kind of registration number. The first letter of an aircraft's registration designates the country (G for the UK, N for the US) and is followed by the aircraft's own series of letters and numbers. The UK registration series numbers, currently prefixed by G–BF, are out of sequence on the Concordes: G–BOAC.

Post-World War II sophisticates equip themselves with VHF radio receivers, picking up the civil waveband (118–136 MHz) to listen to pilots talking to air traffic controllers. Armed with an airways chart, the new-style spotter can plot an aircraft's progress from several hundred miles away.

This guide is designed for everyone who would like to know more about the aircraft they fly in and see parked around airport terminals, or even from cabin windows 35,000 feet up. The following 43 pages tell the story, and point out the unique features, of different aircraft, from piston-engined light planes to Concorde, taking in helicopters, seaplanes, hovercraft and the newest business jets.

Still to be seen are Shorts Sandringham flying boats, in service with airlines in the Caribbean; the Douglas DC-3 which first flew in 1935 and is *still* the most numerous civil airliner in the world; and the very first commercial jet, the Comet, which thrilled the world by flying higher and faster than anything else.

Business jets, some restyled every few years like cars, exhibit the most advanced technological features to be found on civil aircraft. Among airliners, the supersonic Concorde and Tu–144, and the subsonic Airbus A300 are likely to remain the most advanced in service for several years.

Airline fleets are aging, and becoming progressively more uneconomical to run, and the world's airlines are about to embark on their biggest-ever spending spree for new planes to replace thousands of first-generation jets such as Boeing 707s. But it will be at least four years, the time it takes to design a new aircraft and put it into production, before the new generation of jets can be spotted at the world's airports.

Strict limits on noise levels at many airports have increased interest in VTOL (vertical takeoff and landing) aircraft. VTOL aircraft fly above aural range before making a sharp-angled descent, causing noise disturbance over a smaller area of ground than CTOL (conventional takeoff and landing) or STOL (short takeoff and landing) aircraft.

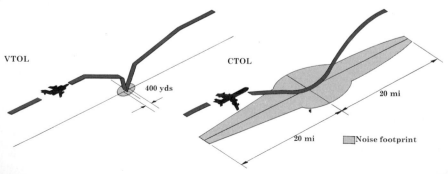

VTOL   400 yds

CTOL   20 mi   20 mi   Noise footprint

Aérospatiale Caravelle

Aérospatiale Caravelle

As the first short-haul jetliner to enter service (1959) the Sud-Est (now Aérospatiale) Caravelle created a stir, despite predictions that it would not sell. The high-flying, long-range Comet was the only jet airliner in service, and it was thought that the Caravelle would be too costly in fuel at low cruising altitudes.

Its design became a classic: to reduce noise the designers mounted two turbojets on the rear fuselage.

The company sold 270 Caravelles, and the concept became so familiar that one Aérospatiale advertisement featured two boys looking at a picture of one of its emulators and saying *"Oh, ils ont copié Caravelle"*.

Aérospatiale
Caravelle 11R

Rear-mounted engines keep jet-blast and noise away from the passenger cabin.

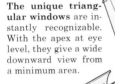

The unique triangular windows are instantly recognizable. With the apex at eye level, they give a wide downward view from a minimum area.

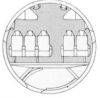

The fuselage cross-section was determined by the shape and size of the nose section.

French designers modelled the Caravelle around the complete nose-section of the British Comet.

The Caravelle, 11R, which first flew in 1967, had a 3-ft fuselage extension forward of the wing incorporating a large freight door, to admit bulky cargo. Six mixed-traffic 11Rs were built.

Wing fences, thin metal strips, keep the airflow straight, reducing drag and improving lateral con-

trol. Spoilers, 20 ft long, can be raised from the upper surfaces to increase drag.

Airbus A300B

The Airbus A300B is the most advanced aircraft currently in airline service. Proposed in 1965 by the British and French governments (the British government subsequently withdrew its support and West Germany joined the team) it is built by companies in five countries and represents Europe's first attempt to break the US monopoly of the market for large subsonic airliners.

The unique wing incorporates supercritical features, now being adopted in advanced military and other civil jetliners. These delay the onset of shockwaves up to high subsonic speeds. The wing took nearly 4,000,000 man-hours and almost 4,000 hours of wind-tunnel tests to perfect. The wing skin panels, some 51 feet long, are milled by computer-guided machines and preformed in gigantic presses. When released, they spring back to the exact aerofoil shape.

The Airbus is the quietest wide-bodied jet, quieter than smaller jets weighing one tenth as much. Unlike other wide-bodied jets, it has only two engines: General Electric CF6-50C (or alternatively Pratt & Whitney JT9D-59A) turbofans which give it the lowest fuel consumption per passenger of any jet in history.

A300B seating configurations can be varied from 345 passengers maximum in charter layout, to a mixed passenger/freight, or all-cargo payload. With an extra centre-section fuel tank, thicker wing roots and Krüger flaps for a sprightly takeoff at "hot and high" airports, the Airbus was converted from a short- to a medium-range airliner in the 1974 B4 version.

No advance sales were made. Air France flew the first scheduled services in 1974, and by mid-1978 production was speeding to four a month, with over 80 sales in the preceding 12 months. This airliner sold itself.

The European Airbus is backed by the governments of France, West Germany, the Netherlands and Spain. The wing was designed and developed by British Aerospace, and the engines are American.

The sophisticated Airbus design means that for a similar passenger capacity, a wide-bodied trijet (superimposed) has an extra engine, 7° more wing sweepback, 27% extra wing area, 60% more tailplane (stabilizer) and 20 tons of additional structure.

Airbus A300B

The A300B carries 20 containers in the hold and, in the A300C4 (convertible), 13 cargo pallets 88 in wide and 125 in long, loaded on to the passenger deck through a large cargo door.

Easily adapted to mixed payloads, the A300B can carry a maximum of 345 tourist-class passengers, or 90,250 lb of cargo. With a full hold of containers and pallets on the main deck, it can still accommodate 145 passengers.

Cargo configuration

Mixed payload configuration

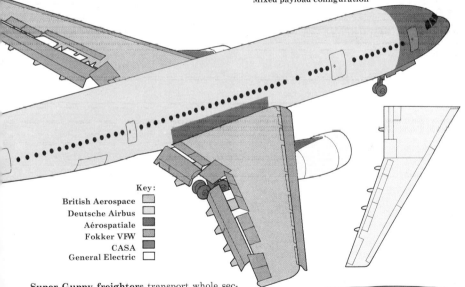

Key:
British Aerospace ▢
Deutsche Airbus ▢
Aérospatiale ▢
Fokker VFW ▢
CASA ▢
General Electric ▢

Super Guppy freighters transport whole sections of the Airbus to the assembly line at Toulouse in France. The Guppy's nose is hinged, so the whole fuselage forward of the wing opens up for loading the huge components.

Super Guppy

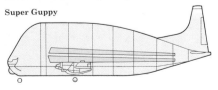

The supercritical Airbus wing has a more convex underside, a flatter top and a down-curved trailing edge so that lift is spread more evenly from the front to the rear section. This advanced design delays formation of sonic shock-waves at high speeds, permitting the wing to be thicker, yet produce no more drag at high speeds than a wing with a conventional section. It is also 2,500 lb lighter and has less sweepback,

The Antonovs/BAC VC10 and Super VC10

One of the leading USSR aircraft design bureaux is led by Oleg K. Antonov, whose design team specializes in high-wing transports for use on second-class, or unprepared, airfields. The 52-seater An-24 (1960) is a short-range twin turboprop, similar to the Fokker-VFW F 27 Friendship. The high wings minimize the risk of propeller damage on the USSR's many unsurfaced landing strips. Aeroflot's vast fleet contains more An-24s than any other airliner; over 1,000 fire-fighting, aerial survey and passenger versions have been built.

Antonov An-24

The An-28 (1969) designed for STOL performance from the most inaccessible "hot and high" airstrips, seats up to 19 passengers. The An-72 (1977) has two powerful turbofan engines mounted above the wing. The blast, directed across large flaps which can be extended sharply downward, hits the ground at a 90-degree angle, reducing the takeoff run.

Antonov An-28

Antonov An-72

BAC Super VC10

Few jets have been as enthusiastically received by passengers and pilots as the Vickers (later BAC) VC10s. Singularly beautiful aircraft, they were custom-built for the national airline, BOAC, but only 54 were sold.

In 1957, within a year of cancelling Vickers' projected successor to the Comet, the VC7, BOAC directors ordered the American Boeing 707, and a new British jet for the short runways of the old Empire routes.

By the 1960s, however, most major airports had extended their runways to meet the needs of the first-generation jets, and the more powerful engines for short-runway operation made the VC10 marginally more costly to run. In 1964 BOAC condemned its new jet as uneconomical.

But the VC10s' four by-pass engines made them quieter than the 707's and efficient Fowler flaps gave a gentler approach speed so that, in the ensuing decade their popularity made them profitable.

BAe One-Eleven

BAe One-Eleven Series 300

Freddie Laker, Managing Director of British United (now British Caledonian) Airways, was the first customer for Britain's successor to the Viscount. A trim 65/89-seater, it was the first modern short-haul twinjet in service in 1965. More than 225 have been sold world-wide, notably in the USA, for which market the Series 400 was specially designed.

Two Rolls-Royce Spey turbofan engines, economical on fuel and able to accelerate from minimum rpm to 95 per cent maximum thrust in only five seconds, enable the One-Eleven to operate from such short landing strips that it is being considered as a replacement for the Japanese NAMC YS-11 turboprop.

The STOL 475 variant, designed to operate from "hot and high" and grass and gravel airfields, has tyres with anti-slush protection and gravel deflectors; glass-fibre skins on the flaps protect them from flying gravel. Quick-change versions can be converted from passenger to cargo layout by four men in less than two hours.

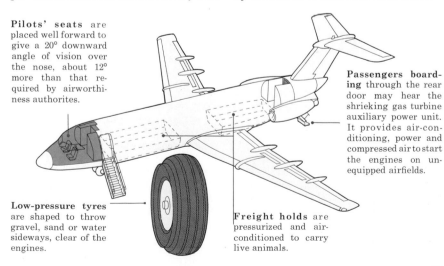

Pilots' seats are placed well forward to give a 20° downward angle of vision over the nose, about 12° more than that required by airworthiness authorites.

Passengers boarding through the rear door may hear the shrieking gas turbine auxiliary power unit. It provides air-conditioning, power and compressed air to start the engines on unequipped airfields.

Low-pressure tyres are shaped to throw gravel, sand or water sideways, clear of the engines.

Freight holds are pressurized and air-conditioned to carry live animals.

Concorde

In January 1976, 29 years after the first aircraft broke the sound barrier, two Concordes took off from Paris and London on the first supersonic passenger service. The westbound flight beat the sun, arriving, as it were, before it had started.

After the Anglo-French Supersonic Treaty was signed in 1962, years of intensive research and over 5,000 hours of wind-tunnel tests proved that the long, streamlined fuselage and slender ogival delta wing finally reconciled good control at speeds as low as 230 mph with low drag up to Mach 2.2 (around 1,300 mph).

The wings, produced by Aéro-spatiale, have elevons which work together as elevators and differentially as ailerons. There are no flaps; control is built into the wings through camber, taper, droop and twist.

Rolls-Royce designed the powerplant — so called because the four Olympus turbojet engines constitute just one part of a complex four-part system made up of air intakes adjustable for high and low speeds, engines with two independent compressors for low fuel consumption at sub- and supersonic speeds, the reheat system to give extra thrust for takeoff and transonic acceleration, and variable geometry exhaust nozzles that also serve as reverse thrust. There could be no margin of error in the powerplant design. Concorde's payload is less than a third of that of a subsonic airliner, so the slightest reduction in engine efficiency is the difference between profit and loss.

The cruising speed was fixed at Mach 2.2, just below the "heat barrier", so the airframe, designed for a life of 60,000 hours, could be constructed in an aluminium alloy resistant to variations in temperature from minus 35 to over 120 degrees Celsius (-31°/248°F). Above this speed rises in temperature demand the use of more costly steel and titanium.

Concorde flies high at 50,000 feet or more, where air density is around one tenth that at sea level, temperatures are low and supersonic engines efficient. She handles easily, pilots report, and the transonic acceleration is unnoticeable. Back in airport takeoff lines, captains of subsonic jets radio in to let her pass for their passengers to see, calling "Speedbird, you're beautiful" to her crew.

Concorde's fuel is pumped between tanks to trim the plane. In supersonic flight, fuel is pumped rearward to keep the nose high.

Concorde's centre of gravity is shifted rearward when the aircraft is landing, but to a lesser extent than when going supersonic.

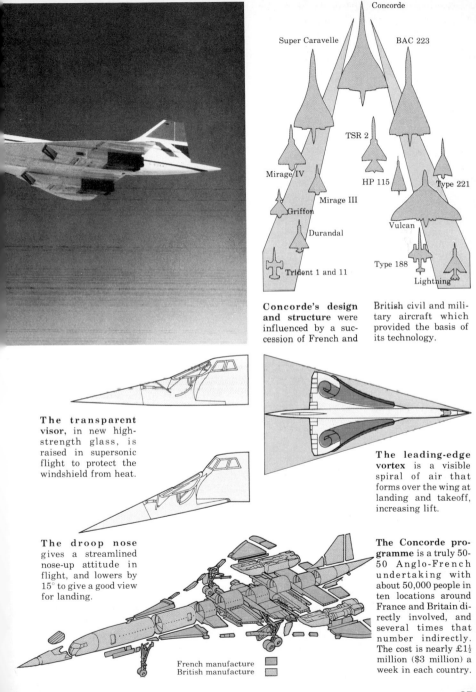

Concorde

Super Caravelle

BAC 223

TSR 2

Mirage IV

HP 115

Type 221

Mirage III

Griffon

Vulcan

Durandal

Type 188

Trident 1 and 11

Lightning

Concorde's design and structure were influenced by a succession of French and British civil and military aircraft which provided the basis of its technology.

The transparent visor, in new high-strength glass, is raised in supersonic flight to protect the windshield from heat.

The leading-edge vortex is a visible spiral of air that forms over the wing at landing and takeoff, increasing lift.

The droop nose gives a streamlined nose-up attitude in flight, and lowers by 15° to give a good view for landing.

French manufacture
British manufacture

The Concorde programme is a truly 50-50 Anglo-French undertaking with about 50,000 people in ten locations around France and Britain directly involved, and several times that number indirectly. The cost is nearly £1½ million ($3 million) a week in each country.

87

Boeing 707

Spare 707 engines can be transported in streamlined underwing "pod-paks" which do not impair the aircraft's handling. With this capability, an airline needs fewer spare engines. The CFM56 engine, projected for the 1980s re-engined 707s, is built, like all modern engines, in modules so that it can be dismantled into small sections and carried inside the aircraft.

The Boeing 707, the first American turbojet airliner, revolutionized post-World War II air transport. Benefiting from de Havilland's experience in designing the first jetliner, the Comet I, Boeing's design provided a model for the first generation of American passenger jets. The 707's cruising speed of over 500 mph, and its 4,000-mile range made intercontinental jet travel a commonplace.

The prototype, developed with $20,000,000 of Boeing's own capital, was unique in having a wing sweepback of 35 degrees, and four engines suspended in pods below the wings. As the 707-121, the first of a whole family of passenger and cargo variants, it was launched on its career by

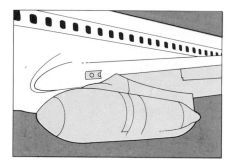

The fuel tanks are mounted inside the wings and in a large central tank between them. Each tank feeds the engine nearest to it. This aircraft can be refuelled in just under half an hour.

The 707 families are identified by "dash" numbers. The original -120, -220 and -720 families (seating up to 180) were domestic models; the stretched -320s and -420s (seating up to 219) were intercontinental versions.

Boeing 707-120B

Boeing 707-320C

Pan Am in 1958 — on the transatlantic route for prestige reasons, although it was designed and subsequently used for medium-range domestic service. It was followed by the intercontinental -320, the largest passenger jet of its era (which flew the first ever round-the-world service in 1959) and the short-range -720.

On 707s only the rudder is power-operated; the other control surfaces, aerodynamically balanced, are moved by spring tabs on the trailing edges. Though criticized for being noisy and excessively smoky, and for needing longer runways than existed at most airports in the 1950s, the 707 quickly overcame all opposition by flying more passengers and cargo faster, farther and more economically than any other passenger plane. Models fitted with turbofan engines were considerably quieter than the early turbojet-powered versions and by the early 1960s, runways at major airports had been extended to accommodate the new generation of jets.

During the two decades of 707 production, almost 2,000 have been built; the -320C is still in production.

The 707's successor, the McDonnell Douglas DC-8, produced in 1958, is so similar that only minor features distinguish the two aircraft.

The cabin air intakes are on the tops of the 707 engines and on either side of the DC-8's nose.

Overwing emergency exits have escape ropes that pull out and hook onto the inboard engine nacelles.

Double-slotted flaps, inboard and outboard, contrast with the DC-8's single flap.

The high-frequency antenna jutting out from the tip of the fin (vertical stabilizer) is peculiar to the 707.

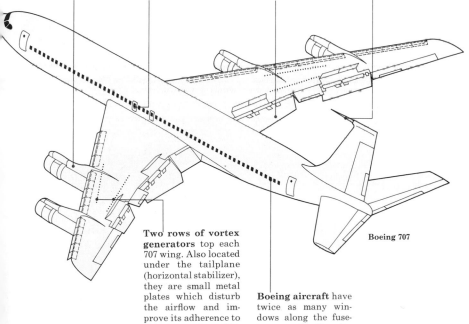

Boeing 707

Two rows of vortex generators top each 707 wing. Also located under the tailplane (horizontal stabilizer), they are small metal plates which disturb the airflow and improve its adherence to the wing surfaces. The DC-8's wings have more curved undersides inboard, adjacent to the fuselage.

Boeing aircraft have twice as many windows along the fuselage as the Douglas jets, usually 2 to each seat row. Douglas designs have larger windows.

Boeing 727

In the late 1950s, Boeing saw a market slot for a short/medium range jet airliner smaller than the 707. The engineers chose a rear-engined trijet, looking just like Britain's Hawker Siddeley Trident. In detail its design is quite different. The wing, with leading-edge slats and the newly-invented Krüger flaps to provide high lift for takeoff from short landing strips, was the most advanced then built. Unlike the 707, the 727 has power-operated control surfaces, but tabs on the primary controls enable the pilot to take over in emergencies. The 727 has a main passenger access at the rear, via a hydraulic stairway beneath the rear fuselage, and a pressure-tight bulkhead door inside, but since 1971, when a hijacker used one to escape by parachute with $200,000 ransom money, these doors have been sealed off on the American 727s. With sales of more than 1,500 since its first flight in 1963, the 727 is the world's best-selling jetliner.

The 727-200 (QC) is a projected quick-change version with seats, galleys and toilets fixed to pallets which are easily removed and replaced with roller floors for all-cargo operations. On the existing -100C (QC) this operation can be carried out in less than 30 minutes.

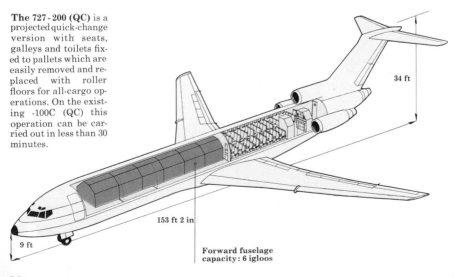

34 ft

153 ft 2 in

9 ft

Forward fuselage capacity: 6 igloos

Boeing 737

Unlike other US jet transports, the 737, Boeing's smallest jet airliner, originated with an order from a foreign customer, Lufthansa. In competition with the McDonnell Douglas DC-9 and the BAe One-Eleven, over 400 were sold in the ten years following its introduction in 1967.

The aircraft has almost the same fuselage cross-section as the longer 707 and 727, giving it a rather stubby appearance, but this design was adopted so that maximum use could be made of 727 tooling and components to keep initial costs low. The aircraft is powered by the JT8D turbofan engine developed for the 727, and has the 727's high-lift system. Wing sweepback tends to increase with an aircraft's speed and range; on the 737 it is 25 degrees and on the fast, long-range 747, 37.5.

Like all Boeing aircraft, the 737 has been developed into a family. There are cargo, convertible, business jet and military variants.

The 737 can be fitted with a "gravel kit", consisting of protective features which enable it to operate from unpaved or gravel airstrips.

A gravel-deflecting "ski" is fitted to the nose-gear, and there are other deflectors on the main gears.

Vortex generators under each engine inlet force air down from the lip to prevent gravel from being sucked into the engines. Glass fibre skins protect the undersides of the lower inboard flaps, the radio antennae are strengthened and the paint is abrasion-resistant.

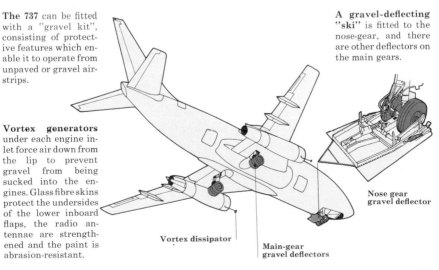

Nose gear gravel deflector

Vortex dissipator

Main-gear gravel deflectors

91

The Boeing 747

Between 1960 and 1966, the number of people travelling by air almost doubled from 100 to 200 million. Fleets had to multiply or aircraft had to be made bigger to meet the demand.

The Boeing 747 had twice the capacity, power and weight of any existing airliner. A completely new factory — arguably the largest building in the world — had to be built near Seattle in the USA to assemble two and a half million components around a fuselage big enough to have contained the Wright brothers' first flight. There was no prototype; number one was first off the production line. At a Paris Air Show, the power of the engines was forcibly demonstrated when the 150-mph jet blast 100 feet behind the aircraft blew the runway sidelights out of their holders.

Less than a year after the first flight, on January 22, 1970, Pan Am began scheduled services. Up to 500 passengers disembarking at once (a Qantas 747 evacuated a record 674 people after a hurricane in Darwin) caused chaos at air terminals. But fears about the runway lengths needed to take off with two and a half times the capacity of a 707 proved unfounded, thanks largely to the wing's high-lift devices. Big, trailing-edge flaps fan out to increase the wing area; slots permit the air to flow smoothly through. And the unique variable camber slats on the leading edge curve to the most efficient high-lift profile as they extend.

The huge 747 has room for six galleys costing $100,000 each, 16 toilets, 6,190 cubic feet of cargo and baggage space and 146 Arctic suits carried as part of the emergency equipment on polar flights. Repainting costs £20,000 ($40,000) and adds 1,000 pounds to the weight. The 747F cargo version has a cargo area the size of two tennis courts.

The weight of the 747 demanded 4 sets of 4-wheel bogies, like giant rollerskates, to land safely. The tubeless tyres are designed like modern car tyres to eject runway water through channels on either side.

The four turbofan engines, 8 ft in diameter, usually chosen for the 747, are versions of Pratt and Whitney's JT90, which powered a 747-200B to a world record takeoff weight of over 366 tons. Since they burn a gallon of fuel in under 2 seconds, a 747 carries more fuel than any other aircraft—over 39,000 gals (47,000 US gals).

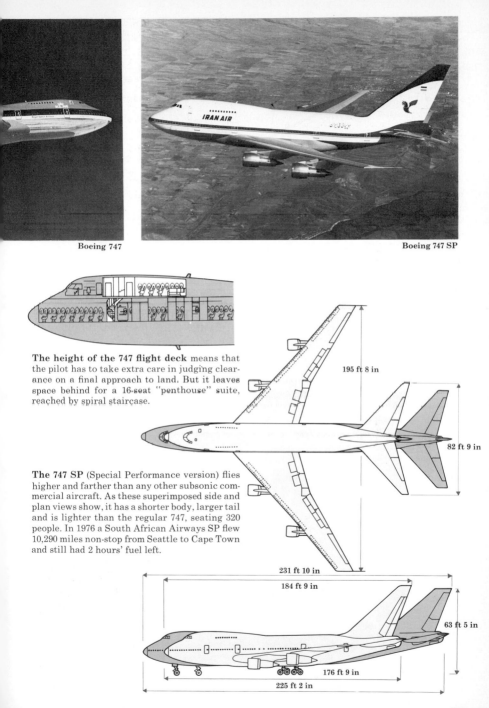

Boeing 747

Boeing 747 SP

The height of the 747 flight deck means that the pilot has to take extra care in judging clearance on a final approach to land. But it leaves space behind for a 16-seat "penthouse" suite, reached by spiral staircase.

The 747 SP (Special Performance version) flies higher and farther than any other subsonic commercial aircraft. As these superimposed side and plan views show, it has a shorter body, larger tail and is lighter than the regular 747, seating 320 people. In 1976 a South African Airways SP flew 10,290 miles non-stop from Seattle to Cape Town and still had 2 hours' fuel left.

195 ft 8 in

82 ft 9 in

231 ft 10 in

184 ft 9 in

63 ft 5 in

176 ft 9 in

225 ft 2 in

93

Britten-Norman Islander and Trislander

Britten-Norman Trislander

At a 1966 air fair, the Britten-Norman Islander took off inside the runway threshold markings. This, and its uncomplicated design, became its biggest selling-points: about 900 have been sold in over 100 countries. In Scotland it flies the world's shortest air route, from Westree to Papa Westree in less than two minutes. This utility aircraft has no central aisle, so the body is narrow, reducing weight and drag. It has bench seats for nine passengers, and two side doors. The aircraft is produced in the UK, Belgium and the Philippines, and costs under £50,000 ($100,000). The first Trislander, seven and a half feet longer to seat 17 passengers,

appeared in 1970. It has a redesigned tail with a third engine mounted at the top of the fin. Like the Islander, it can be fitted with skis, floats or four-wheel landing-gears, and adapted for fire-fighting, ambulance work, photographic survey assignments, executive transport, agricultural operations and fish-spotting.

Dowty-Rotol's new ducted propulsor, which may soon be seen on may new STOL aircraft, is now being tested on an Islander. A seven-blade variable-pitch fan inside a duct similar to that on a high by-pass ratio turbofan, it is driven by a 250 to 500 hp piston engine, and is much quieter than any conventional propeller.

Trislander: commuter layout

Trislander: cargo layout

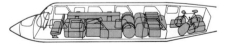

Trislander: executive layout

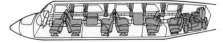

Raked-back wingtips increase the overall span to 53 ft and can house an extra fuel tank to supplement the main wing tanks, allowing an additional 2 hours' flying time.

The Islander has an optional 4-ft nose extension, standard on the Trislander, which can contain up to 28 cu ft of extra baggage. An optional ski-rack can be fitted in the rear baggage bay.

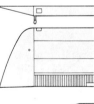

The Trislander is versatile in layout: 17 passengers can board through 5 large doors, stow their baggage at the back and enjoy the view from the large windows. Removable seats allow 24 ft of extra cargo space, or a 10-seat executive suite.

Business jets:
Canadair Challenger/Cessna Citation

Canadair Challenger

Canadair Challenger

68 ft 5 in

The Canadair Challenger 600 represents the ultimate in business jets. Big enough to be a 30-seater airliner, its cabin is more than eight feet wide and six feet high. The advanced supercritical wings, on which it cruises at 554 mph, hold more than 14,000 pounds of fuel giving it an intercontinental range of 4,600 miles, farther than any other business jet can fly. The Challenger, with motorized seats throughout, is one of the most luxurious private jets. At $6,000,000 it is also the most expensive. Yet in an intensely competitive field it had earned an unprecedented $1,000,000,000 in sales before the first flight.

Canadair Challenger: interior

Cessna Citation

The Cessna Citation I, a mass-produced "family" bizjet, sells well at just over $1,000,000. Cruising at around 400 mph over a range of 1,537 miles, it will not fly as fast or as far as other private jets, but low speeds and straight wings give this thrifty aircraft a quietness and ease of handling that permit its owners to land within 3,000 feet on runways too small, and at airports too noise-restricted, for many other jets.

The Citations change little in basic design, but become bigger and more powerful with every model: Citation III (1981) with a range of nearly 3,000 miles, will cost three times as much as Citation I.

Citation I seats up to 6 in a cabin only 5 ft wide, 4 ft 4 in high and 17½ ft long **left.** Citation II, 4 ft longer, seats up to 11 and has 5 in more headroom. Citation III has 1 ft 2 in more length for up to 13 passengers.

Falcon 20

Falcon 50

France's Dassault-Breguet Falcon 20 was chosen by Charles Lindbergh in 1963 for Pan Am's new Business Jets Division. In 1967 it was selected for US Coast Guard service. Priced at under $4,000,000, it has been adapted for cargo transport, ambulance work, scientific, navigation and calibration research, cartographic, aerial photography and military uses.

The prototype Falcon 50 broke the bizjet speed record by averaging 555 mph on its way from New Jersey, USA, to the 1977 Paris Air Show. With the front and centre fuselage sections of the Falcon 20, three TFE731 turbofan engines and a new supercritical wing, it flies 3,900 miles. The smallest Falcon, the 10, is almost as fast.

Gates Learjet 28/29 Longhorn prototype

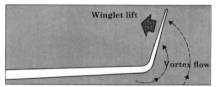

The winglets, developed by Dr Richard Whitcomb of NASA, emerged from tests for a device to reduce the wing-tip vortex on large transport aircraft. They unwind the vortex to give notable fuel savings. By inclining them at an angle of 15° above the wing and 30° below, 40% of their parasite drag can be offset.

The first Learjet was designed in Switzerland by Bill Lear (creator of the Canadair Challenger) who, in 1962, moved operations to Kansas. Seating six in a slim fuselage, their size was based on the premise that "no-one walks about inside a Cadillac". In the Longhorns, Gates Learjets replaced the traditional wing-tip fuel tanks with rakish winglets which improve fuel consumption when cruising. Longhorns will cruise at 51,000 feet, higher than any other FAA-certified commercial jet.

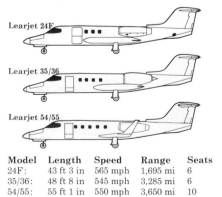

Model	Length	Speed	Range	Seats
24F:	43 ft 3 in	565 mph	1,695 mi	6
35/36:	48 ft 8 in	545 mph	3,285 mi	6
54/55:	55 ft 1 in	550 mph	3,650 mi	10

Grumman Gulfstream II

Hawker Siddeley (BAe) HS 125.700B

The Grumman Gulfstream II, designed by a famed American builder of warplanes, is the fastest business jet, cruising at 581 mph. A much modified turbofan version of the long-range twin turboprop Gulfstream I, the first executive aircraft certificated to fly at 30,000 feet, the 200th Gulfstream II was delivered in 1977. Future models will have winglets.

The Hawker Siddeley (now British Aerospace) HS 125 first flew in 1962 — as the de Havilland 125. This pioneer executive jet was the first to be certificated, with no modifications, for landing on grass and gravel airstrips. Roomy, versatile and in the middle price range, it has had world-wide success; 450 have been sold in 15 years of commercial production.

MBB HFB 320 Hansa

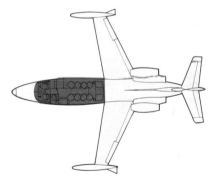

The unique swept forward wing configuration permits the main structural inter-spar box to pass behind the cabin, leaving a spacious interior to seat 12 passengers: 4 at the back and 8 in window seats at either side.

The combined might of Messerschmitt-Bölkow-Blohm and Hamburger Flugzeugbau went into the design of the MBB HFB 320 Hansa turbojet which first flew in 1964. The Hansa is unique in having swept-forward wings, which allow a spacious cabin, but because they have a tendency to bend in flight, need additional stiffening. Flying controls are manual, and the main landing-gears fold forward into the fuselage. A parachute brake in the tail is used for short or icy runways. About 50

were built in executive, cargo and quick-change versions.

Its failure to sell widely outside Germany has less to do with its quality — it is just as good as other, big-selling bizjets — than with the reluctance of buyers to invest in any but the most established, especially US-produced, aircraft.

Business jets:
IAI Westwind/Lockheed JetStar/Rockwell Sabreliner

IAI Westwind 1124

Lockheed JetStarII

Israel's IAI Westwinds, with unswept wings mounted in the mid-fuselage, were designed by Aero Commander of Oklahoma, and first flew in 1963. When the company was taken over by North American Rockwell, an anti-trust court ruled that one jet had to go. Israel Aircraft Industries acquired production rights and has delivered about 250.

The Lockheed JetStar, the world's first executive jet, flew just 241 days after design began, in 1957. Redesigned in 1959 it became, and has remained, the only four-engined business jet. Fuel is contained in fixed wing pods. The 1976 JetStar II has more powerful turbofan engines, and a scoop at the base of the fin rams air into the air-conditioning system.

Rockwell Sabreliner 65A

The Rockwell International Sabreliner, designed in 1957 for the US Air Force, was produced by the company that more recently produced the US B-1 supersonic bomber, the most expensive combat aircraft ever built. Civil Sabreliners include the long-range turbofan-powered 65A. The 75A, with a "stand-up" cabin, has square windows, unusual in pressurized aircraft, and a long-span tailplane (horizontal stabilizer); the 80A model (1978) has an aerodynamically improved new wing.

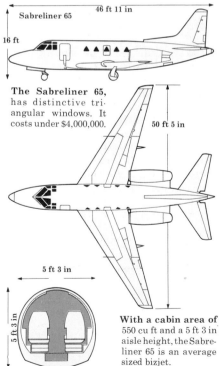

Sabreliner 65

46 ft 11 in

16 ft

The Sabreliner 65, has distinctive triangular windows. It costs under $4,000,000.

50 ft 5 in

5 ft 3 in

5 ft 3 in

With a cabin area of 550 cu ft and a 5 ft 3 in aisle height, the Sabreliner 65 is an average sized bizjet.

Convair 990

Dassault-Breguet Mercure

Convair 340

The Dassault-Breguet Mercure was designed by a team headed by the French tycoon, Marcel Dassault, to fill a market gap for a short-haul "mini-airbus" similar to the Boeing 737 but carrying more passengers and less fuel. Dassault financed factories abroad to handle the expected production programme, but only ten subsidized Mercures were sold.

The turbine engine was not produced in the USA for ten years after World War II, so the Convair 340, produced in 1951, was driven by piston engines. In 1956 Howard Hughes sponsored the Convair 880, so-called because it could fly at 880 feet per second. Elvis Presley's executive version (call sign: Hound Dog One) was fitted with a bed and bathroom and a 52-speaker stereo system. It was followed by the 990, the fastest airliner of its day. These aircraft, technically successful, were commercial failures.

Convair 880

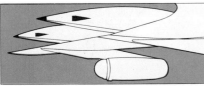

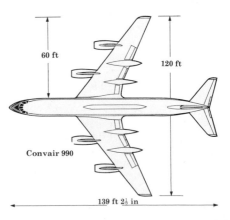

Convair 990

60 ft

120 ft

139 ft 2½ in

Speed bodies, also called "Mach bumps" or "Küchemann carrots" (after the aerodynamicist who conceived them) are prominent features on the CV-990 wings. By increasing the area of the rear part they help to smooth the airflow, delaying the formation of shock-waves.

De Havilland DHC-7 Dash 7/DHC-6 Twin Otter

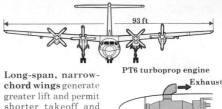

De Havilland DHC-7 Dash 7

Long-span, narrow-chord wings generate greater lift and permit shorter takeoff and landing **above.** To reduce noise, the exhaust pipes are mounted above the engine nacelles **right.**

PT6 turboprop engine

Demand is likely to increase for STOL (Short takeoff and landing) aircraft to serve short-haul commuter routes from airports with short runways in or near city centres. In 1972, de Havilland Canada's expertise in STOL was applied to a 50-seat airliner with large four-blade propellers, geared down to only 1,210 rpm to minimize noise levels.

The Dash 7 can operate from 2,000-foot long runways at city-centre airports in Canada and the USA, where restrictions on noise levels are particularly stringent. The special reduction gears, propellers, pressurized cabin and high-lift system make it an expensive aircraft suitable only for airlines having a clear need for its unique combination of qualities. Four firm orders were taken in 1977, its first year of production, notably from airlines serving "hot and high" airports.

De Havilland DHC-6 Twin Otter

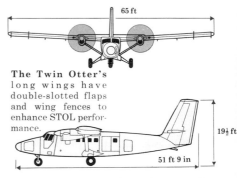

The Twin Otter's long wings have double-slotted flaps and wing fences to enhance STOL performance.

Many remote communities in sparsely populated areas of the world depend upon aircraft that can operate from short, unsurfaced landing strips. De Havilland Canada's success with the Beaver, a small bush transport, and the single-engined DHC-3 Otter (1951) led to the design of the Twin Otter in 1964. Powered by the Pratt & Whitney PT6, the first Canadian turboprop engine, it is an unsophisticated, unpressurized STOL aircraft, able to take off in 820 feet fully loaded, and economical to run.

The Twin Otter can be fitted with wheels, skis or floats, and has proved its versatility in a number of roles, including ice reconnaissance over the Greenland coast, police, forestry and fishery patrols, military transport, ambulance work, search and rescue. Many link city STOL airports without using the main runways. More than 500 have been sold.

Douglas DC-3

Douglas DC-3

By far the most important civil airliner in aviation history, the Douglas DC-3 (sometimes known by its military name, the Dakota) evolved from a proposition made by TWA, in 1932, that Douglas should build a three-engined successor to the Fokker and Ford trimotors. With only two engines on a cantilever wing, the resulting DC-1 (Douglas Commercial 1) flew in 1933. Its advanced design included retractable main wheels, flaps, fully-cowled engines, variable-pitch propellers and all-metal stressed-skin construction. The 196-mph DC-2, an improved version, provided the first non-stop flights over the Newark/Chicago routes.

American Airlines commissioned an enlarged DC-2 for its transcontinental sleeper services. In September 1936 it made the eastbound journey in 16 hours. The daytime version, the 21-seat DC-3, was already flying the New York/Chicago route.

A total of 448 models of this fast, reliable and economical aircraft had been delivered by 1939. During World War II military versions took the total to 10,691 (discounting thousands made under licence in the Soviet Union). Its multi-spar wing construction enabled it to fly for up to 90,000 hours without dangerous fatigue, and over 500 examples of this classic of aviation are still in service.

The Douglas Sleeper Transport, fitted with 21 seats and convertible to 14 bunks, was commissioned by American Airlines in 1935 to fly passengers in comfort on the 16-hour US transcontinental route.

Commodious in its day, the DC-3 carried up to 36 passengers in its 30-foot-long cabin. Its successor, the DC-10, carries 10 times as many passengers.

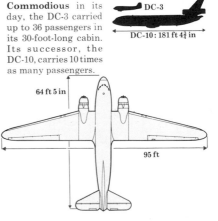

DC-3

DC-10: 181 ft 4¾ in

64 ft 5 in

95 ft

101

Douglas DC-4/DC-6/DC-7

Douglas DC-4

The 204-mph DC-4, the first of a series of four-engined airliners that were to pioneer long-range routes during the 1940s, flew the Atlantic from New York to Hurn (for London) in 23 hours 48 minutes, with two stops.

Douglas DC-6

The 315-mph DC-6, the first civil airliner to be designed after World War II, could fly up to 108 passengers on United Air Lines' transcontinental route, with a scheduled eastbound time of about 10 hours.

Douglas DC-7

The 310-mph DC-7 was the first airliner to fly coast to coast across the USA non-stop. Beginning services on November 29, 1953, it was scheduled to take about 8 hours eastbound and 8 hours 45 minutes westbound. The enlarged, more powerful DC-7C Seven Seas was the first airliner capable of flying the transatlantic route, from New York to London, non-stop. This service, initiated in 1956 by Pan Am and augmented by BOAC, reduced the journey time by half to about 12 hours.

Douglas' first four-engined airliner, the DC-4, could fly 3,500 miles, 1,375 miles farther than the legendary DC-3. Its long-range capability with low fuel consumption spelt the end of the flying boats' supremacy on the world's transoceanic routes.

The early DC-4E, a 52-seat airliner and the first large aircraft to have retractable tricycle landing-gears, was rejected as uneconomically large by the US airlines that had ordered it. The smaller DC-4, designed with the long tubular fuselage characteristic of the modern airliner, eventually flew in 1942 — painted olive-drab and designated C-54 Skymaster by the US Army. When production ceased in 1947, 1,242 had been built, of which hundreds served to re-equip civil airlines during the first postwar years. About 100 are still in use.

The DC-4 was one of the first airliners to be followed by a succession of stretched versions, with increased payload and speed. The DC-6 was a stretched, pressurized DC-4 (yet perversely, it had square windows, less suitable for a pressurized aircraft than the oval windows of the DC-4). The DC-6B, fitted with 2,500-hp engines with paddle-blade propellers, doubled the payload of the DC-4. Fast, economical and reliable, it became the airliner of its day. Of the 705 produced up to 1958, more than 100 are still in airline service.

The DC-7 introduced in 1953 the 3,250-hp Curtiss-Wright turbocompound engine, in which the exhaust gas was made to spin three turbines, compounding the thrust with no additional fuel consumption. The DC-7B had extended engine nacelles made of the new titanium, and contained extra fuel tanks, increasing the range to over 4,000 miles. In 1958 the 121st DC-7C was the 2,284th four-engine, propeller-driven Douglas transport, and the last of the piston-engined airliners.

McDonnell Douglas DC-8

In 1955, the Douglas Aircraft Company took a risk and gambled the company's net worth on the DC-8, which followed the Boeing 707 as America's second jet airliner. Originally powered by the same Pratt & Whitney JT3 turbofans as the 707, it had a fractionally more slender body, less wing sweep, and fully powered flight controls. To reduce drag and avoid stress between wing and fuselage, the aerofoil changes shape toward the root, becoming flatter on top and more curved beneath.

There are four main families of DC-8s: unlike Boeing, Douglas made the first five versions the same size, differing only in power and fuel capacity. A DC-8-40 became the first jet airliner to exceed the speed of sound when, in 1961, it reached Mach 1.012 (667 mph) in a shallow dive.

In 1965, Douglas injected new life into the popular "diesel 8" (as pilots call it) with the first of the Super 60 series. The Super 63 can fly at 600 mph over a 7,700-mile range.

The DC-8 was a great commercial success: 556 built by 1972, when production ended.

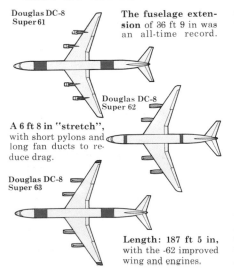

Douglas DC-8 Super 61

The fuselage extension of 36 ft 9 in was an all-time record.

Douglas DC-8 Super 62

A 6 ft 8 in "stretch", with short pylons and long fan ducts to reduce drag.

Douglas DC-8 Super 63

Length: 187 ft 5 in, with the -62 improved wing and engines.

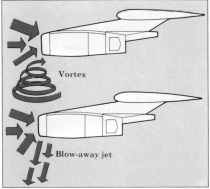

Vortex

Blow-away jet

The blow-away jet was designed by the Douglas Aircraft Company. A device to prevent the formation of air vortices which can suck objects from the ground into the engines, it blows an air jet downward, away from the air intakes.

McDonnell Douglas DC-9

Douglas DC-9 Series 50

Spurred by the penetration of the US market by the British BAe One-Eleven, Douglas flew the first DC-9, America's first rear-engined twin-jet airliner, in 1965. US airlines, needing to absorb the purchase and high running costs of the first generation of jet airliners, made no advance orders. Douglas' own capital was tied up in modifications to the DC-8, so the company reduced the risk by utilizing the DC-8's flight deck, and persuading major suppliers to design and manufacture different parts, receiving payment only as each aircraft was delivered to a customer. De Havilland Canada produced the complete wing, rear fuselage and tail. Later, the Douglas Aircraft Company bought part of their Toronto factory,

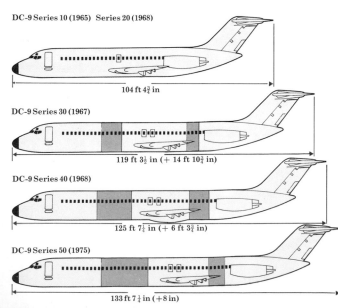

DC-9 Series 10 (1965) Series 20 (1968)

104 ft 4¾ in

DC-9 Series 30 (1967)

119 ft 3½ in (+ 14 ft 10¾ in)

DC-9 Series 40 (1968)

125 ft 7¼ in (+ 6 ft 3¾ in)

DC-9 Series 50 (1975)

133 ft 7¼ in (+8 in)

The 90-seat Series 10 began service only 10 months after first flight; 137 were built. SAS ordered 10 STOL -20s, identical in size but with the -30 wing and -40 engines.

The 115-seat Series 30 with long high-lift wings, was a popular mixed-traffic version; 503 were sold.

The 125-seat Series 40s had more powerful 15,500-lb thrust engines, and increased fuel capacity; 24 were produced for SAS.

The 139-seat Series 50, with 16,000-lb thrust engines, still in production, has increased total sales to over 800.

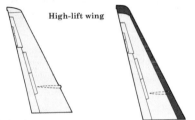

High-lift wing

Basic wing

The basic wing of the DC-9-10, with single-slotted flaps, was modified in the later series to provide high lift for STOL performance. The wing-tips were extended by 4 ft, and full-span leading-edge slats, and double-slotted flaps, were added.

The Super 80, the latest in the series, was announced in 1977 for service from 1980. It seats up to 172 passengers, has an increased 2,000-mile range, and can use 8,000-foot runways.

and continues production there. In 1967, Eastern Air Lines began operating the first of a fleet of 67 long-range DC-9-30s, one of the most popular models. By producing a series of stretched versions, to stay abreast of the demand for larger capacity aircraft, Douglas outsold all competitors in the same category.

Fuselage extensions of 12 ft 8 in and 1 ft 7 in make the Super 80 14 ft 3 in longer than the -50.

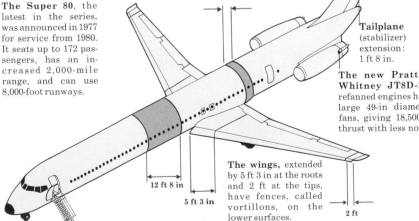

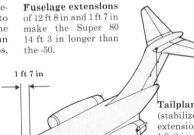

1 ft 7 in

Tailplane (stabilizer) extension: 1 ft 8 in.

The new Pratt & Whitney JT8D-209 refanned engines have large 49-in diameter fans, giving 18,500 lb thrust with less noise.

12 ft 8 in

5 ft 3 in

The wings, extended by 5 ft 3 in at the roots and 2 ft at the tips, have fences, called vortillons, on the lower surfaces.

2 ft

Length: 147 ft 10 in

McDonnell Douglas DC-10

McDonnell Douglas DC-10

McDonnell Douglas was formed in 1967 when the McDonnell Aircraft Corporation, the company that produced the Phantom II supersonic fighter and the Mercury and Gemini space capsules, bought out the 47-year-old Douglas Aircraft Company.

Douglas designed the DC-10 in 1966, competing directly with Lockheed to produce an airbus capable of operating from normal-length runways. By designing the DC-10 around three General Electric CF6-6 turbofan engines, Douglas avoided the financial difficulties encountered by Lockheed with the Rolls-Royce RB.211. In a multi-company manufacturing agreement, Convair produces the fuselage and Aeritalia the fins (vertical stabilizers). The -10 is a short/medium-haul version; the long-range -30 and -40 have an extra forward-retracting main gear, uniquely mounted on the centreline. An aircraft with a fixed wing sweep (the DC-10 wing, designed just before the advanced supercritical form was introduced, is broad and strongly swept) cannot be best for all ranges, but the DC-10's sales record of 250 testifies to its attraction as a sophisticated wide-bodied jet that can fly global routes.

Large windshields and side-panel windows give good flight-deck visibility. Each pilot can see 62° up and 22.5° down, and aft vision of 135° gives a sideways view as far as the wing-tips.

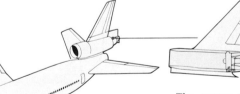

The centre (No. 2) engine is mounted straight through the base of the tail. Changing it involves dismantling the rear fuselage panels.

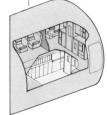

An optional lower galley is connected by two elevators (one for food, one for staff) to a mid-cabin service centre. It can be loaded with up to 600 meals, in container modules, in less than 7 minutes.

The circular cross-section gives 8-abreast tourist (coach) class and 6-abreast first class seating in the mixed-class layout. Baggage can be stowed in an optional centre-line carrier overhead, or the aft cargo hold.

Fokker-VFW F 27

Fokker F 27 Friendship

Conceived in the 1950s, and likely to continue to be produced into the 1990s, the twin-engined Dutch Fokker-VFW F 27 Friendship may be the much sought-for successor to the legendary DC-3. Because of the difficulties of obtaining high-octane fuel for piston engines, old DC-3s are being retired from the small local-route airlines that run them. The classic high-wing F 27, able to fly at almost 300 mph, twice as fast as the DC-3, and carry up to 56 passengers — almost twice as many — is cheaper to run, and the obvious substitute.

The F 27 Friendship is powered, like the BAe 748 and some DC-3s, by Rolls-Royce Dart turboprop engines. In 15 years of steady production these have been increased in power from 1,670 hp to 2,230 hp. The wing, designed for cruising efficiency rather than STOL, was placed above the cabin. The windows are large ovals, a shape having the lowest stress loads in a cylindrical fuselage.

There are many versions of this aircraft, including all-freight, rough-field and troop-carrying versions, as well as the original mixed cargo and passenger configuration; 205 out of 670 sold were made in the USA.

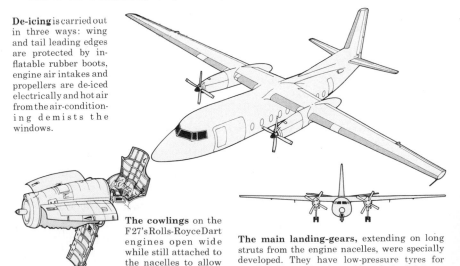

De-icing is carried out in three ways: wing and tail leading edges are protected by inflatable rubber boots, engine air intakes and propellers are de-iced electrically and hot air from the air-conditioning demists the windows.

The cowlings on the F 27's Rolls-Royce Dart engines open wide while still attached to the nacelles to allow easy access.

The main landing-gears, extending on long struts from the engine nacelles, were specially developed. They have low-pressure tyres for rough fields previously usable only by DC-3s.

Fokker-VFW F 28 Fellowship

Fokker-VFW F 28 Fellowship

In 1962, Fokker launched a successor to the F 27. The F 28 Fellowship is a short-haul jet, smaller and lighter than other contemporary twin-jets such as the BAe One-Eleven. Highly manoeuvrable in flight, it is designed for STOL with a wing sweepback of only 16 degrees for good handling at low speed, leading-edge slats and double-slotted flaps. There are no thrust-reversers; instead, the F 28 has powerful air brakes which, uniquely, form the tail end of the fuselage, and highly effective wheel brakes. This aircraft can take off from 6,000-foot long runways, or at altitudes as high as 15,000 feet. It sold well in South America, where it was often the first jet ever seen.

The F 28 was produced in a co-operative risk-sharing programme in which Shorts of Belfast designed the rear fuselage, MBB of West Germany the pods for the Rolls-Royce Spey turbofan engines, and Fokker's German partner VFW, the tail and other fuselage sections. Nearly 150 have been sold in six versions.

The five hydraulically powered spoilers are not used in flight; they are lift dumpers, opened at touchdown to spoil the airflow, causing high drag and throwing the plane's weight onto the wheels, whose especially powerful brakes bring it to a halt.

The Fowler flaps can be extended partially to increase the wing area for lift, or fully, through 42°, to turn lift into drag when landing.

The F 28 has unique air brakes: the whole tail end of the fuselage opens out a variable amount, causing drag. This drastically reduces the aircraft's height and speed without generating buffeting and the high fuel consumption usual at a low approach speed.

108

Hawker Siddeley Comet

On May 2, 1952, the world's first jet airliner, the de Havilland (later Hawker Siddeley) Comet, made history by flying the 6,724 miles from London to Johannesburg at an average cruise speed of 490 mph, in under 24 hours. Hitherto, the fastest airliners had taken nearly twice as long. The four de Havilland Ghost turbojets were mounted in the wing roots, and on later variants additional fuel was stored in streamlined wing pods.

In October 1952, a Comet broke up in flight near Calcutta. Modifications were made, but when, on April 8, 1954, the fifth Comet accident occurred, all Comets were withdrawn from service and production was halted. Salvage and careful investigations showed that fatigue failure of the cabin was the cause of the crashes, and the fuselage was redesigned, but the aircraft's reputation took four years or more to recover. BOAC bought 19 larger, more powerful Comet 4s, and successfully operated the first London/New York jet service from 1958.

Handley Page Herald

The British Handley Page Company designed a promising 44-seat feederliner, the Herald, which first flew in 1955, but made an error of judgement in fitting piston engines. By 1958, when they offered an alternative version powered by Rolls-Royce Dart turboprops, the Fokker F 27 had cornered the market. Of the 48 aircraft produced, many are still in service; British Island Airways' Heralds have black and white propellers, to make them conspicuous.

A radome on the nose of the Herald indicates that the weather radar was fitted after the aircraft was completed.

Corrugations, seen most clearly on the fin (vertical stabilizer) strengthen the skin, reducing the need for internal stiffening. Corrugations are common on light aircraft.

Hawker Siddeley (BAe) 748

The Hawker Siddeley (now BAe) 748 followed the Fokker F 27 and the Handley Page Herald as the last of the twin turboprops designed to replace the ubiquitous Douglas DC-3. About 330 of these popular short-haulers have been sold, including 79 assembled in India from parts manufactured in both countries. Two serve with the Queen's Flight.

This aircraft has a takeoff run of only 2,750 feet, making it particularly useful for rough South American and Indian airstrips. For STOL performance it has a long-span wing, mounted low, with Fowler flaps driven by an electric actuator. The Rolls-Royce Dart turboprops, mounted with their jet pipes above the wings, are rated at about 2,280 hp, though some military versions have 3,200-hp Darts.

Most civil versions of the HS 748 seat 40 to 58 passengers, and some are equipped for freight or passenger/freight operations.

The tabbed Fowler flaps, powered by an electric motor through a clutch and gearbox, have stand-by manual control. They give lift at slow speeds.

The engine nacelles are big enough to accommodate the Rolls-Royce Dart engines and the landing-gears. The "petal" doors give access for repair.

De-icing is by pulsating boots, two sets of rubber tubes which are alternately inflated and deflated to crack ice forming on the leading edges.

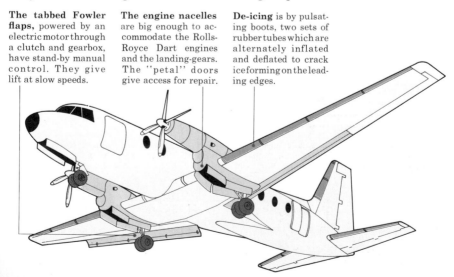

Hawker Siddeley (BAe) Trident

Hawker Siddeley (BAe) Trident

The British Trident began life in 1958 as the de Havilland 121, first of the new rear-engined T-tailed trijets. Designed to cruise at over 600 mph, faster than contemporary civil jets, this aircraft has a squat tail, triplex powered controls (three separate power units driving each control surface) four small wheels on each main landing-gear leg, and an offset sideways-retracting nose gear.

The Trident pioneered truly blind autolanding, and was the first air-liner in the world to be certificated for automatic landing in passenger service, a year after beginning scheduled flights with BEA in 1964. The advanced flight control system, together with the Smiths autopilot, enables the aircraft to lock onto ground radio beams and, using auto-throttle to control airspeed, descend along the glidepath to touchdown.

Over 100 Tridents, including over 30 of the stretched long-range 3B, have been sold.

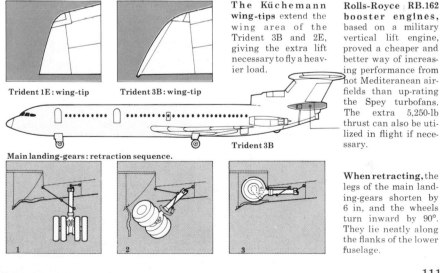

Trident 1E: wing-tip   Trident 3B: wing-tip

Main landing-gears: retraction sequence.

Trident 3B

The Küchemann wing-tips extend the wing area of the Trident 3B and 2E, giving the extra lift necessary to fly a heavier load.

Rolls-Royce RB.162 booster engines, based on a military vertical lift engine, proved a cheaper and better way of increasing performance from hot Mediteranean airfields than up-rating the Spey turbofans. The extra 5,250-lb thrust can also be utilized in flight if necessary.

When retracting, the legs of the main landing-gears shorten by 6 in, and the wheels turn inward by 90°. They lie neatly along the flanks of the lower fuselage.

Helicopters

Bell JetRanger

The Bell JetRanger is one of the most popular helicopters in civil use. Although mass-produced, it is not cheap: the single turboshaft engine alone costs more than a piston-engined helicopter. The five-seat cabin has been increased to accommodate seven in its latest variant, the LongRanger.

Sikorsky S-76

The new streamlined 12-seat Sikorsky S-76 is the first Sikorsky helicopter to be aimed wholly at a civilian market. A special hinge arrangement on the main rotor adjusts blade pitch automatically during turbulence. It is designed for oil-rig supply and search and rescue work.

Mil Mi-8

The Mil Mi-8 is the USSR's most popular helicopter. Used on services to isolated communities all over Siberia, it carries up to 28 passengers. There is a quick-change version, able to carry up to 8,000 lb of cargo, or 24 passengers—or 12 stretchers in an ambulance version. The fuselage can be fitted with a hook for rescue work.

Aérospatiale/Westland Puma

The Aérospatiale/Westland Puma was chosen in 1968 as the tactical transport helicopter of the British Royal Air Force. The newest 20-seat, 168-mph version has glass fibre rotor blades, autopilot, and Doppler radar; it is convertible to VIP travel, broadcasting, rescue and firefighting work.

Helicopter overflies at 500 ft

Helipad location signal

Glideslope signal

Helipad

A helicopter never approaches a heliport landing pad vertically but at an angle of 40° to 60° to avoid descending into its own slipstream, which would affect control.

The Bell 212 is twin-engined for extra safety when flying over water. It also has four flotation bags which inflate automatically in an emergency landing.

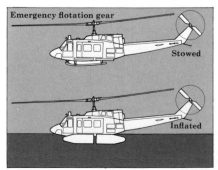

Emergency flotation gear

Stowed

Inflated

Ilyushin Il-86

Ilyushin Il-62

Sergei Ilyushin's design team produced Russia's legendary World War II Stormovik tankbuster, of which a record 41,400 were manufactured. Over 700 Il-18 turboprop airliners were produced from 1957; 100 were exported, and most are still in use. The Il-62 is a 186-seater long-haul jet with four rear-mounted engines like the VC-10; the 1974 62M version could fly from Moscow to Havana non-stop. Colourful textured cabin furnishings replaced the traditional brass, lace and mahogany. The Il-86, the Russian Airbus, was seven years late when it first flew in 1977.

The Il-86, above left, has entrance doors at underfloor cargo-hold level. Here, passengers stow their baggage and climb stairs up to the cabin.

The Il-62, above, the first long-range airliner to be produced in the USSR, has already been exported widely. It flies at 550 mph over a range of 4,000 miles.

Ilyushin Il-18

The Il-62, similar to a VC10 in design, is larger with a taller tail, small doors and short landing-gears, and an 8-ft bullet fairing projecting from the fin.

The Il-18 first flew in 1957 and became Aeroflot's second most numerous purchase.

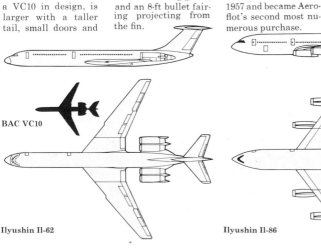

BAC VC10

Ilyushin Il-62

Ilyushin Il-86

Lockheed L-188 Electra

Lockheed L-188 Electra

The Lockheed Aircraft Corporation can claim a number of aviation records. In 1930, Charles Lindbergh set a transamerican speed record in a Model 8 Sirius, and in 1937 Howard Hughes flew round the world in a little under four days, a record, in a Model 14 Super-Electra, claimed to be the fastest airliner of its day.

The L-188 Electra, the first US turboprop airliner, was designed to meet both the challenge of the post-war British jets and turboprops, and the short/medium-haul requirements of American Airlines. By the first flight in 1957, 144 were already on order. Wing modifications followed a series of early crashes, and within five years it was in world-wide use. It could overshoot a runway and circle with two engines on one wing feathered, making it a pilots' favourite.

Only 161 examples of this jet-age turboprop were sold; later Electras were built as freighters. About 14 are still in service in the USA.

The Electra was powered by four Allison D-501 turboprop engines, the first to be manufactured for civil use in the USA. The wingspan was short at 99 ft, but the overall length of 104 ft 6½ in gave room for up to 85 passengers in a cabin 10 ft 8 in wide. Although the Electra's body would fit beneath the wing of a TriStar, it was considered spacious for its day; the domestic version had a rear lounge with seats for six. In addition to the side door, there was an auxiliary entrance at the rear.

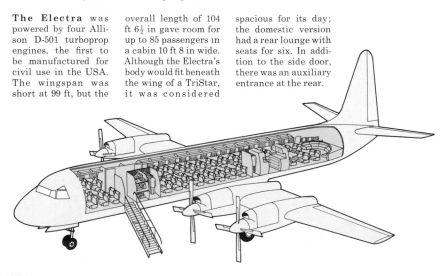

Lockheed L-1011 TriStar

Lockheed L-1011 TriStar

America's second wide-bodied jet, the TriStar, was exhibited at the 1971 Farnborough International Air Show. In this display model, built for Gulf Air, Lockheed surpassed their own reputation for elegant and luxurious interiors. Furnished with extra-large seats and thick carpeting, it had a lounge with a boutique and library.

The TriStar's autoland equipment enables it to land at airports equipped with Category III (zero visibility) landing facilities. Direct Lift Control automatically adjusts lift and pitch through the spoilers, to give smooth tracking during the landing approach.

Despite financial crises within Rolls-Royce, who supply the three advanced RB.211 engines, more than 200 TriStars had been sold by the mid-1970s. There are ten variations, including the short-bodied, long-range 500, seating up to 300 and able to fly the London to Los Angeles route non-stop. Supercritical wings are projected for future TriStars.

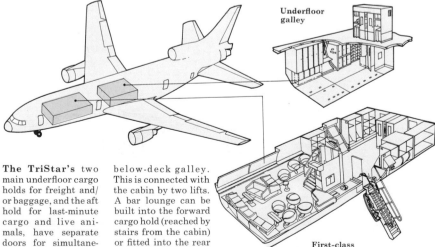

Underfloor galley

The TriStar's two main underfloor cargo holds for freight and/or baggage, and the aft hold for last-minute cargo and live animals, have separate doors for simultaneous loading with the below-deck galley. This is connected with the cabin by two lifts. A bar lounge can be built into the forward cargo hold (reached by stairs from the cabin) or fitted into the rear passenger cabin.

First-class lounge

NAMC YS-11

The NAMC YS-11, the only post-war Japanese airliner, enhanced its country's reputation for cheap but reliable exports. The nose is similar to that of the DC-8, and the overall design very much like a twin-engined Viscount — a concept made practicable by the 3,000-lb Rolls-Royce Dart turboprops, first used on this airliner and twice as powerful as the Viscount's Darts.

A total of 182 YS-11s were built, in 60-passenger, mixed traffic and cargo versions. More than 100 were exported to countries all over the world.

Piper Aztec

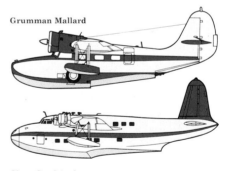

Grumman Mallard

Short Sandringham

Noorduyn Norseman

The Piper Aztec is usually seen with wheels but converts to floats **top** or skis. It seats seven, and thousands are in use as charter planes, air taxis and private planes. The Noorduyn Norseman **above** is a backwoods plane. Though production ended in 1951, it is still much used in Canada and the Arctic, and pre-World War II versions can be found, flown privately or as forest-patrol planes.

The Grumman Mallard, an amphibious flying boat **top,** is still flown on some inter-island services, notably in the Caribbean. About 80 of the smaller Grumman Goose were also operational in the mid-1960s. The Short Sandringham **above** is a civil version of the famous long-range Sunderland flying boat, armed versions of which served as patrol and anti-submarine aircraft during World War II. Many were refitted for civil use after the war, and, as the Empire flying boat, were used on some of BOAC's services. They cruised at 200 mph, and carried 16 to 24 passengers. One is still operated on inter-island services in the Netherlands Antilles.

Shorts 330

The Short Brothers of Northern Ireland made the first floatplane to sink a ship by torpedo in World War I. The success of their STOL Skyvan in the 1960s led them to develop the 330, stretched to meet American requirements for a 30-seat unpressurized airliner. The Skyvan was once called "a shed with wings" and the 330, though redesigned, is hardly beautiful; but it costs a modest $1,500,000 and can take off, fully loaded, from airstrips less than 4,000 feet long, which many aircraft could not use.

Shorts 330

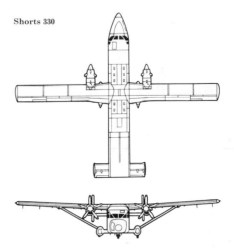

The **Shorts 330** is quieter than most turboprops. It is powered by Pratt & Whitney PT6A-45 engines which, among other features, have an efficient reduction gearbox permitting the propellers to revolve slowly and therefore quietly; fast-spinning propellers are noisy.

Slow-revving propellers are often long, the increased blade area giving the same thrust with lower tip-speeds, in the same way that long oars give more thrust for fewer strokes. But blade area can also be increased by adding more blades. The 330 has five-bladed propellers, 9 ft 3 in in diameter and 2 ft shorter and more compact than those of its competitor, the DHC-7 Dash-7.

The **330** is 58 ft long, and roomy. The cabin, designed by the US consultants responsible for Boeing interiors, offers comfortable big-airliner seating and decor. Pressurization, which would mean radical changes to the square-section fuselage, was not thought justified by commuter flights of 200 miles at 8,000ft. By mid-1978, production of this airliner had reached six per month.

117

Taxi and light aircraft: Beechcraft B99/Cessna/Piper

Beechcraft B99

The US Beech Aircraft Corporation, a major builder of Cadillac-style private and executive aircraft, now has a range of 23 models. Beech planes are sumptuous and correspondingly priced: the Super King Air, with a 2,000-mile range, costs more than $1,000,000. The 99 series (99, 99A and B99 **above**) are airliners seating up to 17 passengers. They were the first aircraft to be designed and manufactured specifically for "third level" (commuter) airlines. From 1968, Beech sold over 160 before ceasing production in 1975.

The Beechcraft B99's 680 hp twin turboprops give this aircraft a speed of 285 mph and an increased range of 520 miles with a full load, reducing the need for refuelling stops. Baggage is stowed in the nose and behind the cabin, and there are air stairs in the door. The unpressurized Airliner B99 can be converted partially or entirely to cargo: there is an optional cargo door and a movable bulkhead; a cargo pod **above** can be clipped to the underside of the fuselage, and takes up to 800 lb weight or 39 cu ft of additional cargo.

Cessna 402

The US Cessna Aircraft Company is the world's largest producer of light aircraft. With output running at about 8,000 a year, this company has sold 150,000 aircraft since it was founded by a pioneer aviator in 1927. Cessnas are the Volkswagens of the aircraft world: cheap, reliable and practical. Cessna concentrate on range and versatility rather than luxury. Among the most popular models, the 402 **above left** is one of a family of light piston-engined twins, seating up to ten, which can fly more than 1,000 miles at 264 mph. The 414 **above right** with a pressurized cabin, has a slightly increased speed and range and can seat seven. In 1976, deliveries began of the 404 Titan **right**, a bigger twin which can carry ten passengers or (unusual in the light aircraft market) comes in a freighter version able to fly a 3,500-lb load out of a 2,530-ft airstrip. It achieves 30% more ton-miles per gallon than a 402.

Cessna 414

Cessna aircraft are often identified by the high-winged, single-engined models with fuel tanks fitted to the wing-tips; but on the 402 these are optional, and on the 414, and the Titan, they were abandoned entirely. Canted wing-tip tanks, no longer fashionable, can improve lift.

Cessna 404 Titan

Cessna 441 Conquest

Piper Navajo

The Cessna 441 Conquest is one of the most luxurious jets of the Cessna range and the first to have been fitted with turboprop engines. Two 625-hp AiResearch TPE 331 engines, with reverse-pitch propellers, drive this 8 to 11-seater aircraft over ranges up to 2,355 miles at speeds up to 339 mph when fully loaded. In appearance the Conquest resembles the Titan, with rather longer wings but, unlike the Titan, has a fully pressurized cabin. Costing under $1,000,000 it is cheaper than other turboprops of similar range and capacity.

The US Piper Corporation, founded in 1931, ranks second in output of general-aviation aircraft. The twin-engined eight-seater Navajo **above** has sold more than 2,000 models since it was first flown in 1964. The Navajo comes in several versions; in the C/R, supercharged Lycoming engines drive counter-rotating propellers, a refinement that helps to reduce torque reaction, causing the air to flow symmetrically around the aircraft, minimizing the need to use the rudder and making handling easier. Pipers, like Cessnas, are modestly priced aircraft.

Piper Cheyenne

Piper Chieftain

The Cheyenne, the first Piper turboprop **above** is among the cheapest of the mass-market turboprops, costing less than $900,000. It seats five to seven, has a pressurized cabin, a cruising speed of around 300 mph (as fast as a Spitfire) and a range of well over 1,000 miles. The Navajo Chieftain **above right** is the biggest member of the family. An unpressurized 10-seater commuter model, rather like a minibus, it can be converted to a business configuration. It flies at around 15,000 ft at a cruising speed of 250 mph over a range of 900 miles. Traditionally such aircraft are produced "green" and transferred to specialist fitting-out organizations for painting, furnishing and equipping with avionics, but Piper purchasers receive a completely finished product. Most Pipers are offered with a number of options, including air stairs, rubber de-icing boots and a choice of radars.

The Piper Navajo Chieftain has luggage compartments in the nose and the cabin, and luggage pods at the back of the engine nacelles on the wings **below**. It is also certified as a cargo carrier, for which an optional utility door next to the passenger door can be fitted.

Tupolev Tu-134/Tu-154

Tupolev Tu-134

Tupolev Tu-154

Andrei Tupolev, a leading Soviet aircraft designer, was imprisoned during the 1930s purges and in the 1940s was awarded the Stalin prize for the Tu-2 bomber. The Tu-104 was the world's second turbojet airliner, beaten only by the Comet 1. The Tu-134 (1964) is a rear-engined trijet, the Soviet counterpart of the BAe One-Eleven, or the McDonnell Douglas DC-9, having "soft-field" twin-axle landing-gears, with legs designed to swing rearward to cushion taxying and landing on rough runways. With a cruising speed of 540 mph, the 80-seat Tu-134 has been one of the most widely exported Soviet airliners.

Tupolev's Tu-114 turboprop was the world's largest airliner until the Boeing 747 was produced in 1970. The sixth and latest Tupolev airliner, the Tu-154, is the world's largest narrow-bodied trijet, Bigger, faster and with a longer range than the Boeing 727 which it closely resembles, it carries fewer passengers. Tupolev designed the 154 with a high-lift wing and six-wheel bogie landing-gears to serve rough 7,000-foot runways. The large number of rough-field airliners now in service with Aeroflot testify to the importance of the aviation industry in the remote areas of the USSR.

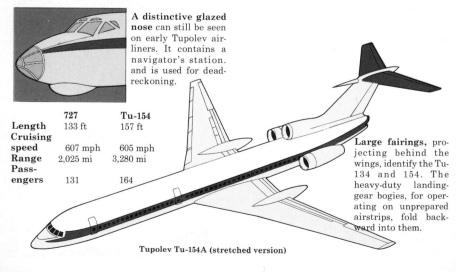

A distinctive glazed nose can still be seen on early Tupolev airliners. It contains a navigator's station. and is used for dead-reckoning.

	727	Tu-154
Length	133 ft	157 ft
Cruising speed	607 mph	605 mph
Range	2,025 mi	3,280 mi
Passengers	131	164

Large fairings, projecting behind the wings, identify the Tu-134 and 154. The heavy-duty landing-gear bogies, for operating on unprepared airstrips, fold backward into them.

Tupolev Tu-154A (stretched version)

Tupolev Tu-144

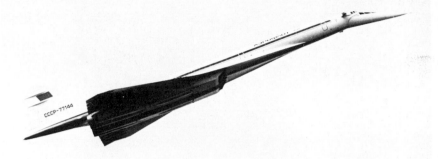

Beating Concorde by a few months, in December 1968, the Soviet Tu-144 was the first supersonic airliner to fly. It was nicknamed "Concordeski" because of its similarities to its Western counterpart (it has similar, though aerodynamically simpler, ogival delta wings and a "droop snoot" nose section with retractable visor), but it is bigger than Concorde, seating 140. It has more powerful Kuznetzov afterburning turbofan en-

gines giving 44,000 pounds of thrust, arranged in two pairs of nacelles, and retractable foreplanes, or canards.

The Tu-144 was first exhibited at the 1973 Paris Air Show, where it suffered a disastrous crash. After major redesign and extensive test flights it was introduced on USSR domestic routes as a cargo-carrier. At least five were known to be in Aeroflot service in 1978, and more than 20 were thought to be built.

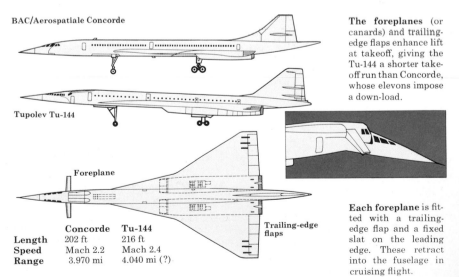

BAC/Aerospatiale Concorde

Tupolev Tu-144

Foreplane

The foreplanes (or canards) and trailing-edge flaps enhance lift at takeoff, giving the Tu-144 a shorter take-off run than Concorde, whose elevons impose a down-load.

Each foreplane is fitted with a trailing-edge flap and a fixed slat on the leading edge. These retract into the fuselage in cruising flight.

Trailing-edge flaps

	Concorde	Tu-144
Length	202 ft	216 ft
Speed	Mach 2.2	Mach 2.4
Range	3.970 mi	4.040 mi (?)

121

Vickers Viscount/Vanguard/VFW-Fokker VFW 614

Vickers Viscount

Vickers Vanguard

Exploiting Britain's World War II lead in the development of the gas turbine engine, Vickers-Armstrong (now BAe) produced the world's first turboprop airliner, powered by four Rolls-Royce Dart engines. Passengers appreciated its smooth 300-mph cruising speed and the panoramic view from the almost elliptical windows. Altogether 438 were sold bet-ween 1953 and 1959; about 150 are still in airline service.

The Vanguard, which followed in 1959, could carry twice the load at higher speeds, but was unable to compete with the 1960s jets. Only 43 were sold. Now, nearly all the surviving examples of these fine aircraft have, like the Lockheed Electra, been converted into freighters.

VFW-Fokker VFW 614

The VFW-Fokker VFW 614 is the only post-war German airliner to have been produced. Nine years elapsed from the beginning of development in 1962 until it reached flight-test stage, but initial response was promising enough to justify the high development costs. A unique feature is the overwing mounting of the Rolls-Royce M45H turbofans. This aircraft can use rough strips only 4,500 feet long. Poor customer response to the high $5,000,000 price meant that only 15 were delivered.

Overwing mounting of the two turbofan engines causes their roar to be shielded by the modestly sweptback wings, making the VFW 614 comparatively quiet when heard from below.

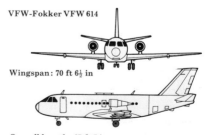

VFW-Fokker VFW 614

Wingspan: 70 ft 6½ in

Overall length: 67 ft 7 in
Engines mounted on above-wing pylons allow the main landing-gear legs to be short and sturdy for rough-field operations. The air intakes are clear of flying gravel, and there is less danger from fire in an emergency landing.

Yakovlev Yak-40/Yak-42

Yakovlev Yak-40

Yakovlev Yak-42

Alexander Yakovlev's design bureau, prominent since 1930, has been responsible for an extraordinarily wide range of aircraft, from gliders and light sportsplanes to fighter-bombers and helicopters. It built few civil transports until 1966 when the Yak-40, the first turbofan-powered feeder-line aircraft, was produced to replace the Li-2 (the Soviet-built DC-3).

Since 1966, more than 500 Yak-40s have been produced to serve Aero-

flot's many thousands of short-haul local services, and the larger Yak-42, a 100-120 passenger trijet which first flew in 1975, is likely to be even more important. With powered flight controls and spoilers, but no high-lift devices on the leading edges of the wings, it is intended for standard use on regional routes, and it is likely that hundreds will serve in the Aeroflot fleet alone. Unlike most Soviet turbofans, the new Lotarev D-36 engines have a high bypass ratio, making this jet quiet.

The Yak-42 has recently been designated "Clobber" in the West, in accordance with established military practice. Since the end of World War II, little official information has been made available about aircraft produced in the USSR, so each new type is allotted a NATO code name.

Proportionally large wheels, and wide, low-pressure tyres enable aircraft to use semi-prepared grass or gravel landing strips.

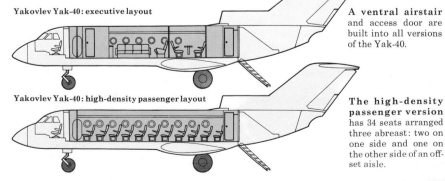

Yakovlev Yak-40: executive layout

A ventral airstair and access door are built into all versions of the Yak-40.

Yakovlev Yak-40: high-density passenger layout

The high-density passenger version has 34 seats arranged three abreast: two on one side and one on the other side of an off-set aisle.

123

Airports

The world's major airports are cities in themselves, designed to serve the needs of travellers, staff, the "meeters and greeters" and those who come to absorb the atmosphere and see the sights of modern air transport. They are interchange points between air services and every form of surface transport. They are also, by their very proximity, closely involved with the local communities and immediate environs.

As aviation has developed, the small grass fields of the "early birds" — centres of local interest and even pride — have expanded enormously, acquired concrete runways and terminal buildings, and changed into propagators of noise and upset in the communities that have grown around them. This Jekyll and Hyde development is typical of the dilemma brought about by technological advance: disadvantages and benefits, side by side.

Now, fortunately, airports are entering a third phase in their progress. The evolution of larger and much quieter aircraft is beginning to reduce noise levels under the flight-paths, while the increased size of aircraft reduces the growth rate in the numbers of takeoffs and landings. Steadily, major airports are on the way to becoming "good neighbours" to their local communities, while continuing to expand their role as centres of trade, travel and employment.

While a modern airport must coexist as harmoniously as possible with the local community and simultaneously look after the interests of air travellers, airlines and its own population of workers, the authorities who plan and run it must concern themselves primarily with providing safe, convenient and regular flights. The airport must, therefore, be so located that the approach and takeoff paths are clear of obstacles and hazards, that the runways are of adequate length and strength, properly lighted and equipped with the essential radio and radar aids, and that taxiways of the necessary width lead to ample parking areas close to the terminal buildings.

After many years of steadily increasing requirements for longer and stronger runways to suit larger and faster aircraft, modern technology has begun to shrink these distances again. For the heaviest aircraft now contemplated for the distant future, up to 500 tons loaded weight, and for the fastest supersonic jets, a runway of 12,000 feet will suffice, even on a hot day when engine power is reduced. The only exceptions are airports located high above sea level, at which safe distances for takeoff and landing are considerably increased because of the thin air.

In catering for the comfort and convenience of increasing numbers of people who use airports (the number of passengers passing through London's Heathrow Airport increased by 10.4 per cent between 1976 and 1977) the authorities' aims are to ensure the best possible access to and from the airport, not only by road and rail, but also by subway and helicopter; adequate parking space for cars

TriStar Approach

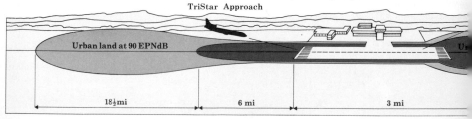

Urban land at 90 EPNdB

18½ mi   6 mi   3 mi

(Chicago O'Hare can accommodate 14,000) and clearly signposted and well-equipped terminal buildings, with a minimal walking distance from arrival point to aircraft. Few airports have *all* these desirable features, but all strive toward them in a steady process of modernization and expansion.

Not only passenger but also air freight traffic has grown immensely in recent years. It is, therefore, essential for airports to provide good cargo-handling facilities and adequate warehouse space for Customs and other formalities.

An airport is a business, and should function efficiently and economically. In the USA most major airports are owned or run by city authorities; in Britain, by the British Airports Authority. In the USSR all airports are owned by the government and run by the state-owned Aeroflot. Airports are expensive to run and one which handles less than about 3,000,000 passengers a year has difficulty in making ends meet. Revenue is collected from airlines through landing and parking fees, and from numerous concessions: renting of office space, duty-free and other shops, and bars and restaurants.

To provide these services and facilities, large airports have a substantial working population, from air traffic controllers, Customs and immigration officials to traffic clerks, loaders, apron staff, caterers, administrators and flight crews. Including aircraft maintenance personnel, this work force may number 50,000 or more. With families included, it represents a dependent community of more than a quarter of a million.

Many of the airport staff live in the immediate vicinity, in the communities that have mushroomed around the airport perimeter as opportunities for employment at the airport and its ancillaries have increased. Most large modern airports have, therefore, become embedded in built-up areas as cities have expanded around them.

Along the flight paths to and from the runways, noise is a major problem affecting nearby communities. It is often aggravated by road congestion. Fortunately, the new aircraft are substantially quieter than the earlier jets which they are steadily replacing. Calculations show that, within ten years from the peak year, 1973, only people who live under the flight-paths to and from the world's major airports will be seriously disturbed by jet noise, about one tenth of those affected today.

These large airports cannot be moved. They must be easily accessible, and it is inconceivable that they will be closed, for the trade, travel, prosperity and leisure activities of the modern world depend upon the services they offer. It is essential, therefore, that the airports are made acceptable to those who live near them. As technology advances, this is indeed happening: the advantages of air transport are rapidly multiplying, the disadvantages are decreasing.

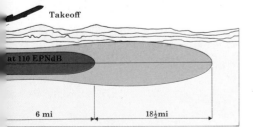

Takeoff

at 110 EPNdB

6 mi   18½mi

A computer-drawn noise footprint is a contour map of the takeoff, approach and landing noise around an airport. It enables airport authorities to direct operations away from areas where nearby communities would be affected. Sound is not recorded in decibels, which measure only noise levels, but in EPNdBs (effective perceived noise decibels) which also measure types of noise. A soft whispering at a distance of two yards will score 47 EPNdBs while a 747 taking off will score 107.

Anatomy of an airport

The world's busiest airport is Chicago O'Hare. It handles more than 43 million airline passengers and almost 750,000 aircraft movements a year. To deal efficiently with such large volumes, a large international airport needs most of the facilities of a town — sewage farms, transport services, medical centres, shops, banks, hotels.

The demand for air transport is growing by around six per cent a year. But many major airports have reached saturation point — Chicago O'Hare has one aircraft movement every 45 seconds. Airports hemmed in by urban sprawl cannot expand.

New airports are designed for expansion. Dallas/Fort Worth in the USA has earmarked a 28-square-mile area — one and a quarter times the size of Bermuda — for future development. It could be the world's largest airport at its planned completion date, 2001.

A site for a large new airport, ideally on inexpensive land within easy reach of the urban centre it is to serve, is hard to find. The area around it should be free of residential communities sensitive to noise and

Hannover Airport in West Germany was planned in the early 1950s to handle over 70,000 aircraft movements and about four million passengers a year. Space has been allowed for future expansion. Located five miles, or 20 minutes, from Hannover, this airport is served by a link road leading to major east/west and north/south European highways and railways.

1

ILS localizers, 1, at either end of the runway, transmit radio beams to guide aircraft onto the runway centreline. The glidepath transmitter, **18**, set to one side of the runway, guides aircraft down at a smooth angle of descent.

A windsock, 2, is a visual guide to wind direction. When the sock is horizontal, the wind speed is 25-30 knots (29-35 mph).

Hangars, leased to airlines for parking and maintenance, **3,8,** may be large enough to take two wide-bodied jets. Other hangars, **14,** may be set aside for executive aircraft and sports-planes.

Emergency services, 4, alerted from the tower, are housed in special units on the airfield.

The flight operations building, 5, contains the central flight planning offices.

The control tower, 6, 148 ft high, gives controllers an unobstructed view across both runways.

The cargo centre, 7, at this relatively small international airport, has an annual turnover of 27,000 tons.

The weather office, 9, is a fully equipped meteorological station.

Parallel runways, 10, 19, are nearly 9,000 ft long. A 13,000-ft long diagonal cross runway is projected.

Highways, 11, and rail links, 13, between passenger terminals and nearby towns, and road access to cargo terminals, maintain the speed advantage of air travel.

Hotels, 12, in or near the airport may provide free transport to and from terminals.

An expansion area, 15, is planned to take future modular extensions of the terminals.

The two passenger terminals, 16, linked to a separate building containing shops and restaurants, can handle 20,000 passengers a day—2,000 an hour at peak times. The long walking distances found in other air-terminal configurations are avoided in a triangular terminal shape. Twelve jetties connect terminals with aircraft parking bays.

An apron area, 17, floodlit at night, adjoins the terminal and connects the aircraft parking and servicing bays with the taxiways.

the airspace above must fit in smoothly with the airways network. Access is vital. France's new Charles de Gaulle Airport at Roissy is sited on the main Paris-Brussels highway, Frankfurt Airport has its own railway station below ground, and London's Heathrow has a subway link.

Modern airports, designed to handle different types of air traffic, vary greatly in size. The largest, for long-haul intercontinental traffic, need runways 12,000 to 15,000 feet long and several passenger and cargo terminals. Smaller airports for medium-range traffic are more common and the smallest are used by local airlines, air taxis or by business and private aircraft owners.

Exploratory plans for future airports encompass ideas for offshore floating air centres, with runways constructed from discs, like chainmail. Planners also envisage land-based airports set in vast parks which will provide a pleasant environment and act as noise-buffers. Industrial and shopping centres, and even residential areas would be included in these complexes.

Airport architecture

Furnished with potted palms and wicker chairs, Heathrow Airport's departure lounge was a tent in the 1940s. Commercial flying, and airports, developed only when the speed, reliability and capacity of passenger planes increased. A gigantic building combining terminal and hangars was built at the first large airport, the Old Tempelhof, Berlin, begun in 1925. It was severely functional in design, as befitted the new mode of transport, and became the model for the first-generation airports such as Croydon, Moscow, Munich, Brussels, Venice, Amsterdam and le Bourget. It stood at the centre of a "snowflake" pattern of runways to minimize taxying, and was designed for slight expansion. In the USA, New York's Newark, La Guardia and Idlewild (now John F. Kennedy) airports were small, single units, not planned for expansion.

Like railway terminals, air terminals were first built with long straight fronts, along which aircraft parked. To accommodate the 1940s growth in air traffic, they were later extended by the addition of piers, flanked by aircraft parking bays.

But long piers mean long walking distances for passengers, and the 1960s saw the evolution of the satellite system. At Los Angeles International Airport, rebuilt in 1961, ticketing buildings are connected to satellites by underground passages.

An event that was important for architecture generally took place in 1956, when the Finnish-American architect, Eero Saarinen, was commissioned to design the TWA terminal at John F. Kennedy Airport. In this building Saarinen broke away from the rectilinear and unadorned "international" style favoured then (and still) for most commercial public buildings. The two cantilevered, wing-like concrete shells forming the roof were an unashamed symbol of flight. Inside, curving pillars, sup-ports and stairways recall the organic lines of the Art Nouveau style.

Saarinen's later terminal at Washington's Dulles International Airport is again typical of the "shell" theme in modern architecture. Light concrete slabs laid on cables slung beneath outward-sloping pillars roof a large area. Passengers are transported to and from parked aircraft by mobile lounges, reducing the need for a long frontage, but the terminal is easily expanded: the 1970 extension was designed by Kevin Roche and John Dinkeloo, architects of New York's Ford Foundation Building.

Reinforced concrete, strong and able to absorb aircraft vibrations, has become an important airport building material.

Recent airport buildings have tended to make grand symbolic statements, especially in developing countries where the national airport, like the national airline, is a source of

Seven satellite terminals ring Terminal 1 at Charles de Gaulle, the newest Paris airport. Passengers reach them on moving walkways that pass through tunnels under the apron.

prestige. And the sheer volume of modern air traffic often forces architects to make airport buildings monumental. The rotunda of the main terminal at Paris/Charles de Gaulle was designed to handle 10,000,000 passengers each year. Its sheer size and complexity make it undeniably imposing.

And at Dallas/Fort Worth Regional Airport, likely to be the world's largest when completed in 2001, semi-circular terminals are threaded like beads on a multilevel highway.

But terminals do not have to overpower the passengers who use them. At John F. Kennedy, where individual airlines or groups of airlines build and operate their own terminals, there is a refreshing variety of styles. Among them, I.M. Pei's National Airlines terminal, opened in 1970, tempers a massive supporting structure with light and airy infill, and a spacious interior.

The central "theme" building at Los Angeles International Airport has 135-ft high concrete arches supporting a bar, restaurant and observation deck overlooking the Pacific.

Eero Saarinen's terminal at Dulles International Airport above is "like a huge, continuous hammock suspended between concrete trees". The pagoda-like control tower follows traditional forms. His TWA terminal at John F. Kennedy left has an external sweep, suggestive of movement.

Minoni Yamasaki, architect of the World Trade Center, New York, designed the terminal and control tower at Dharan Airport, Saudi Arabia right where traditional forms are given a modern interpretation. London's Gatwick Airport left was the first to have aircraft parking piers.

129

Anatomy of an air terminal

From wing-tip to wing-tip the Boeing 747 is nearly 196 feet wide. With the many vehicles that surround it at the gate, it needs a berth about 300 feet wide. Several aircraft docking wing-tip to wing-tip along a terminal building can mean almost a mile of walking for passengers to reach their aircraft, and designers have tried all shapes and sizes of building to try and overcome this inconvenience.

At Paris/Charles de Gaulle and Toronto airports there are circular terminals with integral car parks. The Paris building is surrounded by satellites around which aircraft park; people reach them through tunnels with moving walkways underneath

Medical centres may offer vaccination as well as emergency facilities; large airports may have operating rooms.

Landside restaurants are often open all night to the general public.

Staffed restrooms and nurseries are provided for passenger use at some large airports.

Duty-free shops are usually positioned near the departure gates. Their use is restricted to international passengers with boarding passes.

Banks and foreign exchange counters are found in most air terminals. They may be located on the airside only, and are often subject to local working hours.

An airport information desk, airline ticket sales, a tourist bureau and a hotel reservations desk usually surround the concourse.

A flight information board, with the letter shapes well-researched for clarity, shows flight departure times and gate numbers, and flight cancellations.

Observation decks, with coffee shops, telescopes and loudspeaker guides to aircraft movements, are open to the public, usually for a minimal charge.

Quick-service coffee shops may be located on land and airside.

Bars do not always conform to local licensing laws and are generally available in "dry" Moslem states.

Concourses, usually located on the arrival and departure floors, are scaled to accommodate peak passenger flows, with surge areas allowed for a sudden influx of arrivals, or a sudden hold-up of departures.

Automatic doors are activated by a microwave beam reflected by an approaching person.

Consignes and baggage lockers may not be available at high-security-risk airports. **Insurance** may be bought from machines.

Shopping centres, located away from the passenger flow, make the largest terminals comparable with city shopping centres.

Observation deck

Restaurant

Bar

Restrooms/nursery

Bank

Mail/telegraph office

Duty-free shopping centre

Hotel reservations

FLIGHT INFORMATION

Medical centre

Airline ticket sales

Concourse

Shopping centre

Automatic doors

Information desk

Insurance sales

the taxiways. Aircraft park along the outer curve of the crescent-shaped terminals at Dallas/Fort Worth Airport; a road runs round the inside, and car-parking areas are inside the road curve. Distances from aircraft to cars are only about 150 feet, but people transferring flights could have a long way to go. Alternatively, aircraft may park along piers radiating out from a central terminal, as at Schiphol in Amsterdam, and at Frankfurt. Washington/Dulles and Montreal/Mirabel have small, compact terminals. Planes park out on the airfield and passengers are taken out to them in mobile lounges.

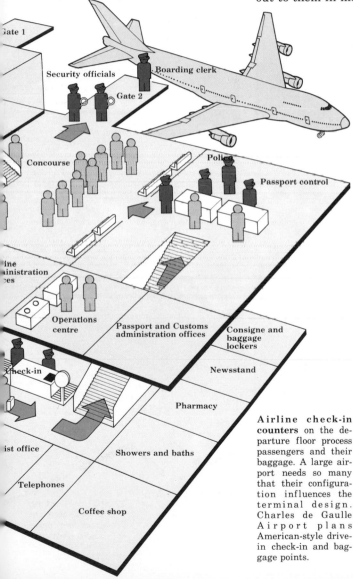

Gate 1

Security officials
Boarding clerk
Gate 2

Concourse
Police
Passport control

ine
ministration
es

Operations
centre
Passport and Customs
administration offices
Consigne and
baggage
lockers

Check-in
Newsstand

Pharmacy

ist office
Showers and baths

Telephones

Coffee shop

Passport control is necessary only for passengers on international flights.

Mail and telegraph facilities exist at most large airports, and some have airside telephones beyond Customs points.

Airlines have their own offices, distinct from the airport administration.

National immigration, Customs and police have offices in every international airport.

The operations centre houses a central computer controlling flight information display units. The central announcements made over the public address system are, in modern terminals, made from computer-operated canned tapes. Here, the airport management monitors activities on closed-circuit TV, liaising with airline personnel.

Airline check-in counters on the departure floor process passengers and their baggage. A large airport needs so many that their configuration influences the terminal design. Charles de Gaulle Airport plans American-style drive-in check-in and baggage points.

Concession areas for newsstands and shops are a source of revenue.

Showers and baths may number among facilities offered.

131

Airport passenger flow

By locating passenger processing points conveniently and in a logical order, air terminal designers aim to keep passengers moving through the system in a smooth flow with a minimum of delay.

But passenger traffic follows an irregular pattern, peaking at certain times of the day and year, so public areas must be large enough to accommodate peak crowds, calculated by quadrupling the estimated numbers of passengers to allow for friends and relatives.

Passengers on long-haul routes tend to arrive well ahead of check-in time, and spend time in shops and restaurants. These must be visible —

At the check-in desk passengers' tickets are verified and their baggage loads totalled. An average allowance is made for the passengers' weights; manual compilation of load sheets is being replaced by computer read-outs to ensure that the aircraft's total weight and CG (centre of gravity) stay within limits. Here, passengers can check that their luggage has been labelled with the correct code for the destination airport. There are various baggage-handling systems. In the illustration conveyor belts carry the baggage to chutes angled at about 21°, which slide it into the sorting areas.

Domestic flights need no Customs procedures but there may be a security check.

Departure lounges (also known as holding rooms) are big enough to hold peak-season crowds, and may have bars and coffee shops.

The gates lead embarking passengers to piers, jetties, mobile lounges or air stairs.

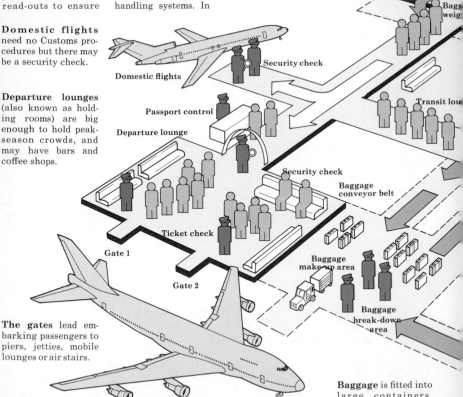

Check-in desk

Bagg weig

Domestic flights

Security check

Transit lou

Passport control

Departure lounge

Security check

Baggage conveyor belt

Ticket check

Gate 1

Baggage make-up area

Gate 2

Baggage break-down area

International departures

Baggage is fitted into large containers. Here, driverless tractors, programmed to a particular route, convey it to the aircraft.

they generate a large percentage of airport revenue — but not sited where they obstruct passenger flows.

A strike can strand thousands of travellers in the departure areas, and a sudden clearance of early morning fog could mean a rapid influx of arrivals. Ten large aircraft arriving consecutively could bring 4,000 passengers in 30-40 minutes. Customs procedures at international airports cause long delays at peak hours and in summer, foreigners may be held up at health and immigration control points, but routine security checks on departing passengers and their baggage are being speeded up by the use of electronic security devices.

Escalators, high-speed elevators and moving walkways reduce long walking distances in large air terminals. Airport buses and taxis wait at ground level, and there may be a car park or rail terminus below ground.

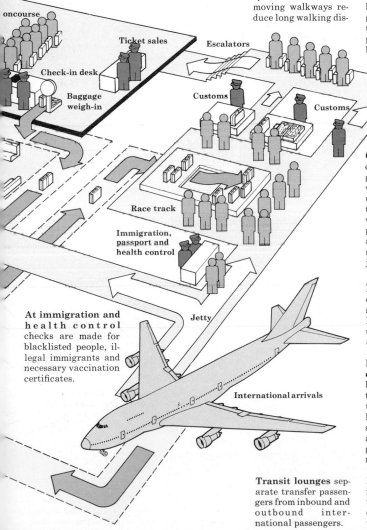

Customs checks for disembarking passengers may be random or work in the widely-used colour coded system where travellers with declarable goods pass into one sector and others pass straight through, subject to random checks.

Inbound baggage is collected from carousels or race tracks. Flight numbers are usually displayed clearly above.

Inbound baggage containers are broken down and taken by conveyor belt to the race tracks. Ideally, baggage should reach the claim area when the passenger does, although this rarely happens.

At immigration and health control checks are made for blacklisted people, illegal immigrants and necessary vaccination certificates.

Transit lounges separate transfer passengers from inbound and outbound international passengers.

Long, narrow jetties reduce the surge of 300 to 500 passengers disembarking from a wide-bodied jet.

133

Flier's Guide to air travel

The permutations of routes, fares, discounts and package deals mean that there is almost always a cheaper way to fly. A reputable travel agent can provide the widest choice of flights and save you the trouble of going to each airline in turn. But insist that he gives you the option of going the cheapest way. Because travel agents get their commission from the operator, not the passenger, they earn more by booking expensive scheduled flights.

Business travel

Most businessmen fly scheduled flights. They are usually more reliable and offer the most flexibility for changes of plan; tickets can be transferred to the next flight, to another airline, or even refunded. Competition for the rich lode of commercial traffic runs high, so many airlines offer special "club" facilities for regular customers. For an annual subscription as low as £13 ($25) you can join TWA's Ambassadors Club or Pan Am's Clipper Club and Frequent Traveller Service; British Airways' Monarch Club and Japan Airlines' Executive Service.

Services vary, but many include private lounges at major airports where coffee, drinks and local telephone calls are sometimes free; the use of small conference rooms for business meetings; check-in facilities that by-pass the main desks and give seat assignments ahead of the staging post at the gate; a generous view of excess baggage and a priority position if some passengers have to be "bumped" through overbooking.

By taking advantage of seasonal prices and excursions, and by plotting the most economical sequence of destinations, the cost of a complex business trip can be cut by 50 per cent of the fare for straight scheduled services; a holiday package which includes the return journey can fre-quently be cheaper than the standard one-way fare. A good travel agent should provide all the information.

Even very large companies have begun to question their travel budgets, so travel agents have been devising plans to adapt vacation fares for business use. IATA-licensed agents sometimes sell to businessmen low-cost travel originally intended to be the basis of bargain holiday packages. This is the kind of money-saver, not generally known and certainly not publicized, which an astute travel agent can find.

In many business circumstances, hiring an aircraft (with or without a pilot) may be an economical consideration. Small aircraft can land at modest uncrowded airports that charge low landing fees, and the flight waits for the passenger, not vice versa. The best place to start enquiries is at a local airport.

Travelling for pleasure

Those travelling for pleasure can take advantage of reduced-rate night flights, and can opt to travel outside peak holiday seasons. The best-known and most straightforward discount service is APEX (Advance Purchase Excursion): by booking and paying three months ahead, passengers are guaranteed a seat at around half the price of standard fares. But APEX tickets are not open; the scheme is designed for holiday-makers who are only interested in travelling between one or two places at set times. IPEX (Instant Purchase Excursion) is cheaper still, but only available for selected stops in Europe and only from certain airlines. Tickets cannot be purchased until the day before departure.

Most airlines offer cheap package holidays which typically include a return flight and a hotel for less than the scheduled one-way flight. Since travellers do not always stay at the hotel provided, some tour operators have been able to cut the prices of some package holidays still further, by-passing international fare regulations by offering air trips as "tour" packages which include poor or merely nominal accommodation.

The wide range of discount fares is worth investigating. Spouse fares give a reduction to one partner if the other pays full fare; group flights can be booked with a group as small as two; there are still youth fares, although these are gradually being phased out under the rash of other budget fares on offer, and student fares, which require an International Student's Union card. Those who do not qualify for a card can join an affiliation group. Groups of people with professional affinity (all lawyers, for instance) or with similar vocational interests, can charter aircraft to fly their members together. A minimum period of membership is usually necessary before such parties can be recognized as qualifying for the low fares.

Cheap travel between the UK and USA is easier since the Skytrain service began. It is cheaper for Europeans to fly to London, or Canadians to New York, to pick up the flight than it is to fly direct from the nearest international airport. There is no guarantee of a seat and you buy a ticket on the day. Skytrain has forced a change of policy for flights between New York and London; some major airlines offer comparably cheap fares on up to 1,000 seats a week. There are no more guarantees of a seat than on Skytrain, but there are more flights per day. Most airlines offering such services have controlled arrangements requiring ticket purchase at set times. Passengers making a last-minute decision to fly on the usual stand-by services pay the full scheduled fare.

Internal flights

Internal commuter or shuttle flights, as casual as bus services, are operated on an increasing number of busy routes. Passengers may board the plane with seconds to spare, and pay in the air. Places are guaranteed: provided that a passenger turns up by check-in time, which is typically only ten minutes before departure, he will fly, even if a back-up plane has to be brought out for him alone. On well-used routes such as New York/ Washington, London/Edinburgh, fares may be lower at weekends or during off-season periods. International shuttles may soon appear in Europe.

The Book of Bargains
The ABC World Travellers' Guide* gives a world-wide survey of flight information: dates, times, fares, special rates and alternative services. Its data allows the flier to calculate his own journey costs:—

Example 1
A London businessman wants to visit Denpasar and Jakarta in Indonesia. The round fare to Denpasar is £872. If he can arrange his itinerary to fit the time restrictions on excursion fares, he can take an APEX fare (to be booked a month in advance) to Singapore and back, costing £372.50, allowing him to return from 14 days to three months later. From Singapore he can either buy a local ticket (where the sale is limited to the country of departure) at a concessionary excursion price of £133 (Singapore $553), which restricts him to ten days to one month of travel, taking in Jakarta and Denpasar, or buy a similar ticket in London at £174 (Singapore $714) with a saving of at least £321. Where tickets can only be bought in the country they apply to, they can be booked from any large travel agency.

Example 2
An American businessman wants to visit three European cities. The round fare to Munich is $736. The APEX fare to Munich allows no stopovers, but he can take an APEX fare for 14-45 days' travel to London, costing $429 and then a non-APEX excursion from London to Munich with a minimum of six nights' travel, allowing two stopovers at, for instance, Amsterdam and Brussels, costing $193, a saving of $114.

*Published by IPC Business Press, London, England; distributed in the USA by Eastern News and San Francisco Warhouse.

Ticket check

Air tickets, transferable between all IATA airlines, are standard in form. The first page is torn out at check-in, at which point passengers are given their boarding passes and, usually, a seat assignment. The second page, reproduced here, should be checked by the passenger.

1 Endorsements: here are recorded any non-transferable APEX and other flights restricted to a certain time on a certain day.

2 Name: should correspond to name on passport. Tickets are transferable to another flight or airline, *not* to another name. Check the spelling.

3 Coupons not valid: an unused ticket can be refunded or renewed up to 30 days after the expiry of the (365-day) period of validity, and thereafter at the airline's discretion.

4 Good for passage: check departure and destination points are correctly entered.

5 Conjunction tickets: if your trip involves more than four stopover points, reference numbers for additional tickets are entered here.

6 Issued in exchange: could be a PTA (prepaid ticket advice) if the ticket is paid for in foreign currency. Details entered below.

7 Ticket designator: single-class Concorde ("R" code) or staff discount flight ("sub law") entered here.

8 Tour code: check tour number for your package-deal holiday is entered here.

9 Departure date: must be correct date for the flight number.

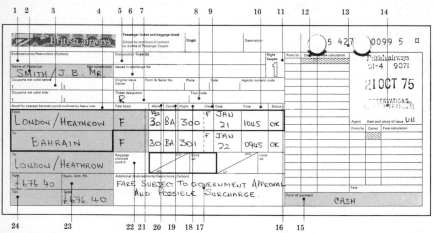

21 Fare basis: check. "F"=first class; "Y" = economy (coach).

22 Baggage checked: weight and number of items checked in. Compensation is not payable on items not entered. **Unck'd:** hand baggage is not checked.

23 Equivalent fare: local equivalent of the fare if paid in foreign currency.

24 Airport tax: not always charged. **Total:** fare plus tax.

17 Additional endorsements/restrictions: comments such as the example filled in should not show on page 2 if not applicable to return trip.

18 Flight number: is always the same for the same route. Check against date and time.

19 Carrier=airline.

20 Allow: baggage allowance, different for different classes. US airlines calculate by piece, not weight.

13 Ticket number: the carrier's code number is followed by the ticket number. The single digit is the coupon number.

14 Agent, date and place of issue: the office stamp of the agent or carrier gives the date of issue of the ticket.

15 Payment can be by cash, cheque, credit card or account.

16 Status: query if not marked "OK".

10 Departure time: given in local time. Check in one hour earlier for international flights; half an hour earlier for internal flights.

11 Flight coupon: marked "1" on page 1 for the outward trip (torn off at check-in) and "2" on page 2 for the return journey.

12 From/to; Carrier; Fare calculation: for official use only; intended for revenue accountancy.

136

Booking and paying

Reservations may be made by telephone and confirmed at the same time, but tickets are not issued until paid for in cash, by cheque or by credit card; payment does not have to be in the local currency, but payments in foreign currency will be at the current rate of exchange.

Tickets can be bought by a friend or company in the country of destination and sent by the airline PTA (Prepaid Ticket Advice) to the user. The cost will be the same, but it may be more convenient to pay abroad.

An account with a reputable travel agent is worthwhile for regular air travellers, not only for the credit facilities made available but also for the preferential services. It is standard practice for agents to book their clients on more than one flight to ensure that a seat is available within a given period. The bookings, made at intervals, are computerized under different numbers and will not be cross-checked; if all bookings are made simultaneously to a single airline they will be computerized under a single number. As soon as the first option comes up, the airline will ask the client to confirm one of the bookings. Agents sometimes book several seats on a flight offering stand-by bargains between London and New York to increase the possibility that there will be a seat for a client to use on a stand-by ticket.

If fares increase between payment and departure, the extra may have to be paid, particularly if the airline has endorsed the ticket to this effect to cover itself at times when fare rises are imminent. The carrier has to refund if fares suddenly decrease.

Children usually travel half-fare and babies under two years at ten per cent of the adult fare, or free.

If a scheduled flight has to be cancelled, the ticket is valid for a year, or payment can be refunded by cash, cheque, or a Miscellaneous Charges Order giving credit to the value of the original ticket.

Cancellation of a discount or budget flight, or a package holiday, may mean forfeiting part or all of the money paid. Breaking the conditions of a return discount flight by returning earlier or later than specified may mean paying the difference between the discount and full standard fare. On European routes, cancellation of an APEX booking more than one month from departure date means forfeiting half the price of the fare; less than a month, the whole fare must be forfeited. On routes to the US, cancellation at any time means forfeiting about ten per cent and, on other routes, usually 25 per cent. The only acceptable reason for breaking the conditions of a discount fare is a death in the family, and a full refund is made only on production of the death certificate.

Since airline computers record details of all ticket sales, to fill in an indemnity form and provide proof of identity is all that is required for a replacement ticket to be issued if the original is lost. The purchaser pays twice if the lost ticket is used.

Compensation for cancelled or delayed flights varies. In the US, airlines must provide meals, transport to hotels, overnight accommodation if needed and telephone and telegraph communication costs. Airlines elsewhere may be less generous. No airline is obliged to compensate for lost time; but it must reroute its passengers if a flight is cancelled or a connection missed through delays. Holiday packages should always be checked out for cancellation procedures; there may be a 24-hour money back guarantee.

Airport taxes are not levied by all airports, but may have to be paid at check-in. The carrier, or your travel agent, should be able to inform you of charges on your journey.

Check list

Passport

Check that your passport has not expired — a new one may take several weeks to arrive. Make sure that any additional children have been incorporated and note the number. Report loss or theft to the police and to the passport office. If abroad, your consulate will issue a travelling document. If you forget your passport, you *may* be allowed out for short trips on proof of identity. You will be required to sign an indemnity form protecting the airline from legal responsibility for you. Passports are usually needed to cash travellers' cheques.

Visas

Consult travel agents, airlines or the embassy concerned about whether or not you need a visa for the country you are visiting (visas are required for the US, but an American does not need one to enter Britain). Submit your passport and, if necessary, vaccination certificates to the appropriate embassy or consulate well in advance. Airlines and package tour organizers often take care of visas for their customers, but it is the traveller's responsibility ultimately. Carry extra photographs for any additional visas needed en route.

Medical

It is wise to have polio, typhoid, tetanus and smallpox vaccinations regardless of where you are going. Check with the relevant embassies which certificates you will need to enter their countries. You must be vaccinated even if your stopover in a potentially infectious area is brief. Have the injections well before the trip, in case of side effects.

Take with you any medicines you regularly use. Even aspirin mixtures vary greatly from country to country. There is no vaccination against malaria, so take a prophylactic regularly as long as there is a chance of passing through a malarial country.

Money

Buy travellers' cheques in the most advantageous currency for exchange (local economic crises can make a difference) and list the serial numbers in case of loss or theft. Familiarize yourself with rates of exchange. Make sure that local currency can be taken in — and out — and carry only small amounts.

Insurance

The Warsaw Convention automatically insures all travellers while in the air. Otherwise, you should be covered for money and goods, medical expenses, flight cancellation and personal accident and liability. Residents of countries with socialized medicine can find treatment without it being dismayingly expensive; they should buy health insurance. Airlines insure baggage, but do set limits; so take out additional insurance on valuables. Comprehensive holiday insurance schemes can be had which promise cover for all these things, based on the areas to be visited and the duration of the stay. Selective policies enable the traveller to choose the cover he requires.

Baggage

Baggage allowances vary for economy (coach) and first class. In the US it is calculated by number and size of pieces. All airlines allow additional carry-on items, usually a bag, coat, umbrella, baby food and baby carrier. Half-fare children have a full luggage allowance. Put your name and home address inside your bags, and display your destination address only on the outside, so as not to advertize your departure to professional housebreakers; keep a list of the contents. Excess baggage may be cheaper sent as air freight.

Check-in

Getting there

Your airline, or another one acting for it, will almost certainly have a terminal in town, often associated with a rail station and usually with a baggage check-in facility. Buses or trains then get you to the airport. There will be a recommended check-in time for the terminal (as distinct from the airport check-in time) which may appear on your ticket; if not, the airline clerks will inform you.

If you are leaving your own vehicle at the airport there will probably be a long-term car park, costing a fraction of the short-term rates, where space may be booked in advance.

Although car parks are guarded, do not make things easy for thieves by leaving your parking ticket in a prominent place; hide it in the car or take it with you. Without the ticket, the car can only be removed when ownership has been proved.

Car rental companies have bases at all major airports.

Checking in

If you have had only telephone confirmation of your reservation, go to the airline ticket sales desk for your ticket before checking in. The check-in desk will have the name of the airline, and possibly your flight number, over it. Here baggage intended for the hold will be weighed and passed to the baggage handlers, while your ticket is checked and you are given a boarding pass.

There are good reasons for checking in earlier than the time shown on a ticket. Since scheduled passengers have great freedom to change or cancel bookings, airlines routinely overbook their flights; sometimes passengers with confirmed reservations are denied boarding, or "bumped". Latecomers are most likely, and members of family groups and handicapped passengers least likely to be "bumped". The assertive passenger with a convincing argument will have a better chance of boarding too.

Any IATA airline is obliged to make alternative arrangements to get you to your destination as soon as possible, by another carrier if necessary. Stay at the check-in desk and argue until satisfactory arrangements have been made for you. In some countries, notably the USA, the civil aviation authorities require carriers to compensate passengers when denied boarding. Payments are made only when the delay is substantial, when the passenger has confirmed his reservation and checked in by the required time, and if the flight was not delayed or cancelled.

If a passenger is required to travel economy (coach class) when he booked first class, he is entitled to a refund equal to the difference in fares; he cannot be charged extra if he is upgraded.

When your baggage is checked, the carrier becomes liable for loss or damage up to limits specified by the Warsaw Convention. A baggage check attached to your ticket records the weight of the baggage; make sure you get the check, and that the weight is not understated: compensation is paid by weight. If the baggage contents are worth more than the compensation rates printed on the back of your ticket, you can make a declaration of excess value, pay an extra charge and gain entitlement to greater compensation. Better still, take your valuables in your cabin baggage and arrange your own insurance beforehand.

If your flight is delayed, do not be in too much of a hurry to pass through security, passport and Customs control to the airside: on a fog-hit day the departure lounge is likely to become more crowded than the main concourse, and will have fewer facilities.

Airport facilities

The permanent facilities offered to passengers are usually signposted on terminal concourses in visual symbols. Various attempts have been made to design a set of symbols that will be immediately intelligible to people from any part of the world, but a successful Esperanto of symbols has yet to be established.

Flight announcements

Continually changing information, such as lists of flight arrivals and departures, is displayed on electronically controlled flipboards and TV monitors. In the most advanced system, the boards and monitors are linked to a central minicomputer so that they are always up to date and consistent. The character generators that inscribe the information on the screens can often handle Arabic or Cyrillic alphabets. A parallel system of monitors, unseen by the public, displays the information throughout the working areas of the terminal. The computer can also provide a print-out of flight statistics based on its own announcements.

There is almost nowhere in the terminal where you can find yourself out of range of announcements in several languages from the public address speakers. These may not come from a living announcer, but may be computer-assembled from pre-recorded snippets, like the announcements of a speaking clock. If the concourse becomes noisier, the volume of the announcements is automatically boosted.

At some airports, personnel are alerted to emergencies by coded messages which sound to passengers like routine announcements. Thus alerted, airport staff can begin to take any necessary action without alarming the public.

Passengers who find no announcements in their own language can enlist help from the desk of their national airline; there will probably also be a general enquiry desk administered by the airport authorities, and major tour operators may have their own desks as well.

Meeting and greeting

Newly arrived passengers can usually be met at the exit from which they appear when they have claimed their baggage, and perhaps also passed through Customs. But there are also designated meeting points. Lost friends can be paged over the public address system.

Messages and telegrams can usually be left at a central message desk. If you telephone any such message through to the airline desk, specify not only the passenger's name, but also his point of origin, expected time of arrival and, if possible, his flight number. The staff who take the message can page the person for whom it is intended as he passes through the arrivals section.

Although airlines communicate with their flight crews in flight on a special company frequency, it is not possible to pass a personal message to a passenger on board. In an emergency, an urgent message can be sent to the destination airport by telephone, cable or telex.

Post and telecommunications

A large airport may have its own post office, and philatelic acquaintances may appreciate letters or cards that have been franked with its date stamp. If there is a post office there will also be a telegraphic service, and perhaps telex offices.

Although telephones will be plentiful on the concourse, they cannot always be found on the airside of the terminal. But at some airports, notably in the USA, telephones are provided in the departure lounges and at points all the way to the embarkation gates.

Business facilities
Air terminals and hotels in and around large international airports may offer conference and secretarial facilities for executive travellers.

Animals
Airlines usually insist that pets be carried in the aircraft cargo holds, so it is advisable to search for an airline that is permissive in this respect if you want to carry a pet in the cabin. All pets should be carried in special pet carriers, available from vets and pet shops, and some animals may need to be tranquillized for the trip.

Animals are usually subject to quarantine regulations in force in the destination country. In the UK these are exceptionally strict, in an attempt to keep rabies out of the country. A dog taken out of the UK would be quarantined for six months on its return, at a cost of £2 to £4 ($4 to $8) a day, depending upon its size, dietary and exercise requirements. Other creatures will cost more or less, depending upon the kind of care they will need.

Children
Many airports are equipped with mothers' rooms where babies can be changed and fed, and others have staffed nurseries where older children can be left for short periods, or entertained during long delays. London's Heathrow Airport, for example, has trained nurses on duty in a nursery area where children up to eight years old can play. Frankfurt Airport's nursery handles up to 100 children a day.

Very young children — usually below six years old, although the age varies from airline to airline — will not be accepted on an airline flight unless accompanied by an adult, but older children can fly unaccompanied. Many airlines offer a child escort service. If notified in advance, they will arrange for ground staff to escort young passengers through Customs, passport and security checks, and hand them over to the care of the cabin staff at boarding time. Each child is provided with special documents advising all staff along the route that they are dealing with unaccompanied minors. In-flight they may be given special childrens' meals, and supervised (and entertained if necessary) by the cabin staff. At the destination they are escorted from the plane and through the airport formalities, to be handed over to an accredited collector.

Although airlines generally provide in-flight supervision free of charge, they may levy a charge for their special child escort services. Such services can also be provided for groups of children.

Welfare
Some very large airports — notably Amsterdam's Schiphol and London's Heathrow — have aid centres for receiving passengers who are destitute on arrival, who are emotionally disturbed, unable to contact relatives or friends, or who are lost. Heathrow Airport's "Wel-care" office is staffed by welfare officers who will counsel staff and passengers on any personal problem, from financial difficulties and lost tickets to marriage guidance.

Rest rooms
All airports have lounges, often with bars serving drinks or snacks, but some airports now have rest rooms where passengers can sleep during short stopovers, or during delays. A small charge may be levied.

Chapels
Many large international airports have chapels, usually interdenominational, with regular services, for the use of both passengers and the airport staff.

Airport facilities/2

Airport medical facilities

If it is not immediately obvious where to get medical aid at an airport, ask any member of the airline or airport staff. If there is no doctor permanently employed on the airport, there will certainly be one on call from the surrounding district, and many members of the airport staff have paramedical or first-aid training; at a small airport, the fire or police chief or the ground stewardesses may be the most likely people to approach for initial help. Asthma, coronaries, the effects of overindulgence in flight and unusual tropical diseases are some of the problems that airport medical services have to be ready for. The largest airports have medical centres as fully equipped as small hospitals. Many charge for their services.

Vaccination services

Some countries demand valid international certificates of vaccination before admitting foreigners and many international airports offer emergency immunization and vaccination services for passengers and staff. Because it takes eight days for a smallpox vaccination to become effective, and ten days for a yellow fever vaccination, and because there are often side-effects from vaccinations for cholera and some tropical diseases, it is advisable to have all vaccinations well in advance of a journey. But revaccinations are valid immediately, and have reduced side-effects. Countries may refuse to admit travellers with new vaccinations, or they may keep them under surveillance for a while.

Travellers should remember to take into account the health requirements of the country to which they are returning. The port health authorities may demand certificates of vaccination against diseases prevalent not only in countries visited, but also where stopovers have been made.

Fitness to travel

Few people are so badly disabled, or enfeebled by age, that they cannot travel by air. Scores of thousands of handicapped passengers are transported routinely by every major airline each year. Only people with infectious diseases, the severely mentally unstable and those whose indisposition (such as a bronchial condition) might be worsened by flying, will be refused a ticket.

A traveller with restricted mobility or other health problem, such as a heart complaint, should find out from the travel agent or airline whether a medical certificate of fitness to fly is required. It is the passenger's responsibility to obtain it from a doctor, and it is wise to obtain several copies. Pregnant women should ask for a certificate stating the number of weeks they have been pregnant, and confirming their fitness to travel. Airlines will not usually permit women to fly in the later stages of pregnancy — usually after the 35th week.

Air travellers with health problems should always discuss the medical aspects of flying with their doctor.

Facilities for the disabled

There is usually a limit to the number of disabled people an airline will carry on one flight (governed by a ratio to available escorts) in case of emergency, so book early. It is the disabled passenger's responsibility to arrange for an ambulance or other transport to the airport terminal. He should arrive half an hour or more before the recommended check-in time to allow for delays, especially in negotiating the often long distances between car parks and terminals. Some airports have special parking spaces for disabled travellers, often near to the air terminal and under cover and wider than usual.

Special facilities for disabled

travellers vary considerably between airports, but most air terminals are designed with automatic doors, wide corridors and concourses, and a maximum number of elevators and moving walkways. These are a boon to the disabled traveller. There may also be ramps and extra-wide walkways with non-slip surfaces and handrails, special toilets, drinking fountains, high dining tables, telephone booths and vending machines, and car rental agencies that hire out hand-controlled cars.

All disabled people can ask for an escort through the terminal formalities and onto the plane. Blind passengers *should* do so. They may take their guide dogs, but these will usually have to be carried with other pets in the cargo hold, and will not be exempt from quarantine laws. Deaf passengers can request written instructions and announcements to be provided on the ground and in the air.

Airline and airport staff are usually well drilled in assisting disabled travellers, especially those in wheelchairs. Help with baggage is as important a consideration as personal help; through his carrier, a disabled passenger can book a cart and porter at the points of departure, stopover and arrival. Collapsible wheelchairs will be carried in the cargo hold free of charge, and the airline will provide its own wheelchairs to take disabled passengers to the aircraft while their own are being loaded. Battery-operated wheelchairs can only be carried if the wet-cell batteries are packed separately in the correct way. Some airline or airport authorities operate ambulance services to convey disabled passengers from the terminal airside to the aircraft.

Airlines may also be able to provide special loading devices to lift disabled passengers from the ground to the aircraft. These usually consist of an enclosed room-like unit that protects its occupant from the weather. It is mounted on a crane resembling a fork-lift truck, and can lift a person in a wheelchair, or on a stretcher, to the aircraft door. Because airline aisles are narrow, the passenger will have to transfer to a special chair to be installed in the cabin seat, and because of the time involved in installing a handicapped person in his seat, he will be expected to check in ahead of the other passengers.

Airlines often require handicapped people to be attended, and their attendants will usually be required to pay full fare. Stretcher cases will usually need — and have to pay for — four seats and an attendant, usually at the first-class rate or higher; ambulance services are costly in many countries. Before undertaking any journey, handicapped travellers should make enquiries as to how much the necessary services en route are likely to cost.

Booking special facilities

Airlines and airports can arrange and provide all sorts of special services, not only those listed here, but also special meals and other services in-flight (pages 145-147), but only if passengers give prior notification of their needs. The airline must know at least two days in advance, and preferably earlier, when the booking is made. The longer they have to prepare, the better the service they can provide. Having informed the airline or a travel agent of your requirements, check again shortly before the flight.

Most airports publish publicity sheets detailing the special services they offer, and airlines and travel agents may also be able to provide information. In the Gazetteer (pages 193-233) the special facilities offered to passengers by 500 of the world's major airports are listed for quick and easy reference.

Duty-free goods

Duty-free goods began as a concession to sailors and travellers who needed to stock up on food for long sea voyages. Today, spirits, wines and cigarettes, usually highly taxed, are the fastest-selling items, but, depending on the country and the size of the airport, a wide variety of goods normally subject to duty and taxes may be sold: souvenirs, clothing, cameras, watches and electrical goods *can* be bargains. In Japan, for example, electronic equipment, televisions and cameras are particularly cheap. At the duty-free shop at Amsterdam's Schiphol Airport (the largest in the world, and the cheapest in Europe) antiques (which usually carry no duty) and even cars are sold.

Duty-free goods may perhaps be more accurately termed "duty-reduced" goods. Although the stock sold may be free of excise duty, it is not always free of local taxes, so it is essential to calculate the cost of a prospective buy in your own currency, to ensure that the goods will be cheaper than at home. At Frankfurt Airport's duty-free shop, where VAT is chargeable on sales to EEC passengers, prices are higher than at other duty-free shops; wine can be bought more cheaply at a landside shop.

Profits from duty-free sales play a large part in the revenue of some airports, and this can affect the prices of the goods sold there. Heathrow Airport is thought to take a cut of 35 to 45 per cent of the gross takings and this, supplemented by income from other concessionaires, accounts for a high proportion of the airport's income. The alternative to this practice would be higher landing fees, or airport taxes, both of which would be passed on to the passengers. Schiphol's duty-free shop, on the other hand, runs at a considerable loss, the management having assumed that this will encourage trade in future years.

Seemingly cheap foreign goods may prove expensive once Customs duty and sales tax or VAT is paid in the home country. Check with your national Customs office for details of duty and other taxes on goods you may want to buy abroad. Rules in the USA are complex, so if in doubt, check with the US authorities, the airline, or a travel agent.

Check, also, on what you are allowed to take *into* foreign countries; citizens of the USA frequently have guns confiscated at the UK Customs. Keep receipts for all purchases, and also for any new items you may take abroad, as proof of origin.

The duty-free shop is located on the airside of the air terminal; only passengers who have passed through Customs may shop there, and, once purchased, the goods are put into sealed bags which should not be opened until after you have left the country. If you want to open your duty-free drinks in flight, ask the cabin staff for permission. Some airlines may object, and in some countries, such as the USA, it is illegal. A smaller selection of duty-free goods — usually drinks, perfume and tobacco — may be sold in flight.

Other shops on the airport landside sell a range of goods, generally more expensive than in town: fruit and souvenirs tend to be particularly highly priced. There are sometimes special duty-free shops on the airport landside; in Germany all tourists are entitled to an export discount, and many shops in London will charge tax-discounted prices on goods sent directly out of the country.

Despite the commercial character of duty-free shops, few countries are prepared to let homecoming travellers shop duty-free on arrival. Goods sold free of the country's excise duty are technically for export — you may bring back an allowance, but may not purchase that allowance at home.

Enplaning

Before boarding an international flight passengers must have passed through Customs, passport control and sometimes security checks; there may be a last-minute security check at the boarding gate.

There are restrictions on the amount of currency travellers can take out of some countries, notably some Eastern bloc countries. Convert any excess before leaving for the airport; if there are no exchange facilities on the airport, any currency you have may be confiscated before you leave the country. Receipts for travellers' cheques cashed may be demanded.

Not all airports conduct security checks, and the checks vary considerably in nature and thoroughness. At some, bags are passed through X-ray viewers, and must be opened if unidentifiable objects are seen. At others, all bags are searched by hand. The X-rays used in baggage checks are weak, but they can fog photographic film if the film is subjected to several checks in the course of a journey. They may also present some slight risk to equipment containing electronic circuitry, such as calculators, radios and cameras. Carry such items in the cabin bags or clear plastic bags, and ask the security staff to hand check it. Cameras should not be loaded: they may be opened by security staff.

At many airports, passengers are examined with a metal-detector. This may be a loop that is run over the body, or a walk-through metal frame. It emits no radiation and cannot cause any damage. In particular, it will not damage heart pacemakers or magnetic credit cards.

Flight announcements are usually broadcast all over the terminal — even in the toilets, coffee bars and restaurants and duty-free shops. Listen for the flight number, which will precede every announcement.

In flight

The amount of baggage passengers may carry aboard an airliner is limited, not because it may weigh too much but because excessive amounts of baggage in the cabin could make it uncomfortable and possibly dangerous in an emergency. Generally, passengers are allowed a nightcase, a handbag, a coat and umbrella, a camera or binoculars, reading matter, baby food and a baby-carrier. Stow baggage as quickly and thoroughly as possible after boarding. There are overhead racks, and space beneath the seat in front. Some US planes, catering for hurried executives, have a baggage compartment in the cabin for overnight bags.

Cigarette lighters are permitted in the cabin, but do not take a filled liquid-fuel lighter on board: it may leak at the reduced pressure of the cabin at altitude. Do not carry cans of spare lighter fuel or try to recharge a gas lighter in flight; boxed matches are safer than book matches.

An old cabin staff trick for preventing ears from "popping" during takeoff consists of yawning and swallowing, followed by pinching the nostrils, then closing the mouth and blowing. Sucking the sweets distributed by the cabin staff may help.

In-flight entertainment

Newspapers and magazines, including the airline's in-flight magazine, stationery, toys and children's books are likely to be available on request. If you want to write letters, be choosy about the kind of pen you use: fountain pens can leak at high altitudes.

Portable radios may not be switched on in flight, they could interfere with the aircraft's radio communications. A portable tape recorder causes no such problems and can be listened to through an earphone, and electronic calculators can also be used.

On one domestic US service, the in-flight entertainment begins on the ground where passengers can watch flight-deck activity until after take-off on short-circuit TV. Movies are usually shown on long flights; family and mature films may be shown in different parts of the cabin. The sound track is heard over headsets plugged into consoles on the seat armrests, and these can also be used to listen to music and other entertainment from a choice of around ten recorded channels. Popular and classical music, country and western, children's songs and comedy can all be dialled up. Lufthansa offer a channel giving isometric exercises which the passenger can do without moving from the seat. Some airlines give basic lessons in the language of the destination country.

Children

Baby-care equipment up to about 26 pounds can be carried in addition to the normal baggage allowance. Mothers with small babies or more than one child will be given seats, on request, at the back of the cabin or near the emergency exits, where there is more leg room than in other parts of the cabin. Many airliners have special fold-down tables, and supplies of nappies (diapers) and talcum powder in the toilets for baby-changing. Certain baby foods can be supplied by the airline, or they will prepare those you have brought yourself if you give ample warning.

Unaccompanied minors will be entertained — and given special meals if a request is made in advance — and the cabin crew always will keep an eye on them to make sure that they are not lonely, nervous or bored. Some airlines have clubs for junior travellers, with badges, membership cards and magazines. They may provide log books in which the members have their mileages on each flight recorded by the captain. And there is a chance that on some airlines (other than on US airlines, where it is forbidden) visitors, including children, will be allowed onto the flight deck for short periods.

Caring for the disabled

Wheelchairs are usually carried free of charge, and are stowed in the hold. The airlines provide wheelchairs for deplaning as they do for enplaning; disabled passengers enplane first but deplane last.

Toilet facilities on board the aircraft are the greatest problem for the disabled person. The cabin crew will not take responsiblity for assisting passengers with toilet equipment, so that use of the toilet may be impossible for an immobile, unaccompanied person. Medical advice may succeed in mitigating discomfort, by modifying eating patterns, or prescribing medicines. People who can move around should ask when booking for seats positioned near a toilet — or an exit. Passengers are rarely permitted to use crutches on board the aircraft. They have to be carried in the hold, as they could be very dangerous in turbulence.

Diabetics and people with heart complaints should notify the airline of their condition, and carry their medicines in their hand-baggage where it is accessible. Oxygen must be ordered at least 24 hours in advance; private oxygen supplies can travel as cargo only if properly packed and labelled.

If there is the slightest doubt about a passenger flying, the final decision rests with the captain. Although cabin crews always have emergency and first-aid training, it is standard procedure to ask if there is a doctor among the passengers if any person becomes ill en route.

Catering and service

Special diets (which can include salt-

Deplaning

free, diabetic and dietetic ulcer as well as vegetarian, Moslem, kosher, kedassia, Hindu and slimming meals) should be ordered when booking, or at least 24 hours before departure. Some airlines carry a few special diets in case a passenger may have forgotten or did not have time to make a request. Do not be tempted to eat too much, because pressure changes can cause indigestion in flight. First-class passengers will have more spacious and more comfortable seats than economy (coach) class. On some of the wide-bodied jets there are bar-lounges up or down stairs; on some, first class passengers leave their seats to eat in a dining area. The extra cost of the first-class ticket is reflected in the comfort, service and menu (see pages 64-65). Most airlines offer free drinks and more service in the first-class cabin. Members of airline clubs will benefit from reduced boarding problems and excess baggage fees, but are entitled to no special benefits in flight.

At the other extreme is the "no frills" service offered by many charter operators and on Laker Airways' transatlantic Skytrain. Passengers pay extra for meals on these flights, and often choose to take their own. It is wise to avoid taking sticky, crumbly or smelly foods, and plastic bags should be taken for remains.

Overnight
Blankets and pillows are available for passengers who wish to sleep, and the seats can be tilted back far enough for tolerably comfortable sleep. If the aircraft is flying into the dawn, blinds can be drawn down.

Soap, talcum powder and cologne are provided for use in the morning. Cabin staff will supply electric shavers. Before the aircraft lands the passengers may be given hot towels to help them wake up, unstiffen and face the outside air.

Transit passengers changing planes between stages of an international journey do not always pass through a baggage claim, Customs or passport control, but they may be subjected to a security check before boarding the next flight.

If your bags are damaged or lost in transit, act immediately. Get a property irregularity report (PIR) from the airline that handled the latest stage of your journey, fill it in, return it to them and keep a copy for yourself. That carrier is responsible for carrying your claim through to its conclusion, even if another carrier is responsible for the damage or loss.

The PIR is not a claim. You must make a claim for damage within seven days, and for loss within 21 days. The airline must provide you with the necessary claim forms; if they fail to do so, write them a detailed letter, specifying the contents of your baggage.

Immigration control may demand evidence that your visit is really for its declared purpose (holiday, business or study), and that you have the financial means to support yourself during your stay. Return air bookings, hotel reservations and invitations to stay with friends are all useful. The landing cards filled in by foreign arrivals to many countries are collated with the records of departing passengers, so there is a record of those who overstay.

Customs officials have the right to search your baggage, and to require you to unpack and repack your bags. Goods on which duty must be paid are impounded until they are paid for. If you are returning to your home country, you should have receipts available for anything you have bought abroad, as well as any valuables you took with you, to prove they were not purchased abroad. Before you leave the air terminal, reconfirm any return or onward booking.

Health hints

Air travel today is more comfortable and more streamlined than ever before. But even the most experienced traveller can fall prey to various disorders. These range from air sickness or fatigue to the now renowned executive bugbear known as jet-lag. All these problems can, however, be either prevented or at least greatly eased.

Fatigue
During or after a flight fatigue is common. It is caused by the length of the journey and also frequently by pre-flight anxiety or excitement. Rest and relax before flying. See to preflight preparations such as immunization and vaccination well in advance, and avoid too hectic a schedule on the day before the flight.

Air sickness
Caused by a bumpy ride (and by anxiety and excitement) sickness is sometimes experienced in aircraft, just as it is in cars and boats. Because modern aircraft fly above bad weather, it is now an infrequent ailment, affecting probably not more than one in a thousand travellers.

But turbulence can upset the labyrinth mechanism of the inner ear — part of the organ of balance — and cause sickness. Keep the head as still as possible on the headrest. Avoid fried and fatty foods, excess alcohol and smoking. Ask a doctor's advice on sickness tablets, particularly in pregnancy. The effective drugs include hyoscine, cyclizine, diphenhydramine, meclozine and promethazine.

Pressurization problems
An aircraft cabin is a communal space suit; air is pumped in to keep the pressure at the outside equivalent of 8,000 feet altitude. For technical reasons it is not possible to achieve ground-level pressure in the aircraft, and the difference can cause discomfort when gases in the body, especially in the intestines, expand.

Palliatives are not to overeat, to avoid carbonated drinks and to wear loose clothing and shoes. Change of pressure during takeoff or landing can affect the ears. A popping sensation is common, or earache or even temporary deafness. These can all be overcome by constant yawning or swallowing. Babies achieve the same end by crying noisily. Anyone with a heavy cold or sinus trouble is prone to sinus pain or earache during a flight, particularly during the descent. Nose drops help but, if possible, avoid flying. Smokers in particular may be affected by the cabin atmosphere as they have a small amount of carbon monoxide in their blood. As the oxygen decreases so this amount increases, sometimes causing a headache or a feeling of being "one degree under". The remedy is to cut down smoking.

Dehydration
The aircraft's pumped-in atmosphere is slightly dry. As a result dehydration can occur. Combat this by drinking as much fluid as possible. Alcohol increases dehydration, so avoid it in flight and be particularly abstemious on long flights to hot countries; dehydration is a serious problem in hot climates.

Swollen ankles
Sitting in the same seat on a long flight puts continuous pressure on the veins in the thighs. People with varicose veins are most affected and their feet and ankles may swell slightly. Wear loose roomy shoes, preferably lace-ups, and walk up and down the cabin periodically.

Jet-lag
This affects travellers flying east-west or west-east journeys in which they change time zones. Biological

rhythms have a programme of around 24 hours, and jet-lag is the failure of the body to adjust its own routine to a clock that may, for instance, bring darkness — and bedtime — ten hours earlier or later than usual. Eating, sleeping and excreting may all be uncomfortably affected and mental reactions may also slow down considerably. The effects of jet-lag seem to be greater on eastbound flights than on westbound. Reactions can be slowed for two days following a ten-zone trip westward, and for three days after a similar eastward trip.

Some companies ban their executives from taking major decisions within 24 hours of a five-hour time change. At least one airline instructs its crews to keep their watches on home time regardless of what time zone they are in. The most cautious medical advice is that one full day of recovery is needed for each five-hour time change. Travellers should try to go to bed as near as possible to their usual bedtime on the first night after arriving; quick-acting aperient pills can allay constipation until the bowels become accustomed to a new daily routine.

The short-stay traveller, such as the businessman continually on the move, is most at risk from jet-lag; the long-stay traveller on holiday has enough time to acclimatize. Babies of up to three months are the most fortunate — their eating and sleeping cycles seem to be unaffected.

Medical problems

All the previous forms of discomfort can temporarily affect the healthy traveller but can be prevented or overcome easily. Diabetics should eat their flight meals at the same time as meals at home; the elderly and anyone with heart trouble should avoid smoking. Above all anyone who is in doubt about his state of health should consult a doctor before flying.

The air traveller's commandments

1. Plan the flight well in advance, taking a day flight if possible, and/or arriving when it is bedtime in the zone of origin; adapt gradually.

2. Lead as quiet a life as possible during the 24 hours before the flight.

3. Cut smoking before and while flying.

4. Drink little alcohol in flight.

5. Avoid the temptation to overeat during the flight.

6. Drink plenty of non-alcoholic, non-sparkling fluids during the flight.

7. Wear loose-fitting, comfortable clothes and shoes.

8. Have a 24-hour rest period after a five-hour time change.

9. Never attend important functions, nor take important decisions, after an east/west or west/east flight.

10. Consider taking a mild aperient and mild, quick-acting sedative if crossing time zones.

Buley's formula

ICAO calculate the number of days of rest needed to overcome jet-lag as:

$$\frac{T/_2 + (Z-4) + C_d + C_a}{10}$$

T = hours in transit

Z = number of time-zones crossed*
  (take this as 0 if X is 4 or less)

C_d and C_a are the departure and arrival coefficients listed in the table below.

Time of day	Departure coefficient	Arrival coefficient
0800–1159	0 = good	4 = bad
1200–1759	1 = fair	2 = fair
1800–2159	3 = poor	0 = good
2200–0059	4 = bad	1 = fair
0100–0759	3 = poor	3 = poor

Example

A traveller leaves Montreal at 1800 hours local time (C_d = 3), spends nine hours travelling, and arrives in Paris at 0800 hours (C_a = 4) having crossed five time zones. The number of days' rest he needs is:

$$\frac{\frac{9}{2} + 1 + 3 + 4}{10} = 1.25 \text{ days}$$

Rounded up to the nearest half-day = 1.5 days.

*See page 193 for time-zone map.

Fighting the fear of flying

Twenty-five million Americans are afraid to fly — one in six of the adult population. Some are not only fearful, but phobic. One difference between a fear and a phobia is in the intensity; a phobia is a disproportionate fear, an exaggerated or irrational feeling, beyond mere anxiety or discomfiture. Phobic air travellers see themselves losing control, suffocating, panicking, falling, crashing or (at the very least) making a fool of themselves.

For both the phobic flier and the merely fearful there are three ways of confronting the ghost. The first is education, or enlightenment. The second is relaxation; and thirdly, there are some techniques and tips that can work well for everyone.

Education
"Nothing is to be feared. It is only to be understood." Understand, then, that every day in the USA, 2,500 aircraft fly an average of 650,000 people some 600 miles from more than 400 airports without incident or accident. According to Lloyd's of London it is 25 times safer to travel by air than by car.

Relaxation
A completely relaxed passenger cannot be fearful. Fear and relaxation are opposite states. Tension and fear adversely affect every muscle, organ, gland, nerve and cell in the body. Relaxation shifts the body motor to idle and all the components throttle back. Learning a simple breathing relaxation procedure helps to curb overwhelming anxiety. It also enables fearful travellers to prepare for comfortable flights.

At home, find a quiet place and settle into a comfortable chair with an arm and head rest. People who are frightened of flying try not to put their full weight down, but for the purposes of this exercise it is essential to do this, with feet uncrossed flat on the floor or supported on some kind of stool. Wriggle as far back into the seat as possible. Make sure jaw muscles are loose, teeth are not touching and lips are slightly parted. Nudge intruding thoughts aside.

Begin the first of three deep breaths by inhaling through the nose, mouth, or both. Inhale fully and hold that inhalation while silently counting to three. Then exhale, silently counting to three. Then exhale completely, saying aloud, "Relax, let go". Breathe normally for a few moments and luxuriate in a refreshing feeling of passivity. Take the second deep breath, repeating the same procedure, but inhaling and exhaling more fully. Relax and let go even more. Then breathe normally.

On the third and final inhalation-exhalation, consider increasing the volume of air by consciously extending the diaphragm. On exhaling, contract the diaphragm muscles so that more air is expelled. Exhale tension, stress and fear. Let go.

Practise the exercise several times before going on to desensitize past feelings about flying. If muscular tension persists, try counting from ten to one and slowly letting go of that tension. Think of a pleasant, peaceful place and fantasize being there, unworried and unafraid.

To learn to be comfortable when flying it is essential to confront fear. Relax with the breathing exercises and review a previous frightening experience or an anticipated one as rationally as possible. Stop any time fear begins to reassert itself. The next day it will be possible to recall the experience with less emotional involvement. From a relaxed position, keep examining your feelings about flying until familiarity dispels fear.

Projection
Once past fears have been confronted, conditioning and programming for a

future flight can begin. Go to a deep level of relaxation with the breathing exercise and select some city or area that has a strong appeal for you. Maybe there is someone you would particularly like to visit there. Recall all previous happy, warm thoughts about being there and imagine enjoying the place and the people.

The next conditioning step is to envisage boarding the plane to make the trip and experiencing a mixture of excitement and fear; it will be difficult to differentiate between them. Choose excitement! Remember it is quite normal to be nervous.

Imagine that someone dear to you, who knows you well, is on board. The seat belt sign comes on and the flight becomes slightly choppy. Pretend that the plane is travelling over a cobbled road in the sky. Any feeling of being distraught or overly disturbed, experienced on past flights, will be reduced. It is quite normal to feel uncomfortable, but not unsafe.

Tips

Visit airports. Observe the different makes of aircraft. Park on the perimeter and watch the planes take off and land. Find out what kind you will be travelling on and learn to recognize it. All are safe.

Some people prefer morning flights so they can get up and go without spending the whole day uneasily. Allow a *minimum* of one hour for parking, buying a ticket or checking in, and security screening. Rushing exaggerates anxiety. Buy a magazine as a distraction.

On stepping aboard, tell the flight attendant that you are fearful, uncomfortable or terrified of flying and that you would like to take a peek into the flight deck. Generally, anyone who makes this request is welcomed by a relaxed crew.

After settling into the seat, do the deep breathing exercises. This singular procedure has worked effectively even for the most sceptical. Do it with your eyes closed. Turn inward for the strength that is waiting to be tapped. Some vestige of anxiety and fear is bound to remain but the important thing is that the previously fearful flier will find that his or her perception of flying has been updated.

In the air, listen for the sound of the landing-gears retracting; then the no-smoking sign will be turned off, the engine power will decrease, and the flaps will be retracted, usually in that order. As soon as possible stand up and stretch. Move about the cabin. Experience the triumph: you have conquered the fear of flying.

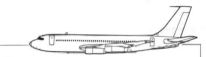

Aircraft noises

Today's jets are quiet. Modern turbofan engines are hardly audible in the sound-proofed cabin, but the bumps, bangs and changes in pitch that can be heard on takeoff and landing should be reassuring noises, evidence of an efficient, sophisticated machine doing its job of flying.

*Engines starting up make a soft purr and tremble. A ground mechanic with headphones on watches them from the ground as they start.

*Taxying out may be bumpy at first if flat spots have formed on the tyres from the weight of the plane at a standstill, and the engines are given a little extra power. Remember that planes moan, groan and grumble when they are taxying. They are birds meant to fly, not to rumble along like an earth-bound bus.

*On takeoff the engines are gently accelerated to full power as the plane moves.

*Less than a minute after takeoff the wheels can be heard (most loudly in the forward part of the cabin) retracting into their compartment in the lower fuselage, before the doors snap closed to make the body smooth again.

*Engines change pitch for landing. A slight jolt may be felt when the landing-gears meet the runway and almost immediately the engines sound louder as the engines' thrust is reversed to slow the plane down

Air cargo

In contrast with passengers, who utilize far more space than is economic for their weight, freight containers require little more space than their own volume. Specially shaped to the contours of modern aircraft, they can be handled quickly, reducing pilferage and insurance rates and easing Customs clearance. They can be packed with all kinds of cargo, which is generally despatched in small consignments.

The organization and operation of air cargo services is now a highly specialized business. Except in remote areas, the days of throwing a mail bag or two in the back of the cabin or baggage compartment are long past. Due to the increase in the size and range of aircraft and the standardization of containers, air cargo carriage worldwide has expanded from a negligible total load in the 1950s to around 18 million ton miles in the 1970s. Although the price per ton mile of carrying goods by air is higher than that for any other form of transport, users of air cargo services value the reliability, frequency, security and particularly the speed of delivery offered by the air carrier. A fast delivery may permit a valuable piece of equipment to commence production earlier, reduce the length of time capital is tied up in stock in transit, and the perishable goods industries dealing in food and flowers depend on it.

Airport cargo terminals are similar to Post Office sorting offices. Full

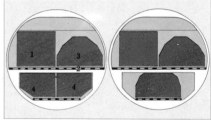

The Boeing 747F, the all-cargo version of the wide-bodied jet, has a hinged nose to permit containerized cargo to be loaded straight in. Standard rectangular containers 1 come in lengths up to 40 ft; pallets 2 are metal sheets on which loads are assembled and held in place by nets; igloos 3 are pallets with rigid sides contoured, like LD3 containers 4, to the fuselage.

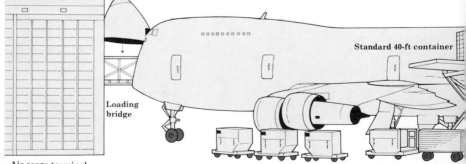

Standard 40-ft container

Loading bridge

Air cargo terminal

automation in the huge cargo centre operated by Lufthansa at Frankfurt Airport means that over 4,500 items can be handled per hour by only 24 men. Goods and mail in a steady stream pass through import and export sections, each overseen by a separate Customs department. The processes along the way: receiving, routeing, stacking while awaiting shipment, recalling and despatching for loading, are controlled with minimum human supervision, by electronics. Computers keep automatic track of every packet that enters the terminal complex. The London Airport Cargo Electronic Data Processing scheme monitors the 500,000 or more tons of cargo handled annually at Heathrow, so that shippers and consignees alike can plan well ahead.

Air cargo terminals provide special facilities for the storage of many different types of cargo, including cages for animals and surveillance vaults for valuables. Vast amounts of valuable cargo such as jewels, travellers' cheques, precious metals, bullion, cigarettes and alcoholic drinks pass through air cargo terminals in small parcels, an easy target for pilferage. Radioactive chemicals are kept in lead-lined inner rooms, fragile cargo is stored on separate racks, and food and perishable goods in cold or refrigerated stores. Dangerous goods such as explosives, corrosives, flammable and toxic materials are carried regularly but are subject to rigorous controls.

Both freighter and convertible 747s have a mechanized cargo-handling system on the main deck. Pallets or containers can be loaded straight in on a motor-driven roller by two men, one at the nose and one inside, who can load and unload the aircraft in as little as 30 minutes.

The enormous capacity of the 747F has revolutionized the air cargo industry. It can carry a maximum payload of about 260,000 pounds 4,000 miles, well beyond transatlantic range, without a refuelling stop.

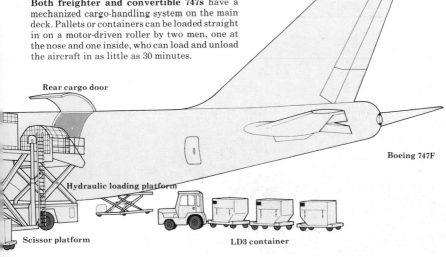

Rear cargo door

Boeing 747F

Hydraulic loading platform

Scissor platform

LD3 container

Air cargo / 2

Cargo consignments are assembled on large pallets – metal sheets ten feet by seven feet, sometimes covered by security "igloos". The whole assembly is bound by stout netting to prevent internal movement in transit. Bulky consignments are loaded in large containers. Mechanized rollers carry the containers from the make-up floor into the aircraft via a truck with a mechanized roller platform.

The airliner will carry as much cargo as the passenger and fuel load will allow. A narrow-bodied Boeing 707 can carry up to 40 tons of freight; the wide-bodied 747 has more space in its lower holds than the entire 707 and can take 16 tons of cargo plus a full passenger load.

The interchangeable passenger/ freighter aircraft, sometimes called a "combi", is designed so that whole blocks of seats mounted on pallets, plus galleys, can be removed, and roller-equipped freight floors fitted in less than an hour. This flexibility makes such an aircraft an attractive proposition. Wide-bodied aircraft are costly to buy, but relatively cheap to operate, and a properly integrated fleet of these and the older all-freight aircraft can be profitable.

Scheduled services are frequently underbooked, and cargo provides the profit. Provided that adequate terminal facilities for rapid unloading, clearance and despatch can be provided at airports in developing countries, there will be no holding the air cargo business.

Redesigned from the Britannia, in 1960 the Canadair CL-44 Forty-four was developed as a troop plane. The unusual tail section of the CL-44D4 cargo version swings aside for straight-in loading, while a long-bodied version carried 214 passengers on north Atlantic services.

Just like the fish from which its name is taken, the Aero Spacelines Super Guppy ingests its cargo whole. This super-freighter has a hold 111 ft 6 in long, 25 ft 1 in wide, and 25 ft 6 in high, making an area of 39,000 cu ft of usable space as compared with 23,630 in the Boeing 747. It can carry whole wings and fuselage sections of Concorde and the Airbus. Developed from the 1940s Boeing Stratofreighter, it is powered by four turboprop engines, and has a 500-mile range fully loaded.

Maintenance and servicing

The rate at which streams of aircraft check in and out of the world's airports is little short of miraculous. Each departure is only the tip of an iceberg of organization designed to ready an airliner for takeoff.

Maintenance is the most important pre-flight activity. The present systems are the result of some 70 years' experience which began with the flimsy, fabric-covered, wire-braced wooden structures in which men first taught themselves to fly. Frequently they were wrecked in the process, to be rebuilt and fly again, perhaps the same day. From these fragile beginnings a system of repair and maintenance has evolved, carried out by aircraft maintenance engineers licensed by aviation authorities. They are trained to overhaul airframes, engines and systems.

Satisfactory maintenance of any advanced machinery originates with the manufacturer. To convince potential customers of the safety of a new aircraft he must satisfy both himself and them that it will be granted a Certificate of Airworthiness by the relevant national authorities. Manufacturers compile maintenance manuals and Service Bulletins to advise on the maintenance of aircraft and their engines when in service, and these are updated from reports from the airline pilots that fly them.

The manufacturer's maintenance schedule lays down the periods in which each part of an aircraft must be inspected, the type and degree of

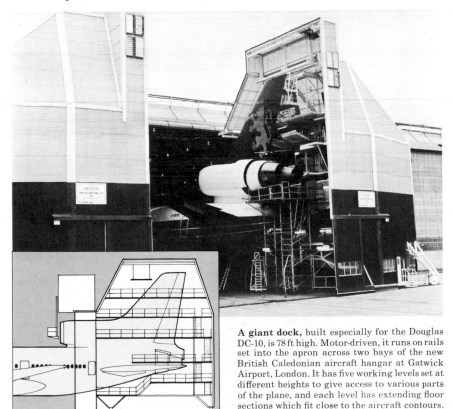

A giant dock, built especially for the Douglas DC-10, is 78 ft high. Motor-driven, it runs on rails set into the apron across two bays of the new British Caledonian aircraft hangar at Gatwick Airport, London. It has five working levels set at different heights to give access to various parts of the plane, and each level has extending floor sections which fit close to the aircraft contours.

inspection necessary, and it also rules on the replacement of individual items according to the number of landings, flying hours, and other criteria. It forms a basis for the proposals for maintaining his fleet which the airline operator must in turn submit to the airworthiness authority. Approval depends on his making satisfactory provision for such matters as suitable hangarage and workshops, tools and test equipment, quality and reliability control, and materials and training.

Enormous hangars are needed to house the wide-bodied airliners. The docks, huge stagings built around the aircraft so that every part is accessible for inspection and repair, are equipped with working platforms at many levels, built-in lighting, and lifts and conveyors for personnel, tools and spares.

The time needed to inspect and overhaul an airliner varies with its size and complexity. Aircraft usually have light checks at 50-60 flying hours, overnight checks at 300-600 hours, and full overhauls, lasting a month or more, every 3,600 flying hours. A total of 84,300 man-hours, three and a half man-hours per flying hour, may be expended in maintaining the aircraft over a ten-year period of about 24,000 flying hours.

Components which will eventually need replacement, particularly the moving parts, must be easy to remove and replace. The BAe One-Eleven's tailplane (stabilizer), for example, is the aircraft's largest moving component and even this can be changed

The **quick turnaround** is essential to airline profitability: an airliner is a vastly expensive piece of capital equipment which must be kept flying for as many hours as possible to earn its keep. Between landing and takeoff it must be unloaded, cleaned, loaded up with passengers, baggage, food, water, duty-free goods and cargo, and refuelled in the shortest possible time.

The **Lockheed Tri-Star** is designed so that 273 passengers and their baggage can be unloaded, and the plane refuelled, serviced and reloaded, within a normal turnaround time of 30 minutes. To do this, 14 or more vehicles may be assembled around the plane at once. Routine maintenance checks of the airframe, engines, tyre pressures, lights, brakes and other essentials take about 25 minutes; minor faults reported by the flight crew are corrected. Refuelling at a rate of about 20 gals a second takes 21 minutes. All the other servicing goes on simultaneously. Auxiliary power units ease congestion on the apron by replacing ground power units, air-conditioning trucks and units for starting up the engines.

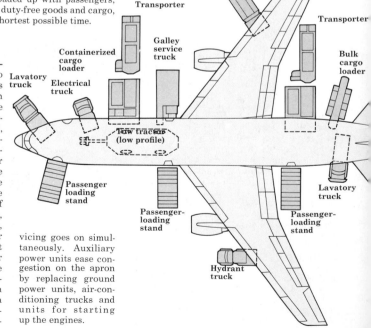

Fuel tanker

Transporter

Transporter

Galley service truck

Containerized cargo loader

Bulk cargo loader

Lavatory truck

Electrical truck

Tow tractor (low profile)

Passenger loading stand

Lavatory truck

Passenger-loading stand

Passenger-loading stand

Hydrant truck

during an eight-hour overnight stop. Condition-monitoring is a system under which an aircraft, its components and systems, are analyzed from pilots' reports of technical delays and unscheduled engine shut-downs, and inspected at predetermined intervals to establish "alert levels" for the future repair and replacement of parts, eliminating all unnecessary removal and dismantling. Non-destructive testing of vital components using X-rays, ultra-sonic and magnetic particle methods detects fatigue-induced cracks before they become serious.

Maintenance programmes for older aircraft especially are dominated by numbers of "lifed" items, each having a "never exceed" time between overhauls. These items are highly stressed and critically important components which may be subjected to corrosion or severe vibration, or both. In all cases fatigue is a major consideration. Wing spars need inspecting at 3,500 flying-hour intervals, and cabin windows and other openings in the fuselage must be inspected every 300 flying hours.

Aircraft performance is affected by dirt deposited on the outer skin in polluted airspace above industrial areas, which raises fuel consumption, so aircraft are washed in giant hangar bays like car washes.

An airliner's structure is designed to be safe to fly at least 30,000 hours in ten years or more without trouble, with a 50 per cent safety factor in addition for critical components.

Servicing connections are designed to international standards and are positioned to ensure a practical distribution of servicing vehicles around the plane. The TriStar was designed for a *fast* turnaround time of 20 minutes, or even less on a short through-stop. A pre-flight inspection, carried out by the crew of all aircraft before a flight, takes the form of a walk-round external check for fuel, oil and hydraulic fluid leaks, and to ensure the security of all removable panels, controls, flaps, landing-gears and so on. Away from the maintenance base, minor repairs can be undertaken on the spot. Even an engine may be changed, and passengers may, occasionally, see an extra engine carried beneath the wing in a pod, for delivery to an overseas maintenance point. The service points on the Lockheed TriStar **right** are as follows:

1 Windshield washer system
2, 3 Oil fillers for air cycle turbine
4 Potable water filling point
5 Pneumatic power units
6 Pressure fuelling points
7 Hydraulic service panel
8 Gravity-fuelling points

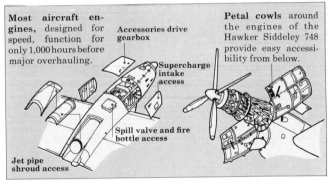

Most aircraft engines, designed for speed, function for only 1,000 hours before major overhauling.

Accessories drive gearbox

Supercharge intake access

Petal cowls around the engines of the Hawker Siddeley 748 provide easy accessibility from below.

Spill valve and fire bottle access

Jet pipe shroud access

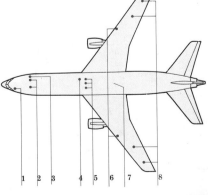

Airport vehicles

A fascinating range of vehicles can be seen at any airport. Some, such as the trucks with conspicuous "Follow me" signs to guide aircraft to their bays, are standard commercial vehicles. Many others are harder to identify.

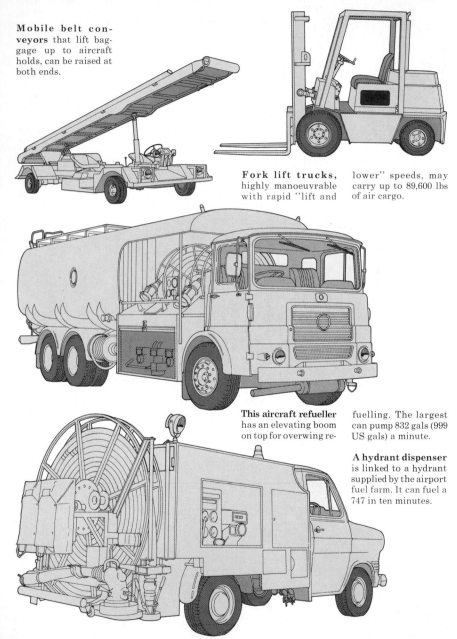

Mobile belt conveyors that lift baggage up to aircraft holds, can be raised at both ends.

Fork lift trucks, highly manoeuvrable with rapid "lift and lower" speeds, may carry up to 89,600 lbs of air cargo.

This aircraft refueller has an elevating boom on top for overwing refuelling. The largest can pump 832 gals (999 US gals) a minute.

A hydrant dispenser is linked to a hydrant supplied by the airport fuel farm. It can fuel a 747 in ten minutes.

This tug carries the aircraft nosewheel on its platform. Its high 40-mph speed is needed on the long taxiways at Charles de Gaulle Airport.

Ground power units (GPUs) are used to start aircraft engines, and to give power to their electrical systems on the ground when the engines are not running. Though useful on busy aprons, they are not needed at airports that supply power from a ring main connected to the power centre, or by aircraft with airborne power units (APUs), auxiliary engines that provide an alternative power supply independent of the main engines.

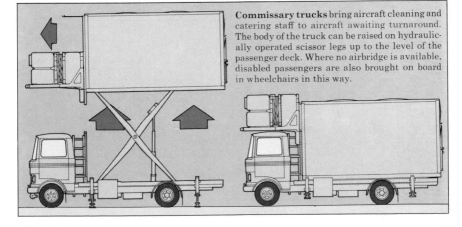

Commissary trucks bring aircraft cleaning and catering staff to aircraft awaiting turnaround. The body of the truck can be raised on hydraulically operated scissor legs up to the level of the passenger deck. Where no airbridge is available, disabled passengers are also brought on board in wheelchairs in this way.

159

Airport vehicles

Self-propelled passenger steps adapt telescopically to any aircraft door height.

Self-propelled aerial platforms give easy access for aircraft maintenance.

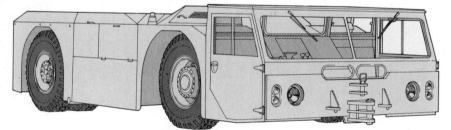

Heavy tugs, weighing an eighth of the 747s they pull, can have a single cab or one at each end. These can be raised and lowered to fit beneath different aircraft fuselages.

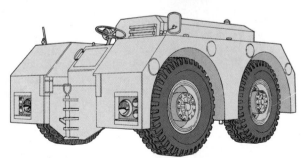

Push - out tugs are used to manoeuvre aircraft backwards into oddly-positioned parking bays by attaching to the nosewheel and pushing it.

Drinking-water supply trucks holding 650 gals (780 US gals) or more can refill an aircraft tank at 20 gals (24 US gals) a minute.

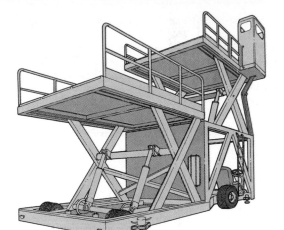

A double deck loader, used to load air cargo pallets, has two scissor-lift platforms. The lower rises to nine ft and the upper deck, mounted on a nine-ft chassis, can extend up to the 18-ft deck height of a Boeing 747. This arrangement facilitates faster air cargo handling. While the top pallet is being unloaded, the next one is readied for collection on the deck below.

This hydraulic platform, used to service and clean inaccessible parts of an aircraft, such as the windscreen, works in two stages. First the cage moves out, and then up to its maximum working height of 33 ft. The controls cannot be accidentally operated.

Mobile lounges, first used in the USA, reduce apron congestion by conveying passengers to aircraft parked away from the terminals. Their extensible and swivelling gangways scissor-lift to enclose any aircraft door—or terminal gate—and so protect their 150 passengers from noise and weather. They travel at speeds up to 20 mph.

Airport fire services

Seventy-five per cent of all aircraft accidents occur within half a mile of an airport. Aircraft fires are rare — London's Heathrow Airport had two in 1977 — but an airport is not permitted to operate without an efficient fire service.

Airport fire services will turn out on full emergency stand-by on the slightest indication that something is wrong with a landing plane: a deflated tyre, a circuit-breaker out in any important system, a warning light in the flight deck. They turn out on average once a day at a major airport, and are always on stand-by in bad weather or fog. During an emergency the fire service provides general emergency help, carrying stretchers and aiding disabled people.

Aircraft burn quickly, giving fire fighters under three minutes to reach them and carry out control and rescue operations. Until the 1960s, airport fire-fighting equipment consisted of little more than modified versions of that used by municipal fire services. Now, every major airport is equipped with rapid intervention vehicles (RIVs) able to reach the runways within two minutes of an alarm. Heavy duty vehicles are designed to cross rough ground to reach a distant runway (by a circuitous route, they cannot drive across runways in use) or the overshoot and undershoot areas where most fatalities occur.

No airport is awarded a licence unless it conforms to national standards based on ICAO recommendations, but each airport is equipped according to its own needs. Some Indian airports have tank-tracked tenders, and Auckland Airport in New Zealand uses hovercraft to negotiate mud flats at low tide.

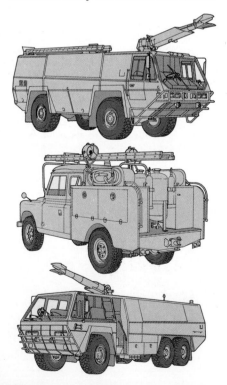

This heavy-duty fire tender can discharge 9,000 gals (10,800 US gals) of water or foam a minute through its monitor, and 900 gals (1,080 US gals) through each of its two handlines, while moving forward or backward.

The light rescue unit carries 330 lb of dry powder sodium bicarbonate in two units pressurized by carbon dioxide. Each discharge pistol can eject powder at the rate of 3.3 lb per second over a range of 39 ft.

This heavy-duty airfield crash truck can be operated by one man, or carry a crew of five. It holds over 3,000 gals of water and over 360 gals of foam, and travels at 60 mph. It throws a 300 ft jet.

The tank holds 200 gals of foam concentrate and is designed so that the base slopes down to a sump.

Two 120-ft hoses of rubberized cloth are folded flat in open trays on each side.

RIVs are fast trucks that carry foam, water, medical and rescue equipment, and lights for use in fog and darkness. Their crews begin holding operations to contain the fire and clear escape routes. Heavy-duty foam tenders follow. They are large, but fast and manoeuvrable, and carry about ten times more foam than the RIVs. Turret-mounted foam guns ("blabbermouths") swivel to project the foam up to 300 feet.

Foam smothers the flames and cools the area around to prevent further outbreak of fire. Water is only really effective as a coolant. Spraying a blanket of foam on the runway to prevent a malfunctioning plane from catching fire on landing is now thought to be a waste of time, but foam is useful for fires that break out during refuelling, when a build-up of static electricity in the tank sparks the fuel. Kerosene is less inflammable than the fuels used by many airlines, but more expensive.

Powder is most effective on localized fires in wheels or tyres, or in electrical apparatus, but it produces toxic fumes on contact with foam. Inert vaporizing gases, such as Halon 1200, attack oxygen and are particularly useful for engine fires.

The emergency services are stationed at various points around the airfield, and are in radio contact with each other, the central station and the control tower.

Airport fire-fighters wear flame-resistant aluminized clothing and are equipped with breathing apparatus against smoke and the toxic fumes produced by burning aircraft furnishings. They train daily, and practise their craft on old fuselages in remote parts of the airfield.

The four-man, four-door cab is made of double-skinned insulated aluminium.

This rapid intervention fire/rescue vehicle is designed to accelerate to 70 mph as fast as a sports car, despite the weight of foam and equipment carried. It carries 200 gals (240 US gals) of a concentrated, ready-mixed water and foam solution, first aid and rescue equipment which is used to contain the fire and keep aircraft escape routes open until the main fire-fighting force arrives. This six-wheeled model carries an aluminium ladder. The versatile chassis can be fitted with stretchers and other special equipment, for use as an ambulance.

The pump expels 200 gals of foam a minute.

Special fittings include a crash grid, powerful fog lamps and a searchlight on the roof which can be set up on a tripod.

Keeping runways clear

Two millimetres of snow can affect the braking action of a runway so adversely as to make landing unsafe. Airport authorities in Switzerland and Austria have researched into surface heating to melt the snow as it falls but, using 200 watts of electricity per square yard, this method would be too costly for large areas.

Flush runway lights are easily obliterated by snow, but increasing their intensity may, initially, melt it. The French use the hot blast from a jet engine at Orly Airport to clear a 130-foot-wide path through fresh snow, but compacted snow and slush take much longer to clear. The system can also be used for de-icing and drying wet runways.

Powdery snow can be compacted and spread with hot sand or gravel to make a runway safe, but one inch of damp, heavy snow covering the runway of London's Gatwick Airport weighs 5,000 tons. This kind of snow freezes rock-hard when temperatures fall, and has to be cleared at once.

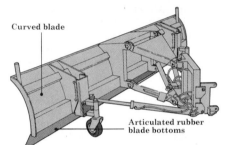

Curved blade

Articulated rubber blade bottoms

A runway snowbrush, below, can clear a heavy snowfall in one operation. Angled up to 45°, the 14-ft-long brush scatters snow up to 50 yds to either side. Variable speed control can be set to slow speeds for sweeping surface dirt, up to 550 rpm to clear heavy slush. By means of an air deflector, snow is thrown high to be carried away by the wind, or low to avoid blowback.

Snow cutters, top, clear snow drifts using rotating blades. Snow chips are directed into an ejection outlet in each drum, swept into the chutes by centrifugal force, and discharged to one side.

Snow ploughs, above, are specially shaped, and adjustable to left or right, to roll the snow and throw it to either side. The articulated rubber blades are designed to clear runway lights.

Mechanical clearance is the only solution to persistent heavy snowfall.

Snow clearance operations are carried out by chains or "congas" of vehicles. First, a high-speed runway sweeper makes swathes through the snow. Snow ploughs follow, moving the loose snow aside, and finally, snow blowers blow it clear.

Some airports have ice-alert systems to give visual and aural warning of the onset of freezing conditions. Anti-icing is carried out using polyglycol fluid dispensed from a vehicle with booms extending some 50 feet. About 500 gallons (600 US gallons) of fluid are needed to cover Gatwick's runway, at a cost of £2 ($4) a gallon, and the treatment takes about half an hour. Some runways are slightly cambered so that icemelt or rain can flow away, and flanked by loose gravel shoulders for complete drainage. Others have porous friction surface courses, or are banded with quarter-inch-deep grooves to break the surface film of water.

Snow-clearance machines are costly, but losses in revenue sustained by an airport closed by snow for one day would almost pay for the equipment needed to clear it. Snow sweepers have a dual role in clearing runways of debris that may be ingested into engines, or puncture tyres. Tyre rubber sticks to the lenses of flush runway lights, and these have to be cleaned by specialized machines with high-pressure water jets, or semi-automatic suction machines. The blast of jets at takeoff blows runway dust away, but at desert airports keeping the runways clear of sand is a major problem.

City street-cleaning trucks are sometimes used to clear runways and apron areas, and magnetic sweepers pick up stray pieces of metal around aircraft servicing bays.

Bird strike

A flock of birds sucked into a jet engine at takeoff can cause a dangerous stall, while a single large bird, hitting an engine with the force of a bullet, may smash a fan blade that costs around £2,000 ($4,000) — the cost of a car to replace. A tailplane hit by a bird at speed may be weakened initially, and torn off by resulting aerodynamic forces. Airframe and engine manufacturers test the resistance of fuselages and turbine blades, and aircraft windshields are built to resist a four-pound chicken carcass fired at a velocity of over 400 mph.

Amplified bird distress calls, as well as dead and decoy birds, are only partially effective. Flares, loud noises and shellcrackers are a more successful harassment.

The use of falcons and other birds of prey is proving a strong deterrent in tests in the UK, but the long-term answer seems to be starvation. Rubbish dumps are covered up, insects and earthworms controlled and small mammals discouraged.

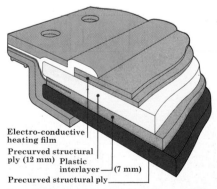

Electro-conductive heating film
Precured structural ply (12 mm) Plastic interlayer—(7 mm)
Precured structural ply

This flight-deck windshield, made especially for a Boeing 747, is one and a half inches thick. Made of special laminated glass, interfaced with plastic, it can withstand an impact of over 50 tons. This type of windshield was the first to exceed 10,000 hours service.

Airport medical services

Tense, nervous passengers become accident-prone at airports. They shut their fingers in doors, fall down stairs, walk into plate glass doors, drink too much, develop toothache and migraine and produce babies while waiting for their flights.

Airport medical staff deal with a surprising variety of cases. At Heathrow Airport they handle an average of 40 fatal coronaries, and a few strokes, every year, and they may also have to deal with inbound passengers suffering from over-indulgence in flight. Some provide last-minute vaccinations for outbound passengers, and airline services based at large airports treat airline flight crews.

Medical services provided at airports differ enormously. The smallest airports may not have so much as a first aid kit, and may be entirely unmanned until the local first-aid-trained fire service comes out from town to meet the daily flight. In contrast, large airports will have round-the-clock stand-by emergency services. John F. Kennedy Airport in

the USA has two operating rooms and a medical centre that can handle up to 1,000 cases. Frankfurt's medical centre has operating facilities and a remedial pool.

No international body compels airports to provide medical services. Although London's Heathrow Airport has a fully-staffed 24-hour emergency service, and free facilities for airport users, the CAA stipulates only that to be granted a licence, an airport must arrange for local doctors and hospitals to be on 24-hour call.

And in the USA, the National Transportation Safety Board, which investigates accidents, frequently criticizes the FAA for its lack of attention to airport medical facilities. Airline pilots' associations are strongly pressuring ICAO and their national aviation authorities to recommend that a full simulated disaster drill be carried out once every six months at all airports. Airline facilities alone are not intended to handle major disasters, so community fire, hospital and police services are necessary and even, sometimes, the military. An

Flight data recorders, introduced in 1965, were dubbed "black boxes" (a nickname for any electronic "box of tricks") by the media. But they are usually egg-shaped, and painted bright red so that they are easily seen from a distance. The earliest versions recorded only altitude, airspeed, pitch attitude, acceleration and magnetic heading, but current models can record information from up to 60 different sources.

The black box **left** was recovered from a Vanguard which crashed in a snowstorm near Basle, Switzerland, in 1973. The pilot seemed to have lost his bearings while flying on instruments, but the black box contained no voice recorder, so what really happened was never made clear. Modern cockpit voice recorders tape all flight-deck conversation. The tape is "wiped" continuously, so that at any moment the previous half hour's data is stored.

A modern flight recorder **right**, built to resist an impact of 5,000 lb, an acceleration of 1,000 times the force of gravity, and temperatures of 2,012 degrees Fahrenheit (1,100 degrees Cel-

operation of disaster scale has to be planned — a plan is drawn up by the chiefs of the services involved — and rehearsed.

A disaster drill takes place on a site away from the main airport operations. A real aircraft is used, with flight and cabin crews and passengers. Casualties wear realistic make-up. The drill begins with notification from the aircraft to the control tower, from where all emergency services are alerted.

The captain and crew are in command until the fire services take over. Fire crews position their vehicles while passengers are evacuating the aircraft and casualties are lying on the ground. They begin fire control and rescue operations, while medical personnel stabilize the casualties, mark the deceased, and give treatments in inflatable hospital tents until the ambulances arrive.

Police are needed to clear the access roads, and the highways leading to the airport, for ambulances and fire and supply trucks. People descend on major disasters once they have been reported in the media. The influx hampers operations.

An enormous amount of equipment is needed at a disaster. In the USA's first disaster drill at Oakland International Airport in 1971, eight converted cargo trailers were used to transport supplies. The first truck brought electrical equipment for lighting, folding desks for command personnel and a platform for the officer in charge of operations to supervise the action. Telephones and communications equipment were in a second, and others brought medical supplies and stretchers, wheelchairs, water supplies and backboards (narrower than stretchers, used to carry injured passengers along aircraft aisles) which, when laid on wooden horses, make examination tables.

A disaster drill ends when the last casualty has been released from hospital. Photographing, recording and clearing-up operations ensure that the lessons learned are made available to other airports so that passengers receive the same fire and rescue attention at any airport.

sius) for 30 minutes, may be the only part of a wrecked aircraft to remain intact. This recorder can be immersed in sea water for a month; an audio recorder inside enables it to be detected by sonar. Digital information is recorded magnetically, from up to 60 sources, onto fine stainless steel wire. This can be played back through an analogue computer to build up a series of graphs giving a complete picture of the aircraft's flightpath. Data are simultaneously recorded on a non-accident-proofed tape, to be monitored after routine flights.

Used to provide airlines with information on all aspects of flight performance, the flight data recorder helps to solve aircraft design problems, a welcome bonus since it can cost over £40,000 ($80,000) to install a complete data and voice-recording system on a large airliner.

The recorder is usually installed high up in the base of the aircraft's fin since this part of the aircraft, behind the centre of gravity and away from the fuel tanks, is most likely to survive an impact.

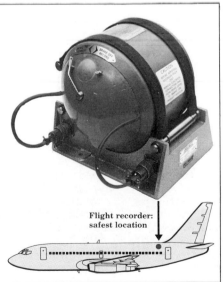

Flight recorder: safest location

Airport security

When smuggling was the major airport crime, the passenger was rarely subjected to the indignity of personal search. The scourge of hijackings by politically-motivated terrorists has changed that. And airports — large, complex and richly-stocked, and vulnerable international frontiers — are prey to thieves and pilferers, illegal immigrants, drug traffickers and smugglers of all kinds.

Airport security starts at the perimeter fence, which will ideally have a ten-foot clear area on either side. Microwave fences, which flash a warning of intruders still some distance away are used for remote boundaries. But because fences have gates, identity cards are issued to airport workers and checked by security guards.

Isolated, as a rule, from the main airport buildings, cargo terminals are targets for thieves and pilferers. Few cargo terminals are as secure as the new one at Singapore Airport, which has armed security guards, closed-circuit TV with zoom lens cameras, videotape recording, and a twin-lock system for high value articles, with one key held by guards and the other by a document acceptance officer. At most airports, bonded stores for duty-free goods, and surveillance cages for valuable cargo, may reduce all but organized pilferage, but will not prevent theft during delivery or loading, or determined armed robbery. Airports have been the scenes of some spectacular thefts. Both London's Heathrow and New York's John F. Kennedy have recorded annual losses in excess of £5 million ($10 million) a year. Heathrow has been dubbed "Thiefrow" by the national press.

Terrorism is the worst threat, and airports and airlines at risk may have air cargo X-rayed or, as at the Lufthansa terminals, containerized cargo is routinely decompressed for 12 hours in remotely-sited chambers,

to reduce the possibility of bombs exploding in aircraft cargo holds.

Ever since a Peruvian Airlines plane was hijacked in 1930, there has been piracy in the sky. Now, this crime has reached epidemic proportions: since 1969 there have been some 400 attempts, half of them successful. Yet 89 ICAO members have not yet accepted the introduc-

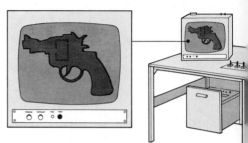

The camera has a zoom control to allow close-up inspection of any suspicious object on the 21-in X-ray monitor. Full pan and tilt control ensure that a suitcase can be minutely examined. Metal shows up densely, other materials as shadows.

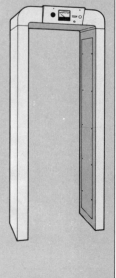

This metal-detection gateway has an electromagnetic field between doorframe-sized metal columns. Ferrous or non-ferrous metal carried through by a passenger disturbs the magnetic field, the disturbance registers on a control panel and an alarm sounds. Sensitivity can be reduced so as not to pick up the metal fastenings on clothes. The machine can be controlled by one person stationed away from the gateway and will not affect heart pacemakers, magnetic recording tape or magnetically-coded credit cards.

tion of world-wide extradition agreements which would eliminate havens.

Because manual searches are undignified, time-consuming and ultimately inefficient, most airports screen passengers through electromagnetic metal-detectors. Hand baggage is visually searched, using low dosage X-ray equipment (which may affect photographic film). At some airports "sniffer" dogs are used to detect explosives or drugs. Searching may take place at the terminal door, or on entry to the departure lounge.

Security depends, eventually, on the observation of well-trained detection-equipment operators, and on experienced security guards.

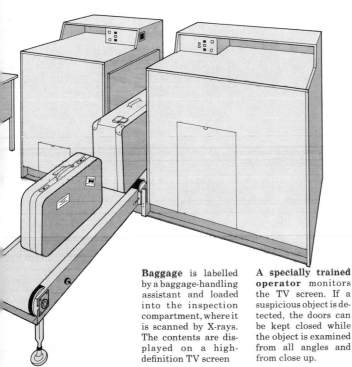

A **combined** check-in desk, electronic weigh unit with digital read-out and X-ray security screening point could replace the airline check-in desk. One monitor can cover several desk points. The system is designed to handle large volumes of passenger baggage rapidly—it takes only eight seconds to clear a passenger's hand-baggage while he is screened by a magnectic metal detector so that frisking and hand-searches are unnecessary.

Baggage is labelled by a baggage-handling assistant and loaded into the inspection compartment, where it is scanned by X-rays. The contents are displayed on a high-definition TV screen

A specially trained operator monitors the TV screen. If a suspicious object is detected, the doors can be kept closed while the object is examined from all angles and from close up.

If the contents are passed, the operator opens the doors to release the baggage. At the press of a button, it is fed, via a small conveyor belt, into the airport's main baggage conveyor system.

A portable explosives detector gives an audible alarm within four seconds of detecting explosive vapour. The probe, inserted into a handbag or suitcase, or passed over hands, clothing or containers, takes a sample of air. This is fed into the briefcase, which contains an electronic sensor unit, a rechargeable nickel-cadmium battery and a bottle containing argon gas, to detect and register the contents. The detector can respond to explosive vapour concentrations of one part per several million parts of air, and can detect traces of explosive on any material hours after contact, but it will ignore vapours from lighter fuel and cleaning fluid.

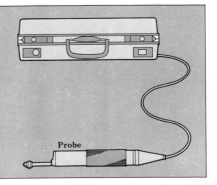

Probe

Economics of air travel

Commercial aviation is big business. The world's airline operators, large and small, cargo and passenger, had a turnover of over £100,000 million ($200,000 million) in 1977. The 110 companies belonging to IATA have a total of 840,000 employees. Many thousands more people work for air charter and taxi companies or at airports, or in building, servicing and supplying the aircraft. Around a quarter of Amsterdam's one million inhabitants depend directly or indirectly on work generated by Schiphol Airport.

Investment

The capital investment is impressive. A short-haul airliner such as the Fokker F28, carrying only 79 passengers, costs over £5 million ($10 million). A 400-seater Boeing 747 can cost about £30 million ($60 million). Modern airliners have service lifetimes of around 15 years, during which they are repeatedly overhauled and rebuilt. When the machine is retired, there may be little of its original fabric left in it. Large airlines sell many old, but perfectly airworthy, airliners to smaller operators; at present, over half of the world's jet airliners are more than ten years old.

Costs

Short-haul routes are considerably more expensive to fly than intercontinental routes. The short-range airliner has to spend nearly as long on the ground during turnaround as the long-distance jet, as long in the stack waiting to land, and often has to pay the same landing charges per ton and per passenger. It is subject to the bans on night-time flying operated by many airports, while intercontinental flying continues day and night. Over the year, aircraft on routes in Europe are used for about 2,500 hours, or about seven hours per day. Intercontinental jets are used 12 hours a day or more. For all these reasons, roughly half of Europe's air traffic goes by charter (which can be cheaper than scheduled services).

A Boeing 747 uses about 3,100 gallons (3,700 US gallons) an hour when cruising. But because it flies so fast and carries so many passengers it is as economical to run as a family car. Modern jet airliners use about 7.7 gallons (9.25 US gallons) per flying hour per seat. After allowing for empty seats and the plane's cruising speed, on short-haul European flights scheduled services fly about 20 passenger-miles per gallon (17 per US gallon). Charter planes, which fly only if they are full, achieve about 31 passenger-miles per gallon (26 per US gallon).

On intercontinental flights, because of the greater average speed, the scheduled services achieve about 36.5 passenger-miles per gallon (30 per US gallon); charter flights achieve 45 per gallon (38 per US gallon).

Profit

The load factor, the percentage of total capacity that is actually sold, is crucial to the profitability of a service. An aircraft with 150 seats that takes off with 90 passengers has a seat load factor of 60 per cent. The overall load factor is the percentage of passengers and cargo combined. Standard weights for passengers and baggage are used in the calculation. At the break-even load factor total cost equals revenue.

The load factor in aviation has been around 55 per cent for the past few years. Few routes can rival the load factors of over 90 per cent on the Concorde's Europe-USA routes.

Aviation load factors compare well with those for mass transport on the ground. Trains and inter-city bus services have load factors under 40 per cent in many countries. Increasingly, airliners are being designed as "convertibles" so that the passenger space can quickly be turned into cargo space, and vice versa.

Expenditure

The airliner incurs large charges every time it lands and takes off. It is charged by its weight, by the number of passengers it is carrying, sometimes by the distance it has flown, and according to the time of day. The charges vary widely according to the size of the airport and are usually revised every six months. But typical charges for an international TriStar flight at peak times at a major airport could include: a £200 (nearly $400) landing charge (with no separate charge for takeoff); a £2.50 ($5) charge for each passenger arriving — which can total £1,000 (about $2,000) or more for a fully loaded 747; and passenger fees, which are paid on departures as well. A runway movement charge can be over £100 (nearly $200), and must be paid both on landing and takeoff. Charges for security checks must be paid for each passenger, and parking charges for excess time spent by the aircraft on the stand. At off-peak times these charges may be halved, and they are also reduced for domestic flights. Light planes carrying a few passengers may pay well under £100 ($200), even at peak times.

In one survey of large US airports it was found that landing charges and services provided to airliners on the airfield represented about a third of the total revenue, another third came from services provided to airlines in the terminal, and the rest came from concessions, such as restaurants.

Revenue

In the end the user pays – whether he sends a letter, a package or a piece of equipment, or travels himself. The pricing of air tickets is a complex matter, decided internationally and agreed to by governments. In general, the air traveller pays more the more flexible his arrangements are. The standard first-class and economy fares offer the passenger the most freedom: he can buy an open-date ticket, or he can make a firm reservation that guarantees him a seat on a certain flight, while retaining the ability to change his travel plans many times; he can change to another airline, make stopovers at intermediate airports, or divert to other destinations within a certain total distance from his starting point. He can even fail to show up at all. Tickets remain valid for one year, and the changes are without charge. All these uncertainties help to push up fares.

In addition, a large variety of reduced fares are available on many routes. By booking a long way ahead and limiting the period during which he can return, a passenger can make substantial savings. Some of the cheapest scheduled fares are only a little more expensive than charter fares. But the cheapest way of flying is still by charter, with or without accommodation and ground travel arrangements included. The passenger is then committed to fixed travel dates. If not enough passengers book, the flight may be cancelled.

Years when airlines lose money often alternate with those when they are profitable. Airline travel and profits slumped temporarily after the oil price rises of 1973, but manufacturers and operators are confident air travel will boom in the 1980s.

Commercial aviation is said to be a marginal industry, always working close to the borderline between profit and loss. Yet in 1976–77 Singapore Airlines earned over £12 million ($24 million) on revenues that grew nearly ninefold in nine years to some £250 million ($490 million).

The flight crew

The captain

A 747 lifts off from runway 09 Right at Miami International en route to Chicago O'Hare. Suddenly there is a power drop on number three engine, the inboard flaps refuse to retract, and as the main gears rise, fire erupts in the nose-gear bay. This will be a long and arduous flight. The cabin pressurization will fail; so will a VHF receiver and the gear hydraulics. Fire will disable number one engine and an oil pressure drop on the troublesome number three will force its shutdown as well. Thus the already hard-pressed crew must make an instrument approach and landing into the world's most congested airport with two of their aircraft's four engines inoperative. They will do a fine job; if not, they will just have to do it all over again.

Pilots sometimes leave the simulators which stage such dramas shaking and soaked in perspiration.

But they may be required to go through the experience twice a year so that their reactions to a set of catastrophes, more than they are likely to meet in their whole flying career, can be measured. A pilot can lose his licence if he fails a simulator test but, in practice, his three years' basic training even before being accepted by an airline ensures that this is rare. Licences are more likely to be lost for medical reasons. A senior pilot undergoes a rigorous medical every six months and a commercial pilot's licence holder, every 12, and twice as often over the age of 40. Half the applicants to training colleges are rejected for eyesight reasons alone.

No pilot can become a captain on any kind of airliner until he has flown as a co-pilot first. Promotion usually depends on seniority. In Britain, there is enough flexibility to take into account a pilot's ability and qualifications as well as experience

but, in the USA, the system is more rigid and a pilot may fly for years before becoming a captain. Only the pilot in command may wear a cap with "scrambled egg" on the peak. A 747 captain is usually fiftyish with 30 years of flying behind him, often partly in the air force. Not many pilots are women – there are just two or three working for major British airlines, for example.

The bigger the aircraft the higher the captain's pay. Captains of wide-bodied jets can earn about £17,500 a year in Britain and around $80,000 in the United States. Such salaries reflect the responsibility of the job and the risk of losing it at the six-monthly checks. But it may not be the money that makes him endure 150 pre-flight checks a year and endure the frustrations of passing through Customs three times a week; it may be a love of flying. And, once the doors are closed on the last passenger, the captain's authority is absolute. Any troublesome person, regardless of rank, can be strapped to the floor with no right of redress until touchdown.

An average crew will work between 900 and 1,200 hours a year, including layovers and rest periods. Many pilots use their considerable free time to run other businesses.

The flight engineer
The third man in the cockpit is the flight engineer. He is answerable to the captain for the performance of all the aircraft's systems, from engines to galley ovens. He goes out to the aircraft ahead of the rest of the flight crew, and checks the exterior: tyres, control surfaces, skin condition and so on, and makes sure that the

necessary maintenance and refuelling has been completed. He alone is qualified to pass the aircraft as fit to fly. A large plane may have 600 circuit breakers in its electronic systems, and these, and any backup systems necessary to the aircraft's safety — the second, third and fourth hydraulic systems — for instance, must be in working order. But a flight crew may choose to fly a short haul with a non-essential system, like the air-conditioning, in less than perfect order. In flight, the engineer's territory is a control panel, on the side wall behind the co-pilot, of up to 500 gauges, lights and switches; about 18 alarm bells, buzzers and sirens supplement the visual systems failure warnings. On some aircraft an electric motor on his seat can power it along a railway to the space between the pilots so he can help them in emergencies. He monitors the aircraft's progress, keeping track of its speeds, altitudes and fuel consumption, and listens out for weather broadcasts. At takeoff he has a particularly vital role, calculating the takeoff speeds and adjusting the engine settings if necessary.

It is even harder to become a flight engineer than a pilot: only four per cent of applicants are accepted for training because fewer airlines are still employing them. Besides, only one engineer is needed for every two pilots, and some airlines make do with another pilot in the third seat. This is unpopular with pilots, who dislike being tied to an instrument panel, and may turn out to be expensive on the long-haul flights, because pilots do not have an engineer's Inspection Approval, the all-important licence enabling him to sign out an aircraft for continued flight after a diversion to an airfield which does not have the normal ground maintenance cover.

This flight crew on a training flight in a Trident 3B include the instructor in the foreground, the captain in the left-hand seat and the co-pilot, who in this aircraft carries out the duties of the flight engineer, on the right.

173

Cabin crews/Ground staff

Cabin crews

The opportunity to travel gives an air stewardess's job an aura of glamour, but it is also plain hard work. On a six to twelve week training course, the women, and an increasing number of men, learn to comfort nervous passengers, assist mothers with (and deliver) babies, and cope with belligerent passengers. They are taught how to cope with heart attacks and diabetic comas, and how to recognize the outward signs of cholera (which would cause a captain to radio ahead to warn the health authorities). They will be taught some first aid, the theory of flight, and be drilled in emergency procedure. They serve meals efficiently, mix cocktails, and check sales of duty-free goods so that the stocks can be renewed. Their uniforms may be designed by distinguished couturiers and the airline will advise, at least, on grooming and sometimes rule on make-up, hair length and the wearing of jewellery and accessories.

Educational qualifications may not be high, but candidates are expected to be alert and articulate. Foreign languages are required by some airlines, notably Lufthansa, and not by others, but they are always an advantage on overseas routes. Air stewardesses do not have to be gourmet cooks; aircraft meals are pre-cooked and merely reheated on board. They are judged for qualities which cannot be tested in examinations: confidence, self-reliance, appearance and the capacity to react coolly in tense situations.

The most important part of cabin crew training is toward a skill that most passengers never see: the ability to evacuate up to 500 passengers from a wide-bodied jet in an emergency landing. Cabin simulators, as realistic as flight-deck simulators, are used to train the crew to empty a plane in

The purser: often the senior cabin officer; supervises cabin crew; deals with unforeseen problems; liaises with flight crew.

The co-pilot: shares flying duties with the captain.
The ground stewardess: meets passengers checking in for the flight.

The captain: chooses the route: makes essential flight decisions; has absolute responsibility for passengers and plane.

The flight engineer: feeds technical information to the pilots.
Air stewardesses: responsible for passenger comfort and safety.

two minutes, knowing that a few wasted seconds may turn a minor incident into a major disaster.

A stewardess on a transatlantic flight can expect to walk up to 13 miles during the crossing. If she works for Pan Am, she will have been chosen for the job out of 10,000 applicants a year. In the last decade her average flying life has increased from 18 months to five or six years, largely because she no longer has to remain single or retire at 30. A few go on to retirement age. The pay is comparable with that of a top secretary, but there are travel allowances and expenses, and a great deal of time off, amounting to the equivalent of every other day.

A senior stewardess or steward will be in charge of the cabin crew and will assign responsibilities (the most critical job is in the galley, where expertise with the ovens is vital to good cabin service). On a big jet a purser will direct the staff and on some airlines there may be a cabin service officer, the most senior rank.

Ground staff
A single passenger out of the tens of thousands who pass through a major airport every day will meet very few of the 30,000 or so people employed to see him safely, comfortably and legally on and off the plane. About five per cent of the people who work at an airport are employed by its management; another five per cent will be civil servants — immigration and Customs officers, health unit officers and air traffic controllers. The rest are largely airline staff.

Passenger service begins with the ticket sales and reservation staff. As front-line personnel, they are trained to do more than just write out tickets and hand out boarding passes. They have to master one of up to 2,000 computer terminals the airline may have around the world, all linked to a central computer which not only processes seating information but handles all the airline planning and control, from aircraft scheduling to payrolls. They will also check passports, visas and vaccination certificates, and are trained to defuse aggressive or agitated latecomers, and remain steadfastly cool-headed in the face of nervous air travellers. As the ground equivalent of cabin crew, they may become stewards or stewardesses responsible for liaising with passengers at airports or city terminals, escorting them to the right places at the right times, manning information desks, looking after luggage and making special arrangements for VIPs or invalids. Every large airport has a stand-by medical service, usually consisting of teams of nurses and doctors. These are backed up by airline medical services, primarily for the crew, but they may check on anyone with a condition likely to be aggravated by flying, such as pregnancy. Airlines usually refuse to carry women past their seventh month of pregnancy.

While outbound passengers are processed on the first floor of the terminal, airside crews on the ground-level aprons turn round newly arrived aircraft, refuelling and checking tyres with the urgency of a pit-stop team, beginning as the inbound passengers are still disembarking. The Customs men are first on, to inspect the plane, closely followed by the cleaners ("groomers") who spruce up the inside for the next flight. Catering staff load and unload meals. Maintenance engineers correct any faults reported from the flight deck and perform routine checks on landing-gears, engines, avionics and systems. These engineers have served apprenticeships in the aircraft industry and are experienced specialists in electrical systems, hydraulics, engines, airframes or other fields.

Painting an aircraft

Inside the cathedral-sized spray-painting hall at Toulouse, painters on movable staging swing their spray guns back and forth over the sides of a huge Airbus or a Concorde. It can take more than two weeks to paint an aircraft; a BAC One-Eleven needs 25 gallons of top coat.

Paint on an aircraft is not just an expensive cosmetic. Applied to a properly prepared aircraft skin it is a protective, guarding against corrosion and fatigue, which can start from a surface scratch.

Aircraft skins are sometimes polished. The thin aluminium coating is corrosion-resistant, but if it is enthusiastically buffed away during the course of polishing, the dull alloy surface beneath can become corroded. The affected surface then has to be reskinned, an expensive remedy. The same problem applies to internal metal parts which, if poorly protected, will also become corroded. Each piece of metal, down to the smallest nut, is given the appropriate priming coat or plating before assembly, and a proper finish afterwards.

Painting aircraft has not changed much over the years except in the chemical composition of the paint and the evolution of airline liveries almost into an art form. Brushes are still used for small jobs but the spray gun is the only practical way of covering an aircraft like the Airbus A300, with a surface area more than the size of six tennis courts.

Until the 1940s the use of paint was restricted largely to sombre camouflage colours; from about 1948 the use of colour brought a gay profusion of airline liveries. Most aircraft had white fuselage tops, largely to reflect sunlight and reduce cabin temperatures, but the high speeds of high-flying jet aircraft made the synthetic paints then in use crack, peel and strip.

Synthetic and epoxy resin paints have been to a great extent superseded by polyurethane products for top coats and liveries on modern jet aircraft. Epoxy compounds for external finishes become dull and chalky and need to be stripped off after about two years; polyurethane finishes, applied over properly prepared surfaces, may last three times as long.

Paint must retain flexibility and not become brittle to withstand temperature variations and flexure in flight. The top coat must ensure adhesion of the whole paint scheme but not pull the undercoat or primer away from the surface. Paint is tested for seven days in salt water, given bond tests at 32 degrees Fahrenheit (0 degrees Celsius) for flexibility, and given scratch tests for hardness and adhesion. Some are required to withstand immersion in a lubricant for 1,000 hours.

Over a ten-year period, an aircraft the size of a McDonnell Douglas DC-9, if painted with epoxy resin throughout and retouched and resprayed from time to time, can gain up to 300 pounds in weight—the equivalent of two passengers. Clearly a single thorough preparation of surfaces, and careful painting to ensure that a single application endures, is an economy.

Cleaning and protecting metal surfaces can be complex. Pre-paint treatments include anodizing (depositing a thin film of metallic oxide), dipping in an acid "pickle" bath, and the application of an etch primer. The priming coat of epoxy is baked or "stoved" on and, where needed, a top coat of polyurethane is added. Suitable painting accommodation is vital for a variety of reasons, the most important being health, safety and cleanliness. Cleaning and chemical pre-treatment take place separately from painting, for which the atmosphere must be clean and at a constant temperature to ensure high quality.

Airline insignia

Aer Lingus Irish Airlines flies an all-jet fleet to Europe and the USA. Each jet is named after an Irish saint.

Aeromexico, the Mexican flag carrier, flies Douglas jets to over 40 local towns, to the Americas and across the Atlantic.

Aeroamerica is an American charter airline operating wide-ranging services from bases in Seattle, Cairo and West Berlin.

AeroPeru, the Peruvian transcontinental airline founded in 1973, is instrumental in promoting the national tourist industry.

Aerocondor is Colombia's second largest international airline, privately owned, with services reaching the USA.

Air Afrique, a multi-national airline founded by 11 former French colonies in 1961, serves 22 African states.

Aeroflot, founded in 1928, is the largest air carrier in the world. The USSR's state airline, it serves all the continents.

Air Algérie links remote Saharan communities with the surrounding African regions, and with East and West Europe.

Aerolineas Argentinas carries the Argentinian flag across the Americas, and over the South Atlantic to Europe.

Air Canada flies its maple leaf insignia on extensive internal trunk services, intercontinental and transatlantic flights.

Airline insignia

Air Ceylon, now Sri Lanka International Airways, has an internal service and links with Asia and Europe.

Air Jamaica, an international airline formed in 1968, links Kingston with the Caribbean islands, the USA and Europe.

Air Djibouti Red Sea Airline provides an important link between East Africa and the Middle East.

Air Madagascar has built up an extensive domestic and regional service since 1962. Intercontinental services fly to Europe.

Air France, first to fly Concorde, and Europe's second largest airline, can trace its history back to 1919.

Air Malawi has a modern jet and turboprop fleet serving Central and southern Africa, the Seychelles and London.

Air India International, founded in 1948 on India's independence, flies to Africa, Europe, the Middle East, Australasia and the USA.

Air Mali connects the land-locked Mali Republic with the surrounding states of Central and North Africa, and Paris.

Air Inter was formed in 1954 to provide a domestic service between the major cities of metropolitan France.

Air Malta, founded in 1973 with the help of Pakistan International Airways, links Malta with Europe and North Africa.

Air Mauritius, founded in 1967, links the islands of the Indian Ocean with major points on three continents.

Air Panama Internacional, the Panamanian flag carrier founded in 1967, links North, South and Central American countries.

Air Nauru has a three-jet fleet serving Pacific islands round Nauru, an eight-mile-square island with a modern airport.

Air Rhodesia, established in 1967, has concentrated on providing domestic flights and services to surrounding countries.

Air New Zealand, with a Maori "koru" emblem, provides inter-island services in Australasia, and international flights.

Air Zaïre, known as Air Congo from 1961 to 1971, serves equatorial and eastern Africa, and Europe. The tail bears a leopard symbol.

Air Niugini, founded in 1973, is the national airline of Papua New Guinea, flying to surrounding islands and Australasia.

Alia — The Royal Jordanian Airline — was named "high-flying" after Hussein's daughter. It serves the East and Europe.

Air Pacific, founded in 1951 by pioneer aviator Harold Gatty, links groups of islands in the South Pacific Ocean.

Alitalia, Italy's flag carrier, has expanded its operations since 1946 to encompass the whole of Italy and all continents.

Airline insignia

Allegheny Airlines' scheduled services cover more than 100 north-eastern American cities and extend into Canada.

Ariana Afghan Airlines, the international Afghan airline since 1955, serves East and Central Asia and also Europe.

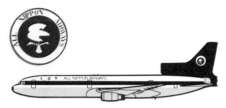

All Nippon Airways, Japan's largest airline, flying domestic and regional routes, has a da Vinci helicopter insignia.

Austrian Airlines has grown rapidly since it was formed in 1957; its services cover East and West Europe and the Middle East.

ALM Antillean Airlines operates an essential service between the Caribbean mainland and South America.

AVIACO (Aviación y Comercio), founded in 1948 as an air cargo company, is now Spain's largest domestic airline.

American Airlines, one of the world's largest carriers, began in 1926. Its vast route system crosses the Pacific.

AVIANCA (Aerovías Nacionales de Colombia) can be traced back to the formation in 1919 of the first airline in the Americas.

Ansett Airlines of Australia, founded by a pioneer aviator in 1936, uses jets and helicopters to serve Australia's states.

Aviogenex is a Yugoslavian charter company offering passenger and charter flights to Europe and the Middle East.

BALKAN
BULGARIAN AIRLINES

Balkan Bulgarian Airlines has an all-Russian fleet flying internal routes, and to East and West Europe and North Africa.

ᗅᗅᗅ Bangladesh Biman

Bangladesh Biman, the national airline of former East Pakistan, flies throughout the Orient, and to London.

BI BRANIFF INTERNATIONAL

Braniff International Airways, set up in 1928 to serve the central USA, now sends its "Flying Colors" to Central and South America.

British airways

British Airways carries more passengers on international scheduled services, and has a larger route network, than any other airline.

British Caledonian Airways

British Caledonian Airways, Britain's second flag carrier since 1970, serves West Europe, Africa and South America.

BMA BRITISH MIDLAND AIRWAYS LTD

British Midland Airways, formed in 1939, is one of the largest domestic airlines in the UK, and serves cities in Europe.

BWIA
International

BWIA (British West Indian Airways), owned by the Trinidad Government since 1967, serves the Caribbean and the Americas.

中國民航

CAAC (Civil Aviation Administration of China), dating from 1929, has a vast domestic, regional and international route map.

CAMEROON AIRLINES

Cameroon Airlines, founded in 1971, has quickly established regional and international services in equatorial Africa.

CAPITOL
INTERNATIONAL AIRWAYS

Capitol International Airways, with a fleet of Douglas DC-8s, is the major US transatlantic charter operator.

Airline insignia

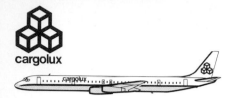

Cargolux Airlines International, established in Luxembourg in 1970, provides world-wide cargo charter operations.

CP Air, a Canadian Pacific rail outgrowth, flies intercontinental routes, and services across the Pacific and Atlantic oceans.

Cathay Pacific Airways is the largest regional carrier in the Far East. It provides passenger and cargo services.

Cruzeiro, Brazil's first airline founded in 1927, has a network covering remote internal states and the surrounding regions.

China Airlines, flying the flag of the Republic of China, operates transasian and transpacific routes from Taipei.

CSA (Ceskoslovenské Aerolinie), the state airline of Czechoslovakia, flies to Europe, the Orient and the USA.

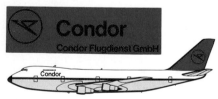

Condor Flugdienst, founded by Lufthansa in 1961, provides world-wide holiday charter and international air taxi services.

CUBANA (Empresa Consolidada Cubana de Aviación) was once owned by Pan Am, and now flies a largely Russian fleet world-wide.

Continental Airlines, based in California, has grown since 1934 into one of the USA's major trunk airlines.

Cyprus Airways has survived the politically turbulent years since 1974. It flies to Greece, the Middle East and Europe.

Dan-Air Services is a major British airline offering domestic services and inclusive tours to Europe and the USA.

El Al Israel Airlines is the national flag-carrier, formed in 1948. It links Tel Aviv with international capitals.

Delta Air Lines began the world's first crop-dusting service in 1924 and now has one of the largest US route systems.

Ethiopian Airlines links remote regions of Ethiopia with the capital, and with Africa, Europe and Peking.

Eastern Airlines, one of the "Big Four" US trunk airlines, began the New York to Atlanta mail service in 1928.

Federal Express, the USA's fifth largest freight carrier, is famous for non-scheduled "small package" services.

Ecuatoriana, Ecuador's national carrier, flies its brightly coloured Boeings on wide-reaching regional services.

Finnair, one of Europe's oldest airlines, was founded in 1924. It runs extensive domestic and international flights.

Egypt Air, known as United Arab Airlines from 1960 to 1971, flies throughout the East, and to Africa, the USA and Europe.

The Flying Tiger Line, the world's largest all-cargo air carrier, was the first all-cargo airline in the USA.

Airline insignia

Frontier Airlines is one of the largest regional airlines in the USA, serving more than 100 cities in 18 states.

Guyana Airways, the national airline of this small South American state, has Douglas DC-3s and DC-6s in its fleet.

Garuda Indonesian Airways has expanded existing inter-island services into a regional network.

Hawaiian Airlines, its fleet bearing Hawaii's classic red hibiscus, has flown inter-island services since 1929.

Ghana Airways began in 1958 with a service to London and has since developed a thriving domestic and regional network.

Hughes Airwest "Sundance Flagships" serve the western USA, Canada and Mexico. In 1970 the company was bought by Howard Hughes.

Greenlandair provides a wide variety of aircraft and helicopter services to remote points on this Arctic island.

Icelandair provides valuable social services to remote communities, and links major cities in the northern hemisphere.

Gulf Air, owned by the governments of Bahrain, Qatar, Oman and the UAE, provides a vital link between the Arabian Gulf states.

Indian Airlines' vast network of services covers the entire sub-continent of India, and its surrounding regions.

Interflug is the German Democratic Republic's national airline, with a fleet of Russian and Czechoslovakian aircraft.

Iran Air numbers pilgrimages to Mecca among its regular domestic and wide-spreading international services.

Iraqi Airways operates a mixed fleet of Russian, American and European aircraft on services west and east.

JAL (Japan Air Lines) flies over the North Pole and the ancient Silk Road on its international network of routes.

JAT (Jugoslovenske Aerotransport), the Yugoslav state airline, serves over 30 international centres with scheduled and air taxi services.

KAC (Kuwait Airways Corporation) provides scheduled services to the Middle and Far East, Africa and Europe.

KAL (Korean Air Lines) covers all major towns in South Korea, and flies to Japan, Taiwan, Hong Kong and Los Angeles.

Kenya Airways, formed in 1977, links Nairobi with seven European cities, and is gradually building up an African and Asian network.

KLM (Royal Dutch Airlines) is the oldest operating airline in the world. Formed in 1919, it serves all the continents.

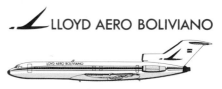

LAB (Lloyd Aéreo Boliviano), one of the world's oldest airlines, founded in 1925, flies throughout South and Central America.

185

Airline insignia

Laker Airways, a British scheduled non-IATA airline, is best-known for its London to New York walk-on Skytrain service.

LOT (Polskie Linie Lotnicze), the Polish state airline founded in 1929, links East and West Europe, the Middle East and the USA.

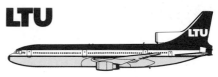

LAN-Chile began as an air mail company in 1929 with Gypsy Moths. It now flies South American and international routes.

LTU (Lufttransport Unternehmen), once a scheduled West German regional airline, is now a general charter company.

Libyan Arab Airlines, a government corporation, links the Middle Eastern capitals with Malta, London, Paris and Rome.

Lufthansa German Airlines has evolved from the world's first passenger service to one of Europe's largest airlines.

Linjeflyg, the Swedish domestic airline, operates aerial ambulance and other services to the northern regions.

Luxair, Luxembourg's national flag carrier, links the Grand Duchy with Europe's major cities and Mediterranean vacation centres.

Loftleider Icelandic Airlines, a non-scheduled operator, offers low-cost flights in the northern hemisphere.

Malév (Magyar Légikozlekedési Vallalat), the Hungarian state airline, has an all-Russian fleet serving 24 countries.

Martinair Holland

National Airlines

Martinair Holland has extended its aerial advertizing and joy-riding services into world-wide charters.

National Airlines, founded as an air mail company in 1934, has a "sunshine" livery known in 15 US states and Europe.

mas
malaysian airline system

new york airways

MAS (Malaysian Airline System) flies to Frankfurt and London, and operates a large domestic and Australasian service.

New York Airways founded in 1949 the first ever scheduled helicopter services in the New York area of the USA.

mexicana
La Primera Linea Aérea de México

NIGERIA AIRWAYS

Mexicana (Compañía Mexicana de Aviación) began with biplanes in 1924, and now serves North and South America.

Nigeria Airways has an elephant insignia advertizing its international services to Africa, the Middle East and Europe.

MIDDLE EAST AIRLINES

NORTH CENTRAL

Middle East Airlines Airliban connects the Lebanon with the Middle Eastern, Eastern and Western European capitals.

North Central Airlines, bearing a mallard duck insignia, links 14 US states and two Canadian provinces.

NEW ZEALAND NATIONAL AIRWAYS CORPORATION

NAC

NORTHWEST ORIENT

NAC (New Zealand National Airways), now part of Air New Zealand, flies between and within the New Zealand islands.

Northwest Orient Airlines, a US air mail company in 1926, links major US cities with the Orient, and is still expanding.

Airline insignia

Olympic Airways, formed in 1957, links the principal Greek cities with five continents. Olympic rings adorn the tail.

Overseas National Airways, a US trail-blazer for the transatlantic charter, now serves four continents.

Ozark Air Lines, named after a central US highland area, has a dense route map covering two-thirds of the USA.

Pakistan International Airlines, Pakistan's only air carrier, serves the Middle and Far East, Europe and the USA.

PAN AM (Pan American World Airways) has a huge 90,000-mile network connecting most of the world's major cities.

Philippine Airlines provides essential inter-island links and intercontinental services between Australasia, the USA and Europe.

Piedmont Airlines' "Pacemakers" provide scheduled services between more than 80 communities in the eastern USA.

PSA (Pacific Southwest Airlines), with a reputation for fast turnaround, offers high-frequency, low-cost services within California.

Qantas Airways, registered in 1920, has a flying kangaroo symbol. Its passenger and cargo routes extend to all the continents.

Royal Air Maroc has extended its internal regional and European routes to North and South America since 1957.

188

Royal Brunei Airlines, founded as the Brunei state airline in 1974, has built up a network of routes in South East Asia.

SAS (Scandinavian Airlines System), founded in 1918, pioneered the first Polar routes to the USA and the Far East.

Royal Iberia, the Spanish flag-carrier linking European, African and US tourist centres, evolved from a 1920s air mail company.

SAUDIA (Saudi Arabian Airlines Corporation) was formed in 1946 and now serves the Near, Middle and Far East, and Europe.

SABENA Belgian World Airlines is one of Europe's oldest carriers, founded in 1923. It serves four continents.

Seaboard World Airlines, one of the foremost transatlantic cargo carriers, took part in the Berlin airlift in 1949.

Safair Freighters, formed in 1969, provides cargo charter and daily freight services throughout southern Africa.

Singapore Airlines, the national flag carrier since 1972, and "Airline of the Year" in 1977, links Asia, Australasia and Europe.

SAHSA (Servicio Aéreo de Honduras), the national airline of Honduras since 1945, has an important South American network.

Somali Airlines, owned by the Somali Republic and Alitalia, has an extensive domestic and Middle Eastern network.

Airline insignia

South African Airways, founded in 1934, has a springbok insignia. The airline links southern Africa with Europe and the USA.

Sudan Airways, the Sudanese flag carrier since 1946, links main East African cities with the Middle East and Europe.

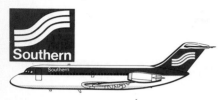

Surinam Airways, the national carrier since 1975, links this South American state with the surrounding region and Amsterdam.

Southern Airways of Atlanta, Georgia, operates jet services in 13 American states, and to Canada and the Caribbean.

Swissair, a pioneering airline founded in 1931, has expanded since 1945 to serve Europe, the Americas, Africa and the East.

Southwest Airlines, based at Love Field, Dallas, has grown since 1967 to be the USA's largest most successful intra-state airline.

Syrianair (Syrian Arab Airlines), government-owned since 1961, links Damascus with Europe, North Africa and the Middle East.

Spantax is a large Spanish charter airline formed in 1959 to serve oil companies prospecting in the Spanish Sahara.

Sterling Airways is an important Danish charter operator providing tour flights to Europe, North Africa and the USA.

TAAG (Transportes Aéreos de Angola) has built up an essential domestic and regional network of routes.

THE AIRLINE OF PORTUGAL

TAP (Transportes Aéros Portugueses), the Portuguese national airline, flies to Africa, Europe and the Americas.

TAROM (Transporturile Aeriene Romane), the Romanian state airline, serves Europe, the Middle East, Peking, the USA and Moscow.

Thai International, Thailand's flag carrier, operates an all-jet fleet to Europe and major oriental cities.

TURKISH AIRLINES

THY (Turk Hava Yollari), the state airline, links Turkey's principal cities with Europe and the Middle East.

TRANS-AUSTRALIA AIRLINES

Trans-Australia Airlines, with the largest network in the southern hemisphere, serves over 150 points across the country.

Trans International Airlines

Trans International Airlines operates world-wide passenger, cargo charter and military services from California.

TRANS MEDITERRANEAN AIRWAYS

Trans Mediterranean Airways, one of the world's major all-cargo carriers, began the first world-wide cargo service in 1971.

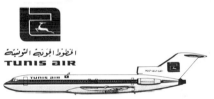

الخطوط الجوية التونسية
TUNIS AIR

Tunis Air's local network of routes has expanded since 1948 to embrace the North African and Gulf states, and Europe.

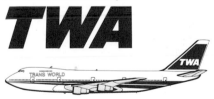

TWA (Trans World Airlines) originated in the 1920s and is the USA's second flag carrier, and the world's seventh largest passenger carrier.

UGANDA AIRLINES

Uganda Airlines carries out charter work throughout the African continent and runs tours to Uganda's game parks.

191

Airline insignia

United Airlines, with over 350 jets, is the world's biggest private airline in terms of total number of passengers carried.

Wardair Canada, founded in 1946 to serve Canada's Arctic regions, now competes in the transatlantic charter market.

UTA (Union de Transports Aériens) is a French airline flying Douglases on African, Far Eastern and transpacific routes.

Western Airlines began as a US air mail company in 1926 and claims to be the USA's oldest continuously operated airline.

Varig Brazilian Airlines, South America's largest airline, flies all around the world serving every continent.

World Airways of Oakland, California, is one of the world's leading non-scheduled airlines flying passenger and cargo charters.

VASP (Viação Aérea São Paulo), founded in 1933, operates a vast network of services throughout the interior of Brazil.

Yemen Airways, the national airline formed in the 1950s, provides scheduled services around the Red Sea region.

VIASA (Venezolana Internacional de Aviación) is Venezuela's international airline serving Europe and the Americas.

Zambia Airways Corporation, founded with Zambia in 1964, serves Central Africa, the Mediterranean and northern Europe.

Airports of the world: gazetteer

How many airports are there in the world? If you count just the airports served by international flights, the number is only about 800, but if you count all those with scheduled domestic and international flights, there are well over 4,000. And if you include airports used by business and private aircraft, there are around 4,000 in the USA alone. The USA, which accounts for more than a third of the world's airline activity, and about 90 per cent of its business and private flying, can muster the impressive total of 12,500 landing places. These range from big, international airports to privately owned grass strips, from heliports to seaplane bases.

In the following 40 pages, just over 500 of the world's major airports are listed, in alphabetical order, country by country (state by state in the USA). Within each country or state the airports with a substantial international traffic, or an annual throughput of not less than 100,000 passengers, are listed under the cities they serve.

Each entry gives the approximate travelling distance to the airport from the nearest town or city; the airport's IATA code (so that passengers may check that their baggage is correctly coded at the point of depar-

ture, and so reduce the possibility that it may be lost) and the telephone number.

Because it may be useful to all fliers to know something of the facilities available at the airports he passes through, and because facilities differ radically from airport to airport, each entry is accompanied by a set of symbols, each representing a different service — from airport buses (or limousine services in the USA) to newspaper sales, from banks to nurseries.

The entries have been compiled from information sent in by the various national airport authorities. Where an entry is marked by an asterisk, the relevant authority did not respond fully to our enquiries, and the information has been drawn from other authoritative sources. Airport facilities are constantly being extended, but airlines and travel agents are kept up to date.

The world is divided into 24 time zones, within each of which all clocks should be set to the same time. In general each zone is one hour ahead of the next zone to the west (except at the International Date Line in the Pacific, where a westbound traveller will go forward by 24 hours). The zones are based on 15-degree divisions of longitude, but have been modified for political convenience. Certain countries introduce daylight saving time; during the summer they put clocks one or two hours ahead of the appropriate setting for their time zone.

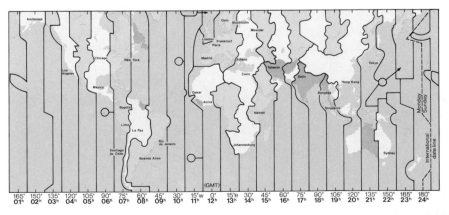

Airports of the world

 Airport bus service

 Train service

 Helicopter service

 Taxi service

 Car rental

 Long term parking

 Hotel reservations

 Airport Hotel

 Bank (landside)

Bank (airside)

 **Post office**

Telephones

Showers

Baths

Paging service

! **Message board**

194

Afghanistan

KABUL: 10 miles (20 min) to Kabul Airport (KBL) Tel: 26341

Albania

*TIRANA: 18 miles to Rinas Airport (TIA)

Algeria

*ALGIERS: 12 miles (30 min) to Dar-el-Beida Airport (ALG) Tel: 76 10 18

Angola

*LUANDA: 2.5 miles to Belas Airport (LAD) Tel: 24141

Argentina

*BUENOS AIRES: 2 miles (20 min) to Aeroparque Airport (AEP) Tel: 773 2066

*BUENOS AIRES: 31 miles (60 min) to Ezeiza Airport (EZE) Tel: 620 0228

Australia

*ADELAIDE: 5 miles (10 min) to

Adelaide Airport (ADL) Tel: 084 32211

BRISBANE: 4 miles (15 min) to Brisbane Airport (BNE) Tel: 268 9511

*MELBOURNE: 13.5 miles (20 min) to Melbourne International Airport (MEL) Tel: 338 2211

*PERTH: 12 miles (20 min) to Perth International Airport (PER) Tel: 277 2466

*SYDNEY: 9 miles (20 min) to Kingsford Smith International Airport (SYD) Tel: 667 0544

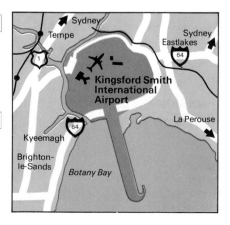

TASMANIA/HOBART: 13.5 miles
(25 min) to Hobart Airport (HBA)
Tel: 48 50 01

Austria

*VIENNA: 11 miles (20 min) to
Schwechat Airport (VIE)
Tel: 77 700

Bahamas, The

FREEPORT: 3 miles (5 min) to
Freeport International Airport
(FPO) Tel: 6020

NASSAU: 8.5 miles (20 min) to
Nassau International Airport (NAS)
Tel: 77281

Bahrain

*BAHRAIN: 4 miles to Muharraq
Airport (BAH) Tel: 21540

Bangladesh

DACCA: 5 miles (15 min) to Tezgaon
Airport (DAC) Tel: 310151

Barbados

BRIDGETOWN: 11 miles (20 min)
to Grantley Adams International
Airport (BGI)

Belgium

BRUSSELS: 10 miles (25 min) to
Brussels National Airport
(BRU) Tel: 511 18 60

Bermuda

*HAMILTON: 12 miles to Kindley
Field (U.S. Naval Air Station) (BDA)
Tel: 3 8111

Bolivia

LA PAZ: 5 miles (30 min) to Kennedy
International Airport (LPB)
Tel: 59310

Brazil

BRASILIA: 8 miles (20 min) to
Brasilia International Airport (BSB)
Tel: 242 6889

Baggage
trolleys

Porters

Baggage
storage

Conference
facilities

Buffet

Bar

Restaurant

Nursery

Medical/
first aid

Vaccina-
tions

Mothers'
room

Rest rooms

Facilities
for disabled

Duty-free
shops

Newsstand

Pharmacy

Airports of the world

Airport
bus service

Train
service

Helicopter
service

Taxi
service

Car
rental

Long term
parking

Hotel
reserva-
tions

Airport
Hotel

Bank
(landside)

Bank
(airside)

Post
office

Telephones

Showers

Baths

Paging
service

Message
board

RIO DE JANEIRO: 12.5 miles
(30 min) to Rio de Janeiro International Airport (RIO) Tel: 398 4132

SAO PAULO: 6 miles (15 min) to
Congonhas Airport (SAO)
Tel: 61 6666

Bulgaria

*SOFIA: 6 miles (15 min) to
Vrajdebna Airport (SOF)
Tel: 45 11 21

Burma

*RANGOON: 12 miles to Mingaladon
Airport (RGN) Tel: 40111

Rio International, opened in 1977, is South America's newest airport, an enlargement of the 30-year old Galeão International Airport (now occupying the new site's south-east corner and detailed for cargo flights). The 160-foot high control tower overlooks the crescent-shaped terminal with its curling access ramps, and the 1,600-vehicle car park.

Cameroon

*DOUALA: 3 miles to Douala Airport
(DLA) Tel: 42 46 93

Canada

MONTREAL: 12 miles (20 min) to
Dorval International Airport (YUL)
Tel: 636 3221

MONTREAL: 33 miles (40 min) to
Mirabel Airport (YMX)
Tel: 514 476 3010

QUEBEC: 12 miles (20 min) to Ste
Foy Airport (YQB)
Tel: 418 872 2304

*TORONTO: 18 miles (30 min) to
Toronto International Airport
(YYZ) Tel: 969 5551

*VANCOUVER: 9 miles (15 min) to
Vancouver International Airport
(YVR) Tel 666 7321

WINNIPEG: 5 miles (15 min) to
Winnipeg International Airport
(YWG) Tel: 786 4105

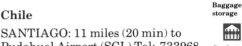

Canary Islands see Spain

Chile

SANTIAGO: 11 miles (20 min) to
Pudahuel Airport (SCL) Tel: 733968

China, People's Republic of

*PEKING: 16 miles to Peking Airport
(PEK) Tel: 555531

Colombia

BOGOTA: 7.5 miles (20 min) to El
Dorado Airport (BOG) Tel: 66 92 100

Cuba

*HAVANA: 11 miles to Jose Marti
Airport (HAV)

Cyprus

*LARNACA: Larnaca Airport (LCA)

Czechoslovakia

*PRAGUE: 11 miles (30 min) to
Ruzyne Airport
(PRG) Tel: 334

Baggage trolleys

Porters

Baggage storage

Conference facilities

Buffet

Bar

Restaurant

Nursery

Medical/first aid

Vaccinations

Mothers' room

Rest rooms

Facilities for disabled

Duty-free shops

Newsstand

Pharmacy

Airports of the world

Airport bus service

Train service

Helicopter service

Taxi service

Car rental

Long term parking

Hotel reservations

Airport Hotel

Bank (landside)

Bank (airside)

Post office

Telephones

Showers

Baths

Paging service

Message board

Denmark

COPENHAGEN: 6 miles (15 min) to Kastrup Airport (CPH)
Tel: 45 01 509333

Dominican Republic

SANTO DOMINGO: 18.5 miles (35 min) to Las Americas Airport (SDQ)
Tel: 687 0421

Ecuador

*QUITO: 5 miles to Mariscal Sucre Airport (UIO) Tel: 241977

Egypt

*CAIRO: 14 miles (30 min) to Cairo Airport (CAI) Tel: 968866

El Salvador

*SAN SALVADOR: 5 miles to Ilopango Airport (SAL) Tel: 27 0025

Ethiopia

*ADDIS ABABA: 5 miles to Bole Airport (ADD) Tel: 447330

Fiji

NANDI: 6 miles (10 min) to Nandi International Airport (NAN)
Tel: 72500

Finland

HELSINKI: 10.5 miles (20 min) to Vantaa Airport (HEL) Tel: 82921

France

BORDEAUX: 9.5 miles (20 min) to Merignac Airport (BOD) Tel: 47 14 47

LYON: 17 miles (30 min) to Satolas Airport (LYS) Tel: 71 92 21

MARSEILLE: 15 miles (30 min) to
Merignane Airport (MRS)
Tel: 89 90 10

MULHOUSE (see also under Basel,
Switzerland) 15.5 miles (25 min) to
Basel/Mulhouse Airport (MLH)
Tel: 44 32 40

NICE: 4 miles (12 min) to Côte d'Azur
Airport (NCE) Tel: 83 19 40

PARIS: 14.5 miles (30 min) to
Charles de Gaulle Airport (CDG)
Tel: 862 12 12

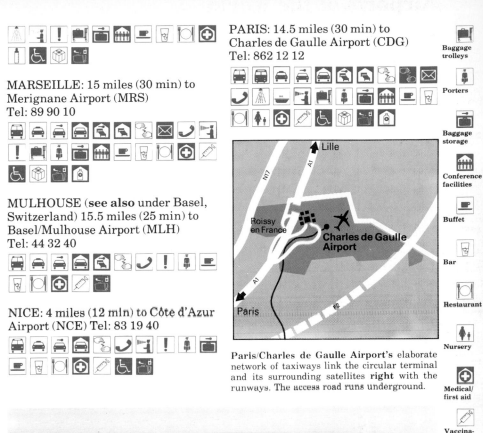

Paris/Charles de Gaulle Airport's elaborate
network of taxiways link the circular terminal
and its surrounding satellites right with the
runways. The access road runs underground.

Baggage trolleys

Porters

Baggage storage

Conference facilities

Buffet

Bar

Restaurant

Nursery

Medical/ first aid

Vaccinations

Mothers' room

Rest rooms

Facilities for disabled

Duty-free shops

Newsstand

Pharmacy

199

Airports of the world

Airport bus service

Train service

Helicopter service

Taxi service

Car rental

Long term parking

Hotel reservations

Airport Hotel

Bank (landside)

Bank (airside)

Post office

Telephones

Showers

Baths

Paging service

Message board

PARIS: 12 miles (40 min) to Orly Airport (ORY) Tel: 587 51 41

TOULOUSE: 6 miles (20 min) to Blagnac Airport (TLS) Tel: 49 30 21

Gabon

*LIBREVILLE: 4 miles to Libreville Airport (LBV) Tel: 71 02 28

German Democratic Republic

*BERLIN, EAST: 12 miles to Schonefeld Airport (SXF) Tel: 67 20

At Paris/Orly Airport, the flat roof of the Orly-Sud terminal provides a magnificent observation deck for visitors. Only five years after completion, this terminal was extended by an additional diamond-shaped satellite at either end, to accommodate a total of nine million passengers yearly.

*DRESDEN: 6.5 miles to Klotzsche Airport (DRS) Tel: 58 941

LEIPZIG: 7.5 miles (20 min) to Leipzig Airport (LEJ) Tel: 2765

Germany, Federal Republic of

BERLIN, WEST: 5 miles (15 min) to Tegel Airport (TXL) Tel: 41011

*COLOGNE: 17.5 miles (40 min) to Cologne-Bonn (Wahn) Airport (CGN) Tel: 40 24 04

DUSSELDORF: 5 miles (12 min) to Lohausen Airport (DUS) Tel: 4211

FRANKFURT: 7.5 miles (20 min) to Frankfurt Airport (FRA) Tel: 0611 690

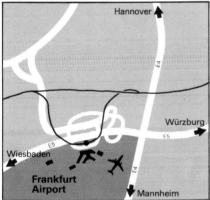

*HAMBURG: 7.5 miles (30 min) to Fuhlsbuttel Airport (HAM) Tel: 5081

HANNOVER: 7 miles (20 min) to Langenhagen Airport (HAJ) Tel: 73051

MUNICH: 6 miles (10 min) to Riem Airport (MUC) Tel: 92111

NUREMBERG: 4 miles (15 min) to Nuremberg Airport (NUE) Tel: 375440

STUTTGART: 9 miles (20 min) to Echterdingen Airport (STR) Tel: 79011

Ghana

ACCRA: 6 miles (15 min) to Kotoka Airport (ACC) Tel: 76171

Gibraltar

GIBRALTAR: 0.5 miles (5 min) to Gibraltar Airport (GIB) Tel: 5984

Greece

*ATHENS: 6 miles (30 min) to Athens Airport (ATH) Tel: 9811 211

Baggage trolleys

Porters

Baggage storage

Conference facilities

Buffet

Bar

Restaurant

Nursery

Medical/ first aid

Vaccinations

Mothers' room

Rest rooms

Facilities for disabled

Duty-free shops

Newsstand

Pharmacy

Airports of the world

 Airport bus service

 Train service

 Helicopter service

 Taxi service

 Car rental

 Long term parking

 Hotel reservations

 Airport Hotel

 Bank (landside)

 Bank (airside)

 Post office

 Telephones

 Showers

 Baths

 Paging service

Message board

CORFU/KERKYRA: 2 miles (10 min) to Kerkyra Airport (CFU) Tel: 34144

HERAKLION: 3 miles (10 min) to Heraklion Airport (HER) Tel: 081 221 401

RHODES/RHODES: 10 miles (15 min) to Maritsa Airport (RHO) Tel: 24302

THESSALONIKI: 8 miles (20 min) to Micra Airport (SKG)

Guatemala

*GUATEMALA CITY: 4 miles to La Aurora Airport (GUA) Tel: 60311

Haiti

*PORT AU PRINCE: 8 miles to Duvalier International Airport (PAP)

Hong Kong

HONG KONG: 4 miles (15 min) to Hong Kong International Airport (HKG) Tel: 3 820211

The landing lights of Hong Kong Airport's main runway stretch out along a causeway built into the harbour. Pilots have to make difficult curved approaches to avoid the hills.

Hungary

BUDAPEST: 10 miles (30 min) to Ferihegy Airport (BUD) Tel: 140 400

Iceland

REYKJAVIK: 28 miles (40 min) to Keflavik International Airport (KEF) Tel: 92 1442

India

BOMBAY: 18 miles (30 min) to Santa Cruz Airport (BOM) Tel: 535461

*CALCUTTA: 12 miles (40 min) to Dum Dum Airport (CCU)

*DELHI: 9 miles (15 min) to Delhi Airport (DEL) Tel:391058

MADRAS: 10 miles (20 min) to Meenambakkan Airport (MAA)

Indonesia

*JAKARTA: 7 miles to Halim International Airport (HLP) Tel: 84071

Iran

ABADAN: 7.5 miles (20 min) to Abadan Airport (ABD) Tel: 32145

TEHRAN: 12 miles (30 min) to Mehrabad Airport (THR) Tel: 641171

Iraq

BAGHDAD: 10.5 miles (20 min) to Baghdad International Airport (BGW) Tel: 551 8888

Irish Republic

DUBLIN: 5 miles (20 min) to Dublin Airport (DUB) Tel: 379900

LIMERICK: 16 miles (20 min) to Shannon Airport (SNM) Tel: 61444

Baggage trolleys

Porters

Baggage storage

Conference facilities

Buffet

Bar

Restaurant

Nursery

Medical/ first aid

Vaccinations

Mothers' room

Rest rooms

Facilities for disabled

Duty-free shops

Newsstand

Pharmacy

Airports of the world

Airport bus service

Train service

Helicopter service

Taxi service

Car rental

Long term parking

Hotel reservations

Airport Hotel

Bank (landside)

Bank (airside)

Post office

Telephones

Showers

Baths

Paging service

Message board

Israel

TEL AVIV: 12 miles (30 min) to Ben Gurion International Airport (TLV) Tel: 299333

Italy

MILAN: 6 miles (25 min) to Linate Airport (LIN) Tel: 710135

MILAN: 29 miles (60 min) to Malpensa Airport (MXP) Tel: 02 868029

ROME: 7.5 miles (30 min) to Ciampino Airport (CIA) Tel: 600021

ROME: 20 miles (40 min) to Leonardo da Vinci (Fiumicino Airport) (FCO) Tel: 601982

*SICILY/CATANIA: 4.5 miles (20 min) to Fontanarossa Airport (CTA) Tel: 340290

TURIN: 10 miles (25 min) to Casselle Airport (TRN) Tel: 57781

*VENICE: 8 miles (30 min) to Tessera Airport (VCE) Tel: 957333

Ivory Coast

*ABIDJAN: 10 miles to Port-Bouet Airport (ABJ) Tel: 368171

Jamaica

KINGSTON: 12 miles (20 min) to Norman Manley Airport (KIN) Tel: 938 7819

MONTEGO BAY: 3 miles (10 min) to

204

Sangster International Airport (MBJ)
Tel: 952 3124

Japan

KAGOSHIMA: 21 miles (50 min) to
Kagoshima Airport (KOJ)
Tel: 09995 8 2111

OSAKA: 12 miles (30 min) to Osaka
International Airport (OSA)
Tel: 06203 1212

TOKYO: 40 miles (90 min) to Narita
Airport (NRT)
Tel: 0476 32 3125

TOKYO: 12 miles (45 min) to Tokyo
International Airport (TYO)
Tel: 03747 3131

Jordan

AMMAN: 5 miles (20 min) to Amman
Airport (AMM) Tel: 51401

Kenya

NAIROBI: 10 miles (25 min) to
Nairobi International Airport (NBO)
Tel: 822111

Korea, Republic of

*SEOUL: 16 miles to Kimpo
International Airport (SEL)

Kuwait

KUWAIT: 10 miles to Kuwait Airport
(KWI) Tel: 710788

Laos

*VIENTIANE: 2.5 miles (20 min) to
Vientiane Airport (VTE)

Lebanon

*BEIRUT: 10 miles to Beirut
International Airport (BEY)

Liberia

*MONROVIA: 38 miles to Roberts
International Airport (ROB)
Tel: 7225

Libya

*BENGHAZI: 18 miles to Benina
International Airport (BEN)
Tel: 3102

*TRIPOLI: 21 miles (45 min) to
Tripoli International Airport (TIP)
Tel: 34 840

Baggage trolleys

Porters

Baggage storage

Conference facilities

Buffet

Bar

Restaurant

Nursery

Medical/first aid

Vaccinations

Mothers' room

Rest rooms

Facilities for disabled

Duty-free shops

Newsstand

Pharmacy

Airports of the world

Legend (left margin)

Airport bus service

Train service

Helicopter service

Taxi service

Car rental

Long term parking

Hotel reservations

Airport Hotel

Bank (landside)

Bank (airside)

Post office

Telephones

Showers

Baths

Paging service

Message board

Luxembourg

*LUXEMBOURG: 3 miles (15 min) to Luxembourg Airport (LUX) Tel: 47911

Madagascar

*TANANARIVE: 11 miles to Ivato Airport (TNR) Tel: 44098

Malawi

BLANTYRE: 11 miles (20 min) to Chileka Airport (BLZ) Tel: 231

Malaysia

*KUALA LUMPUR: 14 miles (30 min) to Kuala Lumpur International Airport (KUL) Tel: 03 760714

*PENANG: 11 miles to Bayan Lepas Airport (PEN) Tel: Bayan Lepas 04 831411

Malta

*VALLETTA: 3 miles (25 min) to Luqa Airport (MLA) Tel: 622910

Mariana Islands

GUAM: 2 miles (3 min) to Agana Field International Air Terminal (GUM) Tel 646 4148

Mauritius

*PORT LOUIS: 18 miles to Plaisance Airport (MRU) Tel: 73531

Mexico

ACAPULCO: 12 miles to Acapulco Airport (ACA) Tel: 4 03 04

GUADALAJARA: 11 miles (25 min) to Miguel Hidalgo Airport (GDL) Tel: 18 27 13

MEXICO CITY: 3 miles (10 min) to Mexico City International Airport (MEX) Tel: 5713478

MONTERREY: 13.5 miles (30 min) to Monterrey Airport (MTY) Tel: 54 34 34

Morocco

*CASABLANCA: 19 miles (60 min) to Nouasseur Airport (CMN) Tel: 339100

*TANGIER: 9 miles (20 min) to
Boukhalef Airport (TNG) Tel: 35720

Mozambique

*MAPUTO: 5 miles to Mavalane
Airport (LUM)

Nepal

*KATHMANDU: 4 miles to
Tribhuyan Airport (KTM)

Netherlands, The

AMSTERDAM: 9.5 miles (25 min) to
Schiphol Airport (AMS) Tel: 511 0432

ROTTERDAM: 6 miles (5 min) to
Rotterdam Airport (RTM)
Tel: 3110 115 860

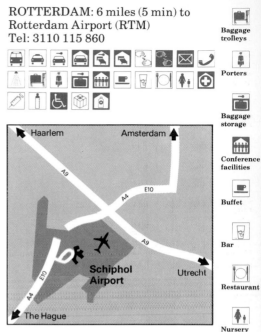

Amsterdam's Schiphol Airport lies below the
site of a famous naval battle fought in 1573; it is
built on a polder reclaimed from the sea, and is
13 feet below sea level.

Baggage
trolleys

Porters

Baggage
storage

Conference
facilities

Buffet

Bar

Restaurant

Nursery

Medical/
first aid

Vaccina-
tions

Mothers'
room

Rest rooms

Facilities
for disabled

Duty-free
shops

Newsstand

Pharmacy

Airports of the world

Airport bus service

Train service

Helicopter service

Taxi service

Car rental

Long term parking

Hotel reservations

Airport Hotel

Bank (landside)

Bank (airside)

Post office

Telephones

Showers

Baths

Paging service

!
Message board

Netherlands Antilles

ARUBA/ORANJESTAD: 2.5 miles (5 min) to Prinses Beatrix Airport (AUA) Tel: 4800

CURACAO/WILLEMSTAD: 7 miles (20 min) to Dr. A. Plesman Airport (CUR) Tel: 82288

***ST. MAARTEN/PHILIPSBURG:** 9.5 miles (20 min) to Prinses Juliana Airport (SXM) Tel: 2160

New Zealand

AUCKLAND: 13.5 miles (30 min) to Auckland International Airport (AKL) Tel: 50 789

CHRISTCHURCH: 7 miles (15 min) to Christchurch International Airport (CHC) Tel: 585029

***WELLINGTON:** 5 miles (30 min) to Wellington International Airport (WLG) Tel: 725659

Nicaragua

***MANAGUA:** 5.5 miles (15 min) to

Las Mercedes Airport (MGA)

Nigeria

***KANO:** 5 miles (30 min) to Kano Airport (KAN) Tel: 3891

***LAGOS:** 13.6 miles (60 min) to Murtala Muhammad Airport (LOS) Tel: 31031

Norway

BERGEN: 11 miles (25 min) to Flesland Airport (BGO) Tel: 522 60 00

OSLO: 6 miles (25 min) to Fornebu Airport (OSL) Tel: 2 12 13 40

STAVANGER: 8 miles (20 min) to Sola Airport (SVG) Tel: 45 50020

Oman

MUSCAT: 22 miles (30 min) to Seeb International Airport (MCT) Tel: 619223

Pakistan

ISLAMABAD: 1.5 miles (3 min) to

Chaklala Airport (RWP) Tel: 62736

KARACHI: 10 miles (15 min) to
Karachi International Airport (KHI)
Tel: 512041

LAHORE: 8 miles (10 min) to Lahore
Airport (LHE) Tel: 371090

Panama

*PANAMA CITY: 17 miles to
Tocumen Airport (PTY) Tel: 661800

Papua New Guinea

*PORT MORESBY: 5 miles (15 min)
to Jackson Field Airport (POM)
Tel: 256611

Paraguay

*ASUNCION: 9.5 miles to Pres. Gen.
Stroessner Airport (ASU) Tel: 22012

Peru

LIMA: 4 miles (10 min) to Jorge
Chavaz International Airport (LIM)
Tel: 52 9570

Philippines, The

*MANILA: 7.5 miles to Manila
International Airport (MNL)
Tel: 831784

Poland

WARSAW: 4 miles (25 min) to Okecie
Airport (WAW) Tel 469670

Portugal

FARO: 4.5 miles (15 min) to Faro
Airport (FAO) Tel: 23081

LISBON: 5 miles (15 min) to Lisbon
Airport (LIS) Tel: 88 11 01

MADEIRA/FUNCHAL: 10 miles
(35 min) to Funchal Airport (FNC)
Tel: 52441

OPORTO: 10.5 miles (20 min) to
Oporto Airport (OPO)

Puerto Rico

*SAN JUAN: 9 miles to Isla Verde
International Airport (SJU)

Qatar

*DOHA: 5 miles to Doha
International Airport (DOH)
Tel: 4881

Baggage
trolleys

Porters

Baggage
storage

Conference
facilities

Buffet

Bar

Restaurant

Nursery

Medical/
first aid

Vaccina-
tions

Mothers'
room

Rest rooms

Facilities
for disabled

Duty-free
shops

Newsstand

Pharmacy

209

Airports of the world

 Airport
bus service

 Train
service

 Helicopter
service

 Taxi
service

 Car
rental

 Long term
parking

 Hotel
reserva-
tions

 Airport
Hotel

 Bank
(landside)

 Bank
(airside)

 Post
office

 Telephones

Showers

 Baths

Paging
service

Message
board

Rhodesia

SALISBURY: 7 miles (15 min) to Salisbury Airport (SAY) Tel: 50422

Romania

*BUCHAREST: 12 miles (15 min) to Otopeni Airport (BUH)

Saudi Arabia

*JEDDAH: 1.5 miles (10 min) to Jeddah International Airport (JED) Tel: 22111

*RIYADH: 15 min to Riyadh Airport (RUH) Tel: 61400

Senegal

*DAKAR: 10.5 miles to Yoff Airport (DKR) Tel: 5118085

Seychelles

MAHE ISLAND/MAHE: 6 miles (20 min) to Mahe Airport (SEZ) Tel: 76553

Sierra Leone

*FREETOWN: 18 miles to Lungi

Airport (FNA) Tel: Lungi 215

Singapore

SINGAPORE: 7 miles (20 min) to Singapore International Airport (SIN) Tel: 888321

South Africa, Republic of

*CAPETOWN: 9 miles (20 min) to D.F. Malan Airport (CPT) Tel: 932767

DURBAN: 10 miles (20 min) to Louis Botha Airport (DUR) Tel: 426111

JOHANNESBURG: 12 miles (25 min) to Jan Smuts Airport (JNB) Tel: 9751185

Spain

ALICANTE: 8 miles (15 min) to Alicante Airport (ALC) Tel: 285011

BARCELONA: 6 miles (10 min) to Barcelona Airport (BCN) Tel: 317 00 08

210

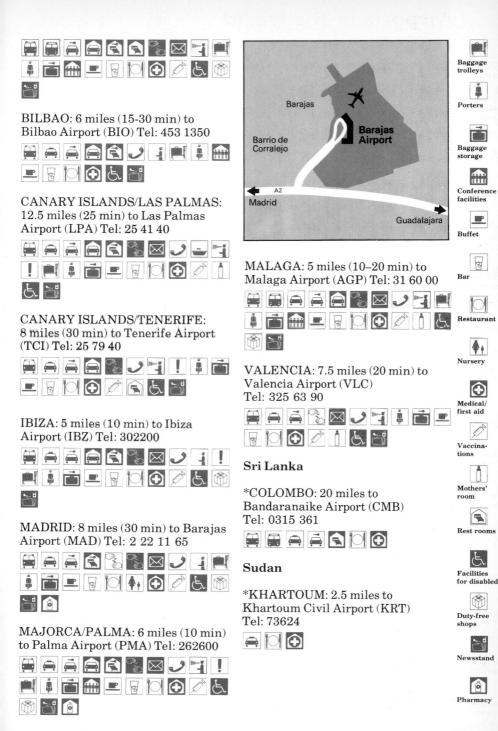

BILBAO: 6 miles (15-30 min) to
Bilbao Airport (BIO) Tel: 453 1350

CANARY ISLANDS/LAS PALMAS:
12.5 miles (25 min) to Las Palmas
Airport (LPA) Tel: 25 41 40

CANARY ISLANDS/TENERIFE:
8 miles (30 min) to Tenerife Airport
(TCI) Tel: 25 79 40

IBIZA: 5 miles (10 min) to Ibiza
Airport (IBZ) Tel: 302200

MADRID: 8 miles (30 min) to Barajas
Airport (MAD) Tel: 2 22 11 65

MAJORCA/PALMA: 6 miles (10 min)
to Palma Airport (PMA) Tel: 262600

Barajas

Barrio de
Corralejo

Barajas
Airport

A2

Madrid

Guadalajara

MALAGA: 5 miles (10–20 min) to
Malaga Airport (AGP) Tel: 31 60 00

VALENCIA: 7.5 miles (20 min) to
Valencia Airport (VLC)
Tel: 325 63 90

Sri Lanka

*COLOMBO: 20 miles to
Bandaranaike Airport (CMB)
Tel: 0315 361

Sudan

*KHARTOUM: 2.5 miles to
Khartoum Civil Airport (KRT)
Tel: 73624

Baggage
trolleys

Porters

Baggage
storage

Conference
facilities

Buffet

Bar

Restaurant

Nursery

Medical/
first aid

Vaccina-
tions

Mothers'
room

Rest rooms

Facilities
for disabled

Duty-free
shops

Newsstand

Pharmacy

211

Airports of the world

Airport bus service

Train service

Helicopter service

Taxi service

Car rental

Long term parking

Hotel reservations

Airport Hotel

Bank (landside)

Bank (airside)

Post office

Telephones

Showers

Baths

Paging service

Message board

Sweden

*GOTHENBERG: 30 min to Landvetter Airport (GOT) Tel: 941100

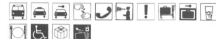

*MALMO: 20 miles (40 min) to Sturup Airport (MMA) Tel: 75040

STOCKHOLM: 27 miles (40 min) to Arlanda Airport (ARN) Tel: 08 780 5000

Switzerland

*BASEL/MULHOUSE: 7 miles to Basel/Mulhouse Airport (BSL)

*GENEVA: 2.5 miles to Cointrin Airport (GVA)

ZURICH: 7 miles (25 min) to Zurich Airport (ZRH) Tel: 8127111

Syria

*DAMASCUS: 18 miles (40 min) to Damascus International Airport (DAM)

Taiwan

TAIPEI: 3 miles (10 min) to Sung Shan Airport (TPE) Tel: 7521212

Tanzania

*DAR-ES-SALAAM: 8 miles to Dar-Es-Salaam International Airport (DAR) Tel: Wageni 221

Thailand

BANGKOK: 15 miles (60 min) to Bangkok International Airport (BKK) Tel: 5237258

Togo

*LOME: 2.5 miles to Lome Airport (LFW)

Tonga Islands

*TONGATAPU/NUKUALOFA: 13 miles to Fua'amotu International Airport (TBU)

Trinidad & Tobago

*PORT OF SPAIN: 16 miles to Piarco Airport (POS)

Tunisia

*DJERBA: 3.5 miles (15 min) to Melita Airport (DJE) Tel: 03 50 223

*MONASTIR: 5 miles (15 min) to
Skanes Airport (MIR) Tel: 03 61 315

TUNIS: 5 miles (10 min) to Carthage
Airport (TUN) Tel: 01 289 000

Turkey

ANKARA: 22 miles (25 min) to
Esenboga Airport (ESB) Tel: 241270

ISTANBUL: 15 miles (20 min) to
Yesilkoy Airport (IST) Tel: 737240

Uganda

*ENTEBBE: 2 miles to Entebbe
Airport (EBB)

Union of Soviet Socialist Republics

KIEV: 24 miles (45 min) to Borispol
Airport (KBP)

LENINGRAD: 10.5 miles (25 min) to
Pulkovo Airport (LED)

MOSCOW: 19 miles (45 min) to
Sheremetievo Airport (SVO)
Tel: 155 5005

United Arab Emirates

ABU DHABI: 12 miles to Abu Dhabi
International Airport (AUH)

DUBAI: 2.5 miles to Dubai Airport
(DXB)

RAS AL KHAYMAH: Ras al
Khaymah Airport (RKT)

SHARJAH: 6 miles to Sharjah
Airport (SHJ)

United Kingdom

ABERDEEN: 5.5 miles (15 min) to
Aberdeen Airport (ABZ) Tel: 722331

BIRMINGHAM: 6.5 miles (30 min) to
Birmingham Airport (BHX)
Tel: 743 4272

Baggage trolleys
Porters
Baggage storage
Conference facilities
Buffet
Bar
Restaurant
Nursery
Medical/first aid
Vaccinations
Mothers' room
Rest rooms
Facilities for disabled
Duty-free shops
Newsstand
Pharmacy

Airports of the world

Airport bus service

Train service

Helicopter service

Taxi service

Car rental

Long term parking

Hotel reservations

Airport Hotel

Bank (landside)

Bank (airside)

Post office

Telephones

Showers

Baths

Paging service

Message board

EDINBURGH: 6 miles (20 min) to
Turnhouse Airport (EDI)
Tel: 334 2351

GLASGOW: 9 miles (20 min) to
Abbotsinch Airport (GLA)
Tel: (041) 887 1111

GLASGOW: 32 miles (60 min) to
Prestwick Airport (PIK) Tel: 79822

LONDON: 28 miles (60 min) to
Gatwick Airport (LGW) Tel: 28822

LONDON: 15 miles (45 min) to
Heathrow Airport (LHR)
Tel: 759 4321

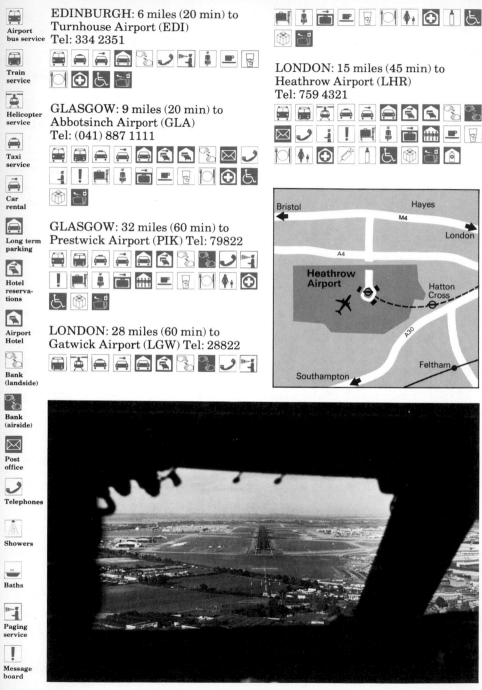

214

LONDON: 30 miles (60 min) to Luton Airport (LTN) Tel: 36061

MANCHESTER: 10 miles (30 min) to Manchester International Airport (MAN) Tel: 061 437 5233

NEWCASTLE ON TYNE: 5 miles (20 min) to Newcastle Airport (NCL) Tel: 860 966

Channel Islands

GUERNSEY/ST. PETER PORT: 3 miles (20 min) to La Villiaze Airport (GCI) Tel: 37682

JERSEY/ST. HELIER: 5 miles (15 min) to Jersey Airport (JER) Tel: 41272

Northern Ireland

BELFAST: 13 miles (30 min) to Aldergrove Airport (BFS) Tel: 29271

London's Heathrow Airport had its beginnings in wartime. It developed from London's first civil airport at Hounslow Heath, in use from 1919, which had been a military airfield in World War I. The airport took a long time to develop, and as late as 1946 the passenger terminal consisted of a cluster of temporary huts and tents **below**. Today, the sprawling complex of buildings seen from an approaching aircraft **below left** accommodates more than 23 million passengers a year, making Heathrow the busiest airport outside the USA. Because more than 20 million of its passengers make international journeys, it now ranks as the world's number one airport for international traffic.

Baggage trolleys

Porters

Baggage storage

Conference facilities

Buffet

Bar

Restaurant

Nursery

Medical/ first aid

Vaccinations

Mothers' room

Rest rooms

Facilities for disabled

Duty-free shops

Newsstand

Pharmacy

215

Airports of the world

Legend (left margin):

Airport bus service

Train service

Helicopter service

Taxi service

Car rental

Long term parking

Hotel reservations

Airport Hotel

Bank (landside)

Bank (airside)

Post office

Telephones

Showers

Baths

Paging service

Message board

United States of America

Alabama

BIRMINGHAM: 5 miles (12 min) to Birmingham Municipal Airport (BHM) Tel: (205) 595 0533

HUNTSVILLE: 11 miles (15 min) to Madison Airport (HSV) Tel: (205) 772 9395

MOBILE: 14 miles (30 min) to Mobile Municipal Airport (MOB) Tel: (205) 342 0510

*MONTGOMERY: 7 miles to Montgomery Municipal Airport (MGM) Tel: (205) 281 5040

Alaska

ANCHORAGE: 5 miles (15 min) to Anchorage International Airport (ANC) Tel: (907) 279 3486

*FAIRBANKS: 5 miles to Fairbanks International Airport (FAI) Tel: (907) 452 2151

*JUNEAU: 7.5 miles to Juneau Municipal Airport (JNU)

Arizona

PHOENIX: 3 miles (10 min) to Sky Harbor International Airport (PHX) Tel: (602) 262 6291

TUCSON: 12 miles (20 min) to Tucson International Airport (TUS) Tel: (602) 294 3411

Arkansas

*LITTLE ROCK: 3 miles to Adams Field Airport (LIT) Tel: (501) 372 3439

California

BAKERSFIELD: 4 miles (15 min) to Meadowsfield Airport (BFL) Tel: (805) 861 2218

BURBANK: 4 miles (10 min) to Hollywood-Burbank Airport (BUR) Tel: (213) 847 6321

FRESNO: 5 miles (15 min) to Fresno Air Terminal (FAT) Tel: (209) 251 6051

*LOS ANGELES: 10 miles (25 min) to Los Angeles International Airport (LAX) Tel: (213) 646 5252

Baggage trolleys

Porters

Baggage storage

Los Angeles Airport was designed as a series of satellites connected by underground channels to the ticketing buildings. The entire complex can be seen from the observation deck of the "Theme" building **centre left**. Concorde, at the satellite in the foreground, visited Los Angeles Airport on its demonstration tour. A proposed new airport for Los Angeles is to be built in the desert at Palmdale.

Conference facilities

Buffet

Bar

Restaurant

Nursery

Medical/ first aid

Vaccina- tions

Mothers' room

Rest rooms

Facilities for disabled

Duty-free shops

Newsstand

Pharmacy

217

Airports of the world

Airport bus service

MONTEREY: 3 miles (10 min) to Peninsular Airport (MRY) Tel: (408) 373 3731

Train service

Helicopter service

OAKLAND: 10 miles (20 min) to Oakland International Airport (OAK) Tel: (415) 562 6600

Taxi service

Car rental

ONTARIO: 3 miles (10 min) to Ontario International Airport (ONT) Tel: (714) 984 1207

Long term parking

Hotel reservations

PALM SPRINGS: 2 miles (8 min) to Palm Springs Municipal Airport (PSP) Tel: (714) 323 8161

Airport Hotel

Bank (landside)

SACRAMENTO: 12 miles (15 min) to Sacramento Metropolitan Airport (SMF) Tel: (916) 929 5411

Bank (airside)

Post office

SAN DIEGO: 3 miles (10 min) to San Diego International Airport (SAN) Tel: (714) 291 3900

Telephones

Showers

Baths

SAN FRANCISCO: 16 miles (30 min) to San Francisco International Airport (SFO) Tel: (415) 761 0800

Paging service

Message board

At San Francisco International Airport, the runway complex **right** extends into the bay, giving aircraft an unobstructed takeoff and approach to landing. The terminal building and its surrounding satellites, visible in the aerial view, is seen in detail **below**, surrounded by DC-8 Super 60s. The terminal design combines a linear arrangement, where aircraft link directly to the main building to give passengers direct access for commuter flights, with satellites, reserved for long-distance flights. Bridges and tunnels connect each satellite with the terminal building. Among the 28 airlines using this airport are the local bay area helicopter services and commuter airlines linking San Francisco with more than 30 Californian cities.

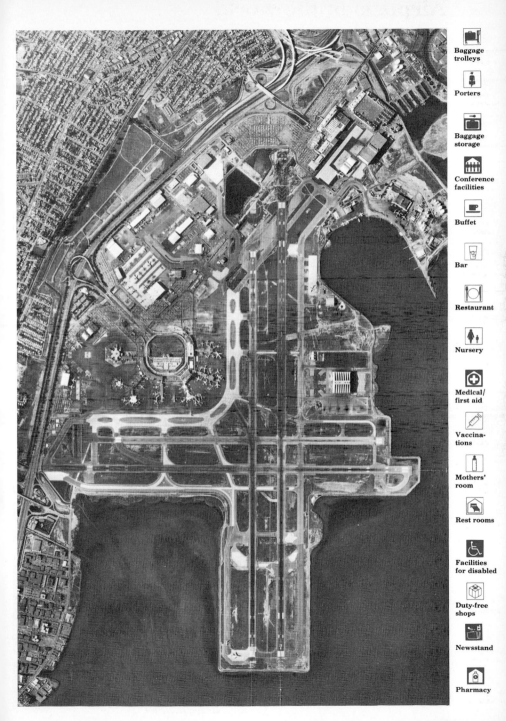

Baggage
trolleys

Porters

Baggage
storage

Conference
facilities

Buffet

Bar

Restaurant

Nursery

Medical/
first aid

Vaccina-
tions

Mothers'
room

Rest rooms

Facilities
for disabled

Duty-free
shops

Newsstand

Pharmacy

219

Airports of the world

Airport bus service

SAN JOSE: 2 miles (5 min) to San Jose Municipal Airport (SJC) Tel: (408) 277 4000

Train service

SANTA BARBARA: 10.5 miles (14 min) to Santa Barbara International Airport (SBA) Tel: (805) 967 7111

Helicopter service

Taxi service

Car rental

Colorado

COLORADO SPRINGS: 6 miles (20 min) to Colorado Springs Airport (COS) Tel: (303) 596 0188

Long term parking

Hotel reservations

DENVER: 5 miles (18 min) to Stapleton International Airport (DEN) Tel: (303) 398 3844

Airport Hotel

Bank (landside)

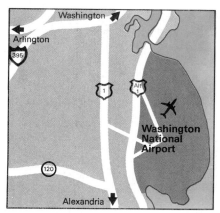

Boulder

Stapleton International Airport

Denver

Denver

Limon

Bank (airside)

Post office

Telephones

Showers

Baths

Paging service

***GRAND JUNCTION:** 4 miles to Walker Field Airport (GJT) Tel: (303) 243 3695

Message board

Connecticut

WINDSOR LOCKS: 13 miles (20 min) to Bradley International Airport (BDL) Tel: (203) 623 3940

District of Columbia

WASHINGTON: 3.5 miles (15 min) to Washington National Airport (DCA) Tel: (703) 557 2045

Washington

Arlington

395

Alt 1

1

Washington National Airport

120

Alexandria

WASHINGTON: 26 miles (45 min) to Dulles International Airport (IAD) Tel: (703) 471 7596

Dulles International Airport, designed by architect Eero Saarinen, was the first civil airport designed specifically to handle jet aircraft. Although it was designed in the late 1950s, the increasing dimensions and capacities of aircraft have caused no serious adjustment difficulties; the air terminal can be elongated by adding further bays.

Florida

*DAYTONA BEACH: 3 miles to
Daytona Beach Regional Airport
(DAB) Tel: (904) 255 8441

*FORT LAUDERDALE-
HOLLYWOOD: 4 miles to Fort
Lauderdale-Hollywood Airport (FLL)
Tel: (305) 765 5910

FORT MYERS: 4 miles (15 min) to
Page Field Airport (FMY)
Tel: (813) 936 3143

GAINESVILLE: 6 miles (10 min) to
Gainesville Regional Airport (GNV)
Tel: (904) 374 2176

JACKSONVILLE: 12 miles (15 min)
to Jacksonville International Airport
(JAX) Tel: (904) 757 2261

Baggage
trolleys

Porters

Baggage
storage

Conference
facilities

Buffet

Bar

Restaurant

Nursery

Medical/
first aid

Vaccina-
tions

Mothers'
room

Rest rooms

Facilities
for disabled

Duty-free
shops

Newsstand

Pharmacy

221

Airports of the world

 Airport bus service

 Train service

 Helicopter service

 Taxi service

 Car rental

 Long term parking

 Hotel reservations

 Airport Hotel

 Bank (landside)

 Bank (airside)

 Post office

 Telephones

 Showers

 Baths

 Paging service

 Message board

*MIAMI: 6 miles to Miami International Airport (MIA) Tel: (305) 526 2000

ORLANDO: 10 miles (20 min) to Orlando International Airport Tel: (305) 855 8841

PENSACOLA: 3 miles (10 min) to Pensacola Regional Airport (PNS) Tel: (904) 436 4315

SARASOTA: 4 miles to Bradenton Airport (SRQ) Tel: (813) 355 2761

TALLAHASSEE: 5 miles (15 min) to Tallahassee Municipal Airport (TLH) Tel: (904) 575 0666

TAMPA: 4 miles (15 min) to Tampa

International Airport (TPA) Tel: (813) 883 3400

WEST PALM BEACH: 3 miles (10 min) to West Palm Beach International Airport (PBI) Tel: (305) 683 5722

Georgia

ATLANTA: 8 miles (10 min) to Atlanta International Airport (ATL) Tel: (404) 766 2772

AUGUSTA: 7 miles to Bush Field Airport (AGS) Tel: (404) 798 3236

COLUMBUS: 3 miles (5 min) to Columbus Metropolitan Airport (CSG) Tel: (404) 324 2449

SAVANNAH: 8 miles (15 min) to
Savannah Municipal Airport (SAV)
Tel: (912) 964 0517

Hawaii

HILO: 2 miles (5 min) to Lyman Field
Airport (ITO) Tel: (808) 935 0809

HONOLULU: 4 miles (9 min) to
Honolulu International Airport
(HNL) Tel: (808) 847 9411

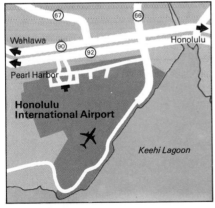

*KAHULUI: 3 miles to Kahului
Airport (OGG) Tel: (808) 877 0078

KAILUA: 9 miles to Ke-Ahole
Airport (KOA) Tel: (808) 329 2484

*LIHUE: 2 miles to Lihue Airport
(LIH) Tel: (808) 245 6301

Idaho

BOISE: 4 miles (10 min) to Gowen
Field Airport (BOI)
Tel: (208) 344 3239

Illinois

ALTON: 5 miles to Civic Memorial
Airport (ALN) Tel: (618) 259 2531

*CHAMPAIGN: 6 miles to University
of Illinois Airport (CMI)
Tel: (217) 333 3204

*CHICAGO: 10 miles to Chicago
Midway Airport (MDW)
Tel: (312) 767 0500

Baggage
trolleys

Porters

Baggage
storage

Conference
facilities

Buffet

Bar

Restaurant

Nursery

Medical/
first aid

Vaccina-
tions

Mothers'
room

Rest rooms

Facilities
for disabled

Duty-free
shops

Newsstand

Pharmacy

223

Airports of the world

Airport bus service
Train service
Helicopter service
Taxi service
Car rental
Long term parking
Hotel reservations
Airport Hotel
Bank (landside)
Bank (airside)
Post office
Telephones
Showers
Baths
Paging service
Message board

*CHICAGO: 16 miles to O'Hare Airport (ORD) Tel: (312) 686 220

*CHICAGO: 1.5 miles to Merrill C. Meigs Field (CGX) Tel: (312) 744 4787

*MOLINE: 4 miles to Quad-Cities Airport (MLI) Tel: (309) 764 9621

PEORIA: 9 miles (15 min) to Greater Peoria Airport (PIA) Tel: (309) 697 8272

*SPRINGFIELD: 3 miles to Springfield Capital Airport (SPI) Tel: (217) 528 7551

Indiana

*EVANSVILLE: 4 miles to Evansville Dress Regional Airport (EVV) Tel: (812) 424 5511

*FORT WAYNE: 7.5 miles to Fort Wayne Municipal Airport (FWA) Tel: (219) 747 6598

INDIANAPOLIS: 7 miles (15 min) to Indianapolis International Airport (IND) Tel: (317) 247 6271

SOUTH BEND: 4 miles (10 min) to Michiana Regional Airport (SBN) Tel: (219) 233 2185

Iowa

CEDAR RAPIDS: 8 miles (10 min) to Cedar Rapids Municipal Airport (CID) Tel: (319) 362 3131

DES MOINES: 3 miles (20 min) to Des Moines Municipal Airport (DSM) Tel: (515) 283 4255

WATERLOO: 6 miles (10 min) to Waterloo Municipal Airport (ALO) Tel: (319) 291 4483

Kansas

WICHITA: 6 miles (15 min) to Mid-Continent Airport (ICT) Tel: (316) 942 8101

Kentucky

LEXINGTON: 4 miles (15 min) to Blue Grass Field Airport (LEX) Tel: (606) 254 9336

LOUISVILLE: 4 miles (15 min) to Standiford Field Airport (SDF) Tel: (502) 368 6524

Louisiana

BATON ROUGE: 5 miles (10 min) to Ryan Airport (BTR)
Tel: (504) 355 0333

NEW ORLEANS: 14 miles (30 min) to New Orleans International Airport (MSY) Tel: (504) 729 2591

SHREVEPORT: 5 miles (10–15 min) to Shreveport Regional Airport (SHV)
Tel: (318) 636 6066

Maine

BANGOR: 1.5 miles (7 min) to Bangor International Airport (BGR)
Tel: (207) 942 4675

PORTLAND: 2 miles (15 min) to International Jetport (PWM)
Tel: (207) 774 7301

Maryland

BALTIMORE: 10 miles (15 min) to Washington International Airport (BAL) Tel: (301) 761 7100

Massachusetts

BEDFORD: 3 miles (10 min) to Hanscom Field Airport (BCD)
Tel: (617) 274 7200

BOSTON: 2 miles (10 min) to Logan International Airport (BOS)
Tel: (617) 567 5400

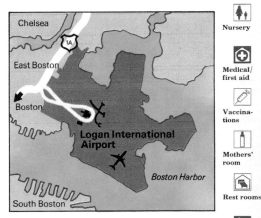

Michigan

BATTLE CREEK: 3 miles (15 min) to W.K. Kellog Regional Airport (BTL)
Tel: (616) 966 3470

DETROIT: 6 miles (15 min) to Detroit City Airport (DET)
Tel: (313) 224 1300

Baggage trolleys

Porters

Baggage storage

Conference facilities

Buffet

Bar

Restaurant

Nursery

Medical/ first aid

Vaccinations

Mothers' room

Rest rooms

Facilities for disabled

Duty-free shops

Newsstand

Pharmacy

225

Airports of the world

Airport
bus service

Train
service

Helicopter
service

Taxi
service

Car
rental

Long term
parking

Hotel
reserva-
tions

Airport
Hotel

Bank
(landside)

Bank
(airside)

Post
office

Telephones

Showers

Baths

Paging
service

Message
board

*DETROIT: 17 miles to Detroit
Metropolitan Airport (DTW)
Tel: (313) 278 3910

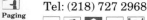

*FLINT: 4 miles to Bishop Airport
(FNT) Tel: (313) 767 4232

*GRAND RAPIDS: 7 miles to Kent
County Airport (GRR)
Tel: (616) 949 4500

KALAMAZOO: 4 miles (10 min) to
Kalamazoo Municipal Airport (AZO)
Tel: (616) 385 8177

*LANSING: 4 miles to Capital City
Airport (LAN) Tel: (517) 371 2020

OAKLAND: 5 miles (10 min) to
Oakland-Pontiac Airport (PTK)
Tel: (313) 666 3900

SAGINAW: 10 miles (15 min) to
Tri-City Airport (MBS)
Tel: (517) 695 5555

Minnesota

*DULUTH: 7.5 miles to Duluth
International Airport (DLH)
Tel: (218) 727 2968

*MINNEAPOLIS: 10 miles to St.
Paul Airport (MSP)

Tel: (612) 726 1717

*ROCHESTER: 8 miles to Rochester
Municipal Airport (RST)
Tel: (507) 282 2328

*ST. PAUL: 1 mile to St. Paul
Downtown Airport (STP)
Tel: (612) 224 4306

Mississippi

JACKSON: 10 miles (20 min) to
Jackson Municipal Airport (JAN)
Tel: (601) 939 5631

Missouri

*KANSAS CITY: 17 miles to Kansas
City International Airport (MCI)
Tel: (816) 243 5200

*ST. LOUIS: 11 miles to Lambert St.
Louis International Airport (STL)
Tel: (314) 426 7777

SPRINGFIELD: 7 miles (15 min) to
Springfield Municipal Airport (SGF)
Tel: (417) 869 7231

Montana

*BILLINGS: 1 mile to Logan Field
Airport (BIL) Tel: (406) 245 3567

226

GREAT FALLS: 5 miles (10 min) to
Great Falls International Airport
(GTF) Tel: (406) 727 3404

Nebraska

LINCOLN: 6 miles (10 min) to
Lincoln Municipal Airport (LNK)
Tel: (402) 435 2925

OMAHA: 4 miles (10 min) to Eppley
Field Airport (OMA)
Tel: (402) 422 6800

Nevada

LAS VEGAS: 7 miles (10 min) to
McCarran International Airport
(LAS) Tel: (702) 739 5211

RENO: 3 miles (20 min) to Reno
International Airport (RNO)
Tel: (702) 785 2375

New Jersey

NEWARK: 3 miles (15 min) to
Newark International Airport (EWR)
Tel: (201) 961 2000

New Mexico

ALBUQUERQUE: 5 miles (15 min) to
Albuquerque International Airport
(ABQ) Tel: (505) 766 7894

New York

ALBANY: 5 miles (30 min) to Albany
County Airport (ALB)
Tel: (578) 869 5312

*BUFFALO: 9 miles to Greater
Buffalo International Airport (BUF)
Tel: (716) 842 5760

NEW YORK: 15 miles (30 min) to
John F. Kennedy International
Airport (JFK) Tel: (212) 656 4444

227

Airports of the world

Airport bus service

Train service

Helicopter service

Taxi service

Car rental

Long term parking

Hotel reservations

Airport Hotel

Bank (landside)

Bank (airside)

Post office

Telephones

Showers

Baths

Paging service

Message board

A Boeing 747 flies over the new microwave landing system installation at New York's John F. Kennedy Airport. The new system will enable aircraft to land with absolute safety in zero visibility.

NEW YORK: 8 miles (25 min) to La Guardia Airport (LGA)
Tel: (212) 476 5000

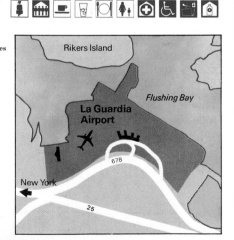

ROCHESTER: 5 miles (15 min) to Monroe Airport (ROC)
Tel: (716) 436 5624

SYRACUSE: 7 miles (20 min) to Hancock International Airport (SYR)
Tel: (315) 454 3263

North Carolina

*ASHEVILLE: 14 miles (25 min) to Asheville Municipal Airport (AVL)
Tel: (704) 684 2226

*CHARLOTTE: 8 miles to Douglas Municipal Airport (CLT)
Tel: (704) 374 2822

FAYETTEVILLE: 5 miles (10 min) to Fayetteville Municipal Airport (FAY)
Tel: (919) 484 7314

*GREENSBORO: 11 miles to Greensboro-Highpoint Regional Airport (GSO) Tel: (919) 299 6896

RALEIGH: 14 miles (30 min) to Durham Airport (RDU)
Tel: (919) 787 4580

North Dakota

BISMARCK: 2 miles (5 min) to
Bismarck Municipal Airport (BIS)
Tel: (701) 223 5900

FARGO: 3 miles (15 min) to Hector
Field Airport (FAR)
Tel: (701) 235 4100

Ohio

AKRON: 7.5 miles (15 min) to Canton
Regional Airport (CAK)
Tel: (216) 896 2385

CINCINNATI: 12.5 miles to Greater
Cincinnati Airport (CVG)
Tel: (606) 283 3151

CLEVELAND: 13 miles (20 min) to
Hopkins International Airport (CLE)
Tel: (216) 265 6000

*CLEVELAND: 12 miles to
Lakefront Airport (BKL)
Tel: (216) 781 6411

COLUMBUS: 9 miles (20 min) to Port
Columbus International Airport
(CMH) Tel: (614) 422 1116

DAYTON: 12 miles (20 min) to James
M. Cox Airport (DAY)
Tel: (513) 898 4631

TOLEDO: 17 miles (25 min) to Toledo
Express Airport (TOL)
Tel: (419) 865 2351

*YOUNGSTOWN: 10 miles to
Youngstown Municipal Airport
(YNG)

Oklahoma

OKLAHOMA CITY: 9 miles (20 min)
to Will Rogers Airport (OKC)
Tel: (405) 681 5311

TULSA: 7 miles (15 min) to Tulsa
International Airport (TUL)
Tel: (918) 835 8412

Oregon

PORTLAND: 10 miles (30 min) to
Portland International Airport (PDX)
Tel: (503) 233 8331

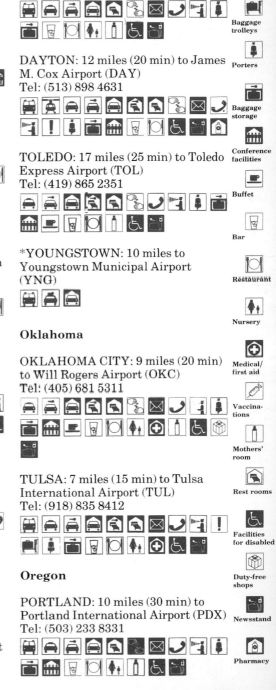

Airports of the world

Airport bus service

Train service

Helicopter service

Taxi service

Car rental

Long term parking

Hotel reservations

Airport Hotel

Bank (landside)

Bank (airside)

Post office

Telephones

Showers

Baths

Paging service

Message board

Pennsylvania

ALLENTOWN: 3 miles (15 min) to Bethlehem-Eastern Airport (ABE) Tel: (215) 264 2831

ERIE: 6 miles (20 min) to Erie International Airport (ERI) Tel: (814) 833 4258

HARRISBURG: 1 mile to Olmstead State Airport (MDT) Tel: (717) 787 7702

PHILADELPHIA: 7 miles (30 min) to Philadelphia International Airport (PHL) Tel: (215) 492 3000

PITTSBURGH: 16 miles (25 min) to Greater Pittsburgh Airport (PIT) Tel: (412) 771 2500

*WILKES-BARRE: 12 miles to Scranton Airport (AVP)

Puerto Rico

SAN JUAN: 7 miles (10 min) to Puerto Rico International Airport (SJV) Tel: 791 4670

Rhode Island

PROVIDENCE: 8 miles (14 min) to T.F. Green State Airport (PVD) Tel: (401) 737 4000

South Carolina

*CHARLESTON: 11.5 miles to Charleston International Airport (CHS)

COLUMBIA: 6 miles (20 min) to Columbia Metropolitan Airport (CAE) Tel: (803) 794 3419

GREENVILLE: 12 miles (20 min) to Greenville-Spartanburg Airport (GSP) Tel: (803) 877 7426

South Dakota

RAPID CITY: 7.5 miles (15 min) to Rapid City Regional Airport (RAP) Tel: (605) 394 4195

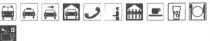

*SIOUX FALLS: 3 miles to Joe Foss Field Airport (FSD) Tel: (605) 336 0762

Tennessee

*BRISTOL: 16 miles to Bristol

230

Tri-City Airport (TRI)
Tel: (615) 323 6271

CHATTANOOGA: 10 miles (20 min)
to Lovell Field Airport (CHA)
Tel (615) 892 1666

KNOXVILLE: 13 miles (30 min) to
Knoxville Municipal Airport (TYS)
Tel: (615) 577 6621

MEMPHIS: 10 miles (20 min) to
Memphis International Airport
(MEM) Tel: (901) 345 7777

NASHVILLE: 6.5 miles (15 min) to
Nashville Metropolitan Airport
(BNA) Tel: (615) 367 3012

Texas

AMARILLO: 9 miles (10 min) to
Amarillo International Airport
(AMA) Tel: (806) 335 1671

AUSTIN: 5 miles (10 min) to Austin
Municipal Airport (AUS)
Tel (512) 472 5439

*CORPUS CHRISTI: 10 miles to
Corpus Christi International Airport
(CRP) Tel: (512) 882 5451

DALLAS: 17 miles (35 min) to Dallas
Fort Worth Airport (DFW)
Tel: (214) 574 3112

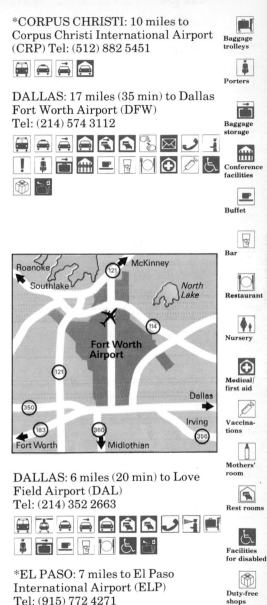

DALLAS: 6 miles (20 min) to Love
Field Airport (DAL)
Tel: (214) 352 2663

*EL PASO: 7 miles to El Paso
International Airport (ELP)
Tel: (915) 772 4271

HOUSTON: 20 miles (30 min) to
Houston
Intercontinental Airport (IAH)
Tel: (713) 443 4731

Baggage
trolleys

Porters

Baggage
storage

Conference
facilities

Buffet

Bar

Restaurant

Nursery

Medical/
first aid

Vaccina-
tions

Mothers'
room

Rest rooms

Facilities
for disabled

Duty-free
shops

Newsstand

Pharmacy

Airports of the world

*HOUSTON: 10 miles (20 min) to William P. Hobby Airport (HOU) Tel: (713) 643 4336

LUBBOCK: 12 miles (15 min) to Lubbock Regional Airport (LBB) Tel: (806) 762 6411

MIDLAND: 9 miles (15 min) to Midland Regional Airport (MAF) Tel: (915) 563 1460

*SAN ANTONIO: 8 miles (15 min) to San Antonio International Airport (SAT) Tel: (512) 824 5335

Utah

SALT LAKE CITY: 7 miles (15 min) to Salt Lake City International Airport (SLC) Tel: (801) 355 6251

Vermont

*BURLINGTON: 3 miles to Burlington International Airport (BTV) Tel: (802) 863 2874

Virginia

NEWPORT NEWS: 10 miles (15 min)

to Patrick Henry International Airport (PHF) Tel: (804) 877 0221

NORFOLK: 8 miles (30 min) to Norfolk International Airport (ORF) Tel: (804) 857 3351

*RICHMOND: 5 miles (10 min) to Richard Evelyn Byrd Airport (RIC) Tel: (804) 222 7361

*ROANOKE: 4 miles (10 min) to Roanoke Municipal Airport (ROA) Tel: (703) 981 2531

Washington

SEATTLE: 5 miles (10 min) to Boeing Field International Airport (BFI) Tel: (206) 344 7380

SEATTLE: 12 miles (20 min) to Tacoma Airport (SEA) Tel: (206) 433 5385

SPOKANE: 6 miles (15 min) to Spokane International Airport (GEG) Tel: (509) 624 3218

West Virginia

*CHARLESTON: 3 miles (5–10 min)

to Kanawha Airport (CRW)
Tel: (304) 346-0707

*HUNTINGDON: 9 miles (20 min) to
Tri-State Airport (HTS)
Tel: (304) 453 3481

Wisconsin

*GREEN BAY: 5 miles (10 min) to
Austin Straubel Airport (GRB)
Tel: (414) 494 2900

*MADISON: 5 miles (10 min) to Dane
County Airport (MSN)
Tel: (608) 241 1251

MILWAUKEE: 6 miles (10 min) to
General Mitchell Field Airport
(MKE) Tel: (414) 747 5300

Upper Volta

*OUAGADOUGOU: 5 miles (10 min)
to Ouagadougou Airport (OUA)

Uruguay

MONTEVIDEO: 12 miles (25 min) to
Carrasco Airport (MVD) Tel: 502261

Venezuela

*CARACAS: 13 miles (25 min) to
Maiquetia Airport (CCS)

*MARACAIBO: 2 miles (5 min) to
La Chinita Airport (MAR)

Viet-Nam

*HO CHI MINH CITY: 4.5 miles to
Ho Chi Minh City Airport (SGN)

Yemen Arab Republic

*SANA'A: 2 miles (5 min) to El-
Rahaba Airport (SAH)

Yugoslavia

BELGRADE: 10 miles (15 min) to
Surcin Airport (BEG) Tel: 601 555

DUBROVNIK: 13.5 miles (30 min) to
Dubrovnik Airport (DBV)

ZAGREB: 10 miles (20 min) to Pleso
Airport (ZAG)

Zaire

*KINSHASA: 15 miles (30 min) to
N'djili Airport (FIH)

Zambia

LUSAKA: 13 miles (15 min) to
Lusaka International Airport (LUN)
Tel:74331

233

Glossary of terms

A

Abort
To abandon a course of action; e.g., to cancel a takeoff already started.

Acceleration
The rate of change of velocity — of speed, or direction, or both at once. (See: **Deceleration**.)

Aerodynamics
The science dealing with air or other gas in motion and its effects on a moving body.

Aerofoil (airfoil)
A suitably shaped structure that generates lift when propelled through the air, such as a wing, propeller, rotor blade or tailplane.

Afterburner (reheat)
A system in which fuel is injected into the jet exhaust and ignited to give extra thrust to supersonic aircraft for short periods.

Aileron
A movable control surface hinged to the trailing edge of each wing, usually near the tip.

Air brake
A hinged surface that increases drag.

Aircraft surface movement indicator (ASMI)
A radar screen in a control tower that shows all objects on the airfield.

Airspeed indicator (ASI)
An instrument that measures the speed at which an aircraft is moving through the air (not generally equal to ground speed).

Airway
A path for air traffic, defined by radio beacons such as VORs or NDBs (q.v.).

Alphanumeric display
Computer "writing" in letter and number characters on a TV-type screen.

Altimeter
An aircraft altitude indicator.

Angle of attack
The angle at which an aerofoil meets oncoming air.

Annular
Ring-shaped.

Aquaplaning
Riding on a thin film of water on the runway.

Artificial horizon
A gyro-stabilized flight instrument that shows the pitching and rolling movements of an aircraft.

Astro-navigation
Traditional navigation using the positions of the sun and stars.

Autopilot
Automatic pilot, a gyroscopically controlled device that keeps an aircraft in steady flight or puts it through pre-set manoeuvres, such as climbing to a chosen flight level.

B

Baffle
A structure that impedes the flow of a fluid, such as fuel in a tank.

Barrette
Closely spaced ground lights that from the air appear as a bar of light.

Bleed air
High-pressure air "bled" from a main engine for cabin pressurization and other services.

Bogie
Four-, six- or eight-wheel truck on a main landing leg.

Boom carpet
The strip of ground along which sonic boom from supersonic aircraft is heard.

Bulkhead
A transverse panel across a fuselage, such as those at the front and rear of pressure cabins.

By-pass engine
A jet engine (q.v.) in which up to about half of the intake air is ducted around the combustion chamber by a fan. When the by-pass ratio is higher the engine is called a turbofan (q.v.).

C

Camber
The curvature of an aerofoil surface.

Canard
An aircraft with main wing at the rear, with a "foreplane" — a horizontal control surface — at the front.

Cantilever wing
A wing supported at the root only, and lacking bracing wires or struts.

Centre of gravity (CG)
The point at which the total weight of an aircraft may be considered to act.

Chord
The distance from the leading to the trailing edge of an aerofoil. The mean chord is the average chord of a tapered wing.

Clean
(Describing an aircraft) having all extensible devices (landing-gears, flaps, etc) retracted — the normal en route configuration.

Clear air turbulence (CAT)
High-level turbulence occurring in clear weather conditions.

Clearway
The area of land or water over which an aircraft may begin its climb in the first few seconds after takeoff.

Collective-pitch control
Control that varies the angle of attack of all the blades of a helicopter rotor simultaneously to make the craft rise or descend. (See: **Cyclic-pitch control**.)

Combi
A transport plane in which the proportion of passengers to cargo can easily be varied by removing or adding seats in order to achieve the most economical combination.

Compressor
A device that compresses (increases the density of) intake air in a piston engine, turboprop or jet engine.

Condition-monitoring
Continuous monitoring of an aircraft's components and systems.

Control surface
A movable aerofoil (such as a stabilizer) or section of an aerofoil (such as an aileron or elevator) that controls an aircraft's flight.

Cyclic-pitch control
Control that varies a helicopter's direction of movement by tilting each blade according to its position in the circle of rotation. (See: **Collective-pitch control**.)

D

Deceleration
The rate of reduction of speed, also called negative acceleration. (See: **Acceleration**.)

Delta wing
A triangular or near-triangular wing; named after the Greek letter corresponding to "D".

Doppler radar
Airborne equipment that determines speed and direction of movement by measuring the changes in frequency of several radar beams transmitted from the aircraft and reflected from the ground. (See: **Radar**.)

Drag
The air's resistance to moving objects.

Drift
The lateral movement of an aircraft away from its desired track; caused by the wind.

Duct
A channel or tube through which fluid passes.

E

Elevator
A horizontal control surface on the tailplane (stabilizer) that controls climb and descent. Many modern jets have pivoted tailplanes and no elevators. (See: **Elevon**.)

Elevon
A control surface on the wing of a tailless aircraft, functioning as both elevator and aileron.

EPNdB
Effective perceived noise decibel, a unit of noise that is intended to represent both its duration and its "annoyance value". (See: **PNdB**.)

F

Feather
To turn the blades of a propeller edge-on to the slipstream when power has been cut off, so that they are not forced to rotate.

Fin (Vertical stabilizer)
The fixed vertical surface at an aircraft's tail that helps to control roll and yaw.

Flame-out
Extinction of combustion in a gas-turbine engine, resulting in total loss of power.

Flap
A movable surface on an aircraft wing that increases lift, or both lift and drag. Most are fitted at the trailing edge, but one type (the Krüger) is on the leading edge. Flaps are extended before takeoff or landing.

Flight director
A flight-deck instrument that tells the pilot whether he should guide the aircraft left or right, up or down, or stay level and on a pre-set heading.

Flight envelope
The limiting accelerations and speeds that an aircraft may fly at. (See: **G-forces**.)

Flight recorder
An airborne device, able to withstand accidents, that continuously records important features of an airliner's flight, such as height, speed, control-surface position, etc.

Floatplane
An aircraft with floats, capable of landing on water, usually called a seaplane in the U.K. (See: **Flying boat**.)

Flutter
An unstable air-induced oscillation of an aerofoil.

Flying boat
An aircraft that can land and take off from water on its boatlike hull. (See: **Floatplane**.)

G

Gas turbine
An engine driven by hot gases, formed by the burning of fuel, which escape through blades that are thereby forced to rotate. Most jet engines, including turbofans, as well as turboprops and turboshafts, are gas-turbine engines.

G-forces
The crew of a plane in a turn or pulling out of a dive experience "centrifugal" forces (that is, forces directed away from the centre of the curved path). These "g-forces" (gravity-forces) give the crew a feeling of increased weight, can cause blackouts, and stress the aircraft.

Gimbals
A mounting that permits an instrument such as a compass or gyroscope to move freely and so maintain a constant orientation regardless of an aircraft's movement.

Glidepath
The path an aircraft follows as it comes in to land; also, the beam in an ILS system giving vertical guidance.

Ground effect
Extra lift experienced by an aircraft very close to the ground. It is caused by the downwash of air striking the surface.

Gyrocompass
A device incorporating gyroscopes that indicates true north.

H

Head-up display (HUD)
Information projected onto an aircraft's windshield, focused at infinity, so that the pilot can see it without lowering his eyes.

Heat sink
Any structure that can absorb a large amount of heat while undergoing only a small rise in temperature.
Horizontal situation indicator (HSI)
Flight-deck instrument that indicates aircraft heading, the distance and bearing of radio beacons and other position information.
Hypersonic
More than five times as fast as sound.

I

Inertial navigation system (INS)
A system incorporating three sensitive accelerometers, which continuously measure changes in an aircraft's speed and direction, and a computer which works out the position from this information.
Instrument flight rules (IFR)
The procedures a pilot must follow when flying without visual cues from the ground.
Instrument Landing System (ILS)
A system that guides a pilot during landing by means of two sets of radio beams transmitted from the ground near the runway.

J

Jet engine
An engine that takes in air, uses it to burn fuel, emits a stream of hot gas, and experiences a reaction thrust. (See: **Gas turbine, Turbofan, Turbojet.**)
Jet-lag
The discrepancy between local time and the time to which an air traveller, recently arrived from another time zone, is adapted.
Jet stream
Clearly defined streams of fast-moving air at high altitudes.

K

Knot
A speed of 1 nautical mile per hour, equal to 1.15 statute miles per hour.

L

Leading edge
The front edge of an aerofoil.
Lift
The force generated on an aerofoil at right angles to the flow of air around it. Usually denotes the supporting force generated by a wing (including a helicopter rotor blade); but the thrust created by a propeller is the same kind of force.
Lift dumper
A surface extended from a wing upper surface immediately after landing in order to "spoil" the airflow and reduce lift.
Loran
Long-Range Navigation, a radio navigation system in which signals from three linked ground stations are automatically compared by

an onboard receiver.

M

Mach number
The ratio of true airspeed to the local speed of sound. Since the latter varies with altitude, a given Mach number does not represent a fixed speed.
Magnetic compass
An instrument containing a magnetized needle showing the direction of magnetic north.
Microwave Landing System
A newly accepted radio landing aid that will replace the Instrument Landing System (q.v.). Aircraft are guided to the runway from many directions by a microwave beam (a type of very short-wave radio beam) that scans a large area of sky. Since aircraft do not have to join a single glidepath, MLS can handle a greater volume of traffic than ILS.

N

Nautical mile
The unit of distance used in air navigation, equal to approximately 1.15 statute miles.
Navaid
Navigational aid.
NDB
Non-directional beacon, radio navaid giving position, but not steering guidance.

O

Omega
A navigation system that employs a world-wide network of VLF (very low frequency) radio transmitters. Their precisely synchronized transmissions are compared by an airborne computer. The entire world is covered by eight transmitters.

P

Phonetic alphabet
An alphabet that uses words instead of letters to prevent confusion over the radio:

A=Alpha	B=Bravo	C=Charlie
D=Delta	E=Echo	F=Foxtrot
G=Golf	H=Hotel	I=India
J=Juliet	K=Kilo	L=Lima
M=Mike	N=November	O=Oscar
P=Papa	Q=Quebec	R=Romeo
S=Sierra	T=Tango	U=Uniform
V=Victor	W=Whiskey	X=X-ray
Y=Yankee	Z=Zulu	

Pitch
The angular setting of a propeller blade or helicopter rotor blade; or up-and-down movements of an aircraft's nose.
Pitot head
Forward-facing, open-ended tube measuring dynamic air pressure (which increases with speed), surrounded by an outer tube with side perforations to measure "static" atmospheric pressure. (See: **Airspeed indicator.**)

PNdB
Perceived noise decibel, a unit of noise that takes account of the annoying quality of the different frequencies present. (See: **EPNdB.**)

Q
QNH
Air pressure at sea level. This figure, which varies, is supplied by air traffic control to aircraft captains so that they can set their altimeters correctly.

R
Radar
Radio Direction and Ranging. *Primary* radar equipment, housed in ground stations, planes or ships, emits ultra-high-frequency radio pulses to determine the position of objects by measuring the time taken for the radio waves to return after being reflected from them, and displays them as glowing "blips" on a TV-type screen. Ground-based *secondary* radar also scans an area with a radio beam, but triggers a transponder (transmitter-responder) in suitably equipped aircraft. The transponder sends a radio pulse to the interrogating station, carrying information about the aircraft's identity, heading, speed, altitude, etc. This information is "written" on the radar display next to the blip representing the aircraft. (See: **Doppler radar.**)

Radio compass
An airborne instrument that indicates true north on the basis of radio signals from ground stations.

Radio Direction Finder (RDF)
An airborne instrument that shows the direction of a ground radio station. (See: **VOR**)

Radio magnetic indicator (RMI)
Flight-deck instrument that shows the magnetic heading of a VOR (q.v) station and the magnetic heading of the aircraft.

Radome
Streamlined protective covering for radar aerials, transparent to radar waves.

Refanned engine
A turbofan (q.v.) that has had its fan blades replaced with larger ones.

Reverse pitch
A setting of aircraft propeller blades at which they exert a backward thrust to slow the aircraft after touchdown.

Reverse thrust
Rearward thrust from a jet engine, achieved by deflecting the jet forward, to slow aircraft after touchdown.

Roger
"Message received and understood".

Roll
Rotation of an aircraft about its nose-to-tail line (longitudinal axis).

Roll-out
The distance an aircraft requires to come to a halt after touchdown.

Rotate
To pull up the nose of an aircraft on the runway and take off.

Rotor
An assembly of moving wings and their hub, usually turning in a horizontal plane, as on a helicopter; or the rotating part of the fan, compressor or turbine in a jet engine.

Rudder
The vertical control surface at the rear edge of the fin.

Runway visual range (RVR)
Visibility along a runway. At major airfields it is measured by automatic equipment.

S
Seaplane
Floatplane (q.v.).

Servomotor
Motor controlled by small inputs, and delivering large outputs; an airliner's control surfaces are driven by servomoters guided by pilot movements or autopilot signals.

Shockwaves
Pressure waves that trail from aircraft travelling at or beyond the speed of sound.

Slat
A small auxiliary wing mounted on the leading edge of an aerofoil. It is extended to increase lift.

Slipstream
Stream of air thrown back by a propeller.

Slot
Gap between a leading edge and slat (q.v.).

Span
The distance from wing-tip to wing-tip.

Spoilers
Control surfaces on the wings of an aircraft that destroy lift by interfering with the airflow. Sometimes they are used as lift dumpers (q.v.) after landing.

Spool
A rotating assembly in a turbine engine, consisting of a turbine, a drive shaft and a compressor or fan.

SST
Supersonic transport aircraft.

Stability
An aircraft's resistance to change in its condition of steady flight, turning or climbing.

Stall
Loss of lift due to excessive angle of attack (q.v.), often caused by insufficient speed.

Standard instrument departure (SID)
A specified route from an airport, marked by radio beacons, that an airliner must follow.

Static dischargers
Metal "prongs" or fine metal-impregnated wicks mounted on an aircraft's trailing edges, which discharge static electricity into the air.

Stator
The stationary part of a machine around, within or alongside which a rotor (q.v.) turns; in a gas turbine or its compressor, a set of fixed blades,

interspersed with rotor blades, that guide the air or gas flow.

STOL
Short takeoff and landing.

Stratosphere
The upper atmosphere lying above the "region of weather", or troposphere.

Streamline
The path of a particle in a moving fluid.

Subsonic
Slower than sound.

Supercharger
An air compressor that increases the power output of a piston engine.

Supercritical wing
A wing designed to delay the build-up of shockwaves (q.v.) at transonic Mach numbers. The top is flatter than a conventional wing's, and lift is more evenly distributed.

Supersonic
Faster than sound. (See: **Hypersonic**.)

T

Tabs
Small movable surfaces fitted to main control surfaces. The large force developed on them by the airstream moves the main control surface.

Tailplane (horizontal stabilizer)
The horizontal aerofoil at the tail that can be fixed or pivoted.

Torque
The twisting reaction force that a propeller or rotor exerts on the aircraft carrying it.

Trailing edge
The rear edge of an aerofoil.

Transonic
Close to (above or below) the speed of sound.

Trim
To adjust the tabs (q.v.) or other control surfaces of an aircraft so that it flies in the correct attitude without manual effort.

Turbofan
A jet engine in which most of the intake air by-passes the combustion chamber and is discharged as a cold jet.

Turbojet
A jet engine (q.v.) in which all the intake air goes through the combustion chamber and none is by-passed; it is also called a straight jet.

Turboprop
A gas-turbine engine that drives a propeller.

Turboshaft
A gas-turbine engine that drives an output shaft — in, for example, a helicopter.

Turbulence
Violent and irregular motion of air.

U

Undershoot area
The unobstructed section of a runway before the threshold, in which a pilot should not land.

V

V_1
A critical speed during takeoff. Below V_1 the takeoff must be abandoned if an engine fails. Above V_1, the takeoff must be continued.

V_2
The speed required by an airliner to climb safely at the desired angle after takeoff.

V_R
"Velocity-rotate," the speed at which an airliner must be travelling along the runway when its nose is pulled up to take off.

Variable-geometry wing
A wing whose sweepback can be reduced for takeoff, landing or cruising, and increased for high-speed flight.

Vector
A directional quantity, such as the distance and bearing of a landmark.

Vertex
A "corner" of a geometric form; a triangle has three vertices, a cone one, and so on.

Visual approach slope indicator (VASI)
A system of light beams projected from lamps near a runway, whose apparent colour indicates to the pilot whether he is on, below or above the correct glidepath.

Visual flight rules (VFR)
The procedures a pilot, usually of a light aircraft, follows when flying without radar guidance from Air Traffic Control.

Volmet
Reports of actual weather conditions at major airports, continuously broadcast on VHF. (French *vol*, flight.)

VOR
VHF omnidirectional range, a system of radio navigation employing a network of radio transmitters whose bearings are determined by receivers in the aircraft.

Vortex
A region of a fluid in rotary motion; a smoke ring is an example. Vortices trail from aircraft wings, increasing drag; but they are deliberately generated on some wings to control airflow or increase lift.

VTOL
Vertical takeoff and landing.

W

Wilco
("Will comply.") Message received and understood; I will obey your instructions.

Y

Yaw
Movement of an aircraft's nose to left or right.

Yoke
The control column of an aircraft.

Acknowledgements

The Publishers received invaluable help from the following people and organizations:
David P. Davies (Chief Test Pilot, the UK Civil Aviation Authority, Airworthiness Division); Captain Hugh Dibley (Training and Technical Management, British Airways); Phil Jarrett (Editor, *Aeroplane Monthly*); John W.R. Taylor (*Jane's All the World's Aircraft*); Anthony Vandyk (IATA); Captain B.O. Walpole (Flight Manager (Technical), British Airways Concorde)

George Anderson (Romana Air Travel); Hugh Cloudsley; Chris Cooper; Antonia Gaunt; Ann Kramer; Freda Parker; Penny Stapley; Ann Tilbury; Daphne Wood

Aeroflot Ltd Soviet Airlines; Aéroport de Paris; ACS Engineering Sales Ltd; Aérospatiale; Air Associates Ltd; Airbus Industrie; Aircraft Engineering; Aircraft Furnishing Ltd; Air France; Air-India; Airside Systems Division, Ludwig Honold Manufacturing Co; Air Transport and Travel Industry Training Board; Air Transport Users Committee; American Science and Engineering Inc; L'Armement Naval de la SNCF; Aviaexport USSR; Avions Marcel Dassault – Breguet Aviation; Avis Rent A Car; BBC "Tonight" Programme; B.P. Trading Ltd; Beaufort Air-Sea Equipment Ltd; Beech Aircraft Corp; Boeing Commercial Airplane Co; Bonser Engineering Ltd; British Aerospace Aircraft Group; British Aircraft Corp Ltd; British Airports Authority; British Airways; British Caledonian Airways Ltd; Bell Helicopter Co; British Hovercraft Corp; British Oxygen Co; Britten-Norman (Bembridge) Ltd; Bunce Ltd; CAA (Civil Aviation Authority); CFM International SA; Canadair Ltd; Canadian Pacific Ltd; Cessna Aircraft Corp; Chelton (Electrostatics) Ltd; Chubb Fire Vehicles Ltd; College of Air Training, Hamble; Thomas Cook & Son Ltd; Combs-Gates Denver, Inc; Davall & Sons Ltd; The Decca Navigator Co Ltd; Decca Radar Ltd; de Havilland Aircraft of Canada Ltd; Donne Security Group; F.L. Douglas (Equipment) Ltd; Dowty Group Services Ltd; Dowty Rotol Inc; The Dunlop Co Ltd; EECO; English Electric Ltd; Equipos Técnicos de Transporte SA; Fairey Britten-Norman Ltd; Fairey Hydraulics Ltd;

F.F. Impulsphysics Corp Inc; US Federal Aviation Administration; Flight International; Flight Refuelling Ltd; Flughafen Hannover-Langenhagen GmbH; Fokker-VFW BV; GEC Overseas Services Ltd (Aviation Services Division); General Aviation Manufacturers & Traders Association; General Aviation Manufacturers & Traders Association; General Dynamics/Convair; Gloster Saro Ltd; Grumman American Aviation Corp; Hamburger Flugzenban GmbH; Harper & Row Publishing Inc (with whose permission Captain Cummings has contributed to this book); HCB-Angus Ltd; Hertz Rent A Car; Hestair Eagle Ltd; Houchin Ltd; Hoverlloyd Ltd; Infoplan Ltd; Institution of Civil Engineers; International Aeradio Ltd; International Air Transport Association; International Civil Airports Association; International Civil Aviation Administration, Canada; International Civil Aviation Organization; The International Paint Co Ltd; Israel Aircraft Industries Ltd; KLM Royal Dutch Airlines; Lockheed Aircraft Corp; Loganair Ltd; Lucas Aerospace Ltd; Lufthansa German Airlines; Manpower Services Commission, Employment Services Division – Heathrow; Marconi Avionics Ltd; McDonnell Douglas Corp; The Meteorological Office, Bracknell; Normalair-Garrett Ltd; Oshkosh; Palmer Aero Products Ltd; Pan American World Airways; Piper Aircraft Corp; Plessey Radar Ltd; Port Authority of New York and New Jersey; Power Lifts Ltd; Qantas Airways Ltd; RFD Inflatables Ltd; Racal-Amplivox Ltd; Romana Air Travel Ltd; Reliance-Mercury Ltd; Rockwell International Sabreliner Division; Rolls-Royce Ltd (Aero Division); L.A. Rumbold Ltd; Sabena Belgian World Airlines; John Schneller & Associates; Secmafer SA; Shell Aviation News; Shell International Petroleum Co Ltd; Short Brothers and Harland Ltd; Singapore Airlines; Skihi Ltd; Smiths Industries Ltd; Southern Meals Supplies Ltd; Sundstrand Data Control Inc; Sweepster Inc; Swissair; C.F. Taylor Ltd; Taylor-Woodrow Construction Ltd; Thorn Lighting; Trans World Airlines Inc; Trepel Airport Equipment; Triplex Safety Glass Co Ltd; UBM Aero Docks; VFW-Fokker International; Vickers-Armstrong (BAC); Wadham Stringer Ltd; The Walter Kidde Co Ltd; Weldwork Cargo Systems Ltd; Westland Aircraft Ltd; Wollard Aircraft Equipment Inc.

Printing: Heraclio Fournier, S.A., Vitoria, Spain
Origination: Colour Workshop Ltd., Herts
Typesetting: Art Reprographic Ltd., London

Picture credits

Cover and prelims: Arnold Desser; p11: Copyright 1978 Jeppesen & Co (Illustration — not to be used for navigational purposes); p13: Crown Copyright; p14: Keystone Press Agency; p15: Lee Battaglia/Colorific Photo Library Ltd, Camera Press Ltd; p18: Camera Press Ltd, Civil Aviation Authority; p19: Civil Aviation Authority, Camera Press Ltd (Sven Simon); p30: British Aerospace/Hawker Siddeley Aviation Ltd, British Aerospace/Aérospatiale; p31: British Aerospace/Aérospatiale; p41: Flight International; p46: K.B. Photographics; p54: British Aerospace, Esso Air World; p55: Esso Air World/Jochen Mönch; p60: Airports International/Sabena Belgian World Airlines; p61: British Aerospace/Hawker Siddeley Aviation Ltd; p64: Airports International; p65: British Aerospace; p67: KLM Royal Dutch Airlines; pp68–69: Aerofilms; p71: Plessey Radar Ltd; p72: British Aerospace; p74: Flight International; p76: Plessey Navaids (Parker PRA Associates Ltd); p81: Air France; pp82–83: Airbus Industrie; p84: Novosti Press Agency, Tass News Agency, British Airways; p85: British Aerospace/BAC; pp86–87: British Airways; p88: Boeing Commercial Airplane Company; pp90–93: Boeing Commercial Airplane Company; p94: Britten-Norman (Bembridge) Ltd; p95: Canadair Ltd, Cessna Aircraft Corp, John W.R. Taylor; p96: Avions Marcel Dassault-Breguet Aviation, Gates Learjet Corp; p97: Grumman American Aviation Corp, Flight International, British Aerospace/Hawker Siddeley Aviation Ltd; p98: Israel Aircraft Industries, Lockheed Aircraft Corp, Rockwell International Corp; p99: Kenneth Munson, General Dynamics/Convair, Avions Marcel Dassault – Breguet Aviation; p100: de Havilland Aircraft of Canada Ltd; p101–106: McDonnell Douglas Corp; pp107–108: Fokker-VFW International BV; p109–110: Flight International; p111: British Aerospace/Hawker Siddeley Aviation Ltd; p112: John W.R. Taylor, Basil Arkell; p113: Novosti Press Agency, Kenneth Munson; p114–115: Lockheed Corp; p116: Flight International, Aviation Photo News; p117: Shorts Publicity Department; p118: Beech Aircraft Corp, Cessna Aircraft Corp; p119: Flight International, Piper Aircraft Corp; p120: Novosti Press Agency, Tass News Agency; p121: Tass News Agency; p122: Vickers-Armstrong (BAC), Rolls-Royce Ltd; p123: John W.R. Taylor; p127: Flughafen Hannover – Langenhagen GmbH; p128: Aéroport de Paris, British Airports Authority/Alan Timbrell; p129: Los Angeles Department of Airports, Barnaby's Picture Library, Camera Press Ltd, Costain International Ltd; p136: British Airways; p152: Lufthansa German Airlines; p153: Pan American World Airways; p154: Flight International, British Aerospace/Hawker Siddeley Aviation Ltd; p155: UBM Engineering Ltd; p164: Schmidt GmbH; p166: Keystone Press Agency; p167: Daval & Sons Ltd; p172: Air Malta; p174: Smiths Industries Photographic Dept; p193: Lufthansa German Airlines "Logbook"; p196: Airports International; p199: Aéroport de Paris; p200: Paul Popper Ltd; p202: General Electric Co Ltd; p207: N.V. Luchthaven Schiphol; p214: Flight International; p215: British Airways; p217: Image in Industry Ltd; p218: Paul Popper Ltd; p219: Airports International; p221: Paul Popper Ltd; p228: John Hillelson Agency Ltd.